THE
SELF-MADE
MAN

THE
SELF-MADE
MAN

Success and Stress—
American Style

BY

ISADORE BARMASH

The Macmillan Company
Collier-Macmillan Ltd., London

To my wife,
Sarah,
and the children

CONTENTS

———— ◆ ————

Contents

PREFACE

———•———

WHEN I decided to write a book on the self-made man, one of the first things I wondered about was how I could avoid the stereotype that has become so deeply imprinted on our national consciousness. We have accepted this caricature much as we have those of the politician, the actor, the doctor, and the athlete.

How to avoid this? I decided to go to the source. Although I had spent two decades as a business journalist, during which I had met an innumerable amount of successful and not-so-successful businessmen, I began the project as though I hadn't met any. Two years later, I had had more than one hundred interviews specifically for this purpose. These formed the core of this book, augmented by other sources and references. Naturally, whether I liked it or not, my attitude and my appraisals of those I interviewed were conditioned by my prior experiences with their species.

I would like to dispose here of three points having to do directly or indirectly with the stereotype.

One, why are so many self-made successes small men physically? Do they attempt to compensate for their size by being excessively aggressive? Psychiatrists say that the answer to this is probably yes, but it is equally true that the small man who is also very successful has the drive and the energy anyway. The fact is, too, that there are plenty of big men who are aggressive and successful, as well as many medium-sized men. And there are plenty of pint-sized men, incidentally, who never become successful, for that matter.

Two, is a self-made man really self-made? The answer here is simpler. Yes, he is, but he obtained help, in various forms. Everyone who has made it had the advice, the enthusiasm, the financial aid, and the forebearance of others, as many of the life-stories in these pages will show, but the will and the abilities of the man himself were by far the first requirements for success. Those who help themselves are likely to get help, life shows. And those who are helped in spite of their indolence probably won't do much with their success so that it eventually slips through their fingers.

Three, is the entrepreneur so full of push and zest that he has lost his sense of humanity? Ah, that is a good question, one of the key ones, and it is explored and answered in detail in the following pages.

These three points aside, another thing that I wondered about when I decided to embark on this book was: Could I do it? One thing that helped me was that I wanted deeply to do it but, like the self-made man, I needed help. To those who spent much time with me, who counseled, who corresponded, who opened doors, who helped with their suggestions and their enthusiasm, I am very grateful.

I approached this project as a reporter or journalist, either term meaning that my intent was not to write a tract or to adopt a viewpoint peculiar to my beliefs. I wanted instead to present a body of facts, and an interpretation of them. That was all. To those few and important businessmen who declined to see me because they had heard that I was a "hard-nosed" reporter, or were reluctant to let me pry beneath the façade, or, once becoming involved, withdrew, I can only say, "Shame on you—but you were only a few."

After all, great success imposes certain responsibilities. The public should know. Americans have raised the very successful businessman to the rank almost of a national hero and they are curious about him, groping, perhaps, for a personal identity with him. Seeing only the gnarled, veined hand holding the strap in the back as the Cadillac brougham slides by is simply no answer to the curiosity of the public.

Finally—unlike the usual disclaimer that any similarity between anonymous persons in this volume and the real-life people is purely coincidental and unintentional—virtually everyone referred to here by name, anonymously, or by description is real and does exist and has or had the successes, the failures, the problems, and the challenges that are appropriately ascribed to them.

ISADORE BARMASH

One

One

MEN AND MOMENTUM

1. FROM NOON TO DAWN

"THE era of the terrible tyrant, the one-man show, who started a business with one machine, a battered table and a broken chair is gone. . . . Like the dodo bird, he gives in to progress—in his case, to the management team, operating the computer, using information retrieval systems, audio-visual sales aids, complex financial controls. . . ."

The slim, dapper man behind the massive desk read no more. As if it soiled his fingers, he allowed the business journal to drop into the heavy, burnished-copper waste-basket. He turned forty-five degrees in his high-backed chair and dictated into a tiny recorder:

"Circulation: Directors, Executive Committee. Subject: Acquisition of the Owens–Bennett Corporation. You may not have heard of this private company. Owners have agreed to sell at a 15 price/earnings multiple, based on telephone agreement yesterday. O–B will add $60 million volume, another

$1.05 a share to our earnings. We will tap our authorized but unissued preference stock. Executive committee meet in my office at 2 P.M., directors at 9 A.M. tomorrow."

Now he pressed a button, summoning his administrative assistant.

"A few things before I go downtown," he told her. "I decided last night that we're going to fight that National Labor Relations Board ruling on our Carolina plant. Tell the legal department to draw up a brief.

"Also," he went on quickly, "tell Smith to meet me here at three. I've decided that he just doesn't fit into our setup. We'll just have to face up to the fact that we need a new executive vice president. After three, I want you to leak his leaving to the 'team.'

"In case anyone tries to pump you before we meet on why we're buying Owens–Bennett, play dumb. Let them find out for themselves by the time we meet, if they can, that O–B has a $5 million tax-loss carry-forward and $27 million in liquid assets—and I mean cash. One of their outside directors steered me to this jackpot. I'm keeping those two little facts in my back pocket in case there's some opposition."

As he arose, he appreciatively patted the woman's firm posterior. She smiled fondly back at him. It was a friendly, nonerotic exchange. He had been doing it for the past twenty-two years and she had been responding in the same way, ever since they had started with little more than a battered desk and a broken chair.

He left, with a high step, a "dodo-bird" on the way out— to a lush, carefree lunch with his admiring bankers.

Less than a half hour later, he sank into a chair at a table in a handsome men's club in the Wall Street area where three others had preceded him and were on their second drinks. One of the bankers was in the midst of a story, and the newcomer immediately recognized the name of the man they were discussing. It was that of a well-known entrepreneur who had lately been in the news because he had quite unexpectedly sold his company.

"I'd say Bill Shanley is one of the sharpest and yet one of the most naive businessmen I ever met," the banker said.

"He conned practically everybody into thinking he was naive—but he's naive like a wolf. Here's a guy who started with nothing and wound up with at least $40 million. He did it by building a business through internal expansion and acquisitions, by wheeling-dealing, and by playing games with taxes. But somewhere along the line he got bored and decided to live the life of leisure."

He paused while they ordered and then he resumed. "So, quietly, Shanley began trying to sell his business. Actually, he had already made so much money on the side, he had so many different profitable investments, that he wasn't even anxious to make a killing. But he wanted to sell the company at a fair price. He didn't want to end twenty years of building it up with a record of having sold it cheaply. But he had problems—its earnings were down.

"One of the divisions was still being paid for by the corporation—they had acquired it only eighteen months before—and its president was a rough guy. This man, Harry Johansen, was always pushing Shanley to buy this company or to buy that company. He had a right to, I guess. His division, which he had founded himself, was earning more than double what the whole rest of the company was and he knew it and that's why he pushed so hard. He only worked an hour or two at the most a day and then went to the race track or played golf.

"Shanley, in the meantime, was offered a few good propositions of companies he could advantageously have bought but he ruled them out because he had made up his mind to sell. He has a wonderful quality—as you know. He's so soft-spoken, even humble, that his anxiety never shows. Everyone thought he's a patsy, a pushover. Some pushover! He was such a pushover that he made me, who never even went close to the line of crookedness, to consider doing things with him that I'm ashamed of. That's how naive and how smooth he really was."

They ate and after a while the narrator continued, "Well, he found a buyer. It was Sam Axelrod, the movies and real estate man, whom everyone considers such a big brain, especially after he paid ten dollars a share under the market price for Shanley's business. But, less than six months after he bought it, he finds that he had been sucked in. First, the Internal Revenue Service began scratching around various divisions because they think there's been a cover-up of some sort. Then, there's an odor of fraud in another division.

"Axelrod blew his top. He cleared out most of the executives who came with Shanley's company, all except Harry Johansen. Harry's division is still the most profitable, even though he's hardly ever there. In fact, Harry is still sitting pretty. He pushed Shanley so hard with the fact that his division's earnings were so high that he insisted Bill do something to show his appreciation. So Shanley bought Johansen a five-hundred-thousand-dollar home in Westchester."

They were at the dessert now and so the banker's kicker was opportune. "Who do you think is paying for Harry Johansen's five-hundred-thousand-dollar home in Westchester?" He demanded with a broad grin. "Sam Axelrod, the great, big, smart businessman, that's who! Shanley had made only a down payment and had committed the company to pay the rest. And what's Shanley doing now? He's living it up in Vegas, the Bahamas, the Riviera, and the other, hot gambling spots around the world."

That evening, a lonely man in a fine, brocaded dinner jacket finished his dinner in his hotel apartment and walked rather heavily into his study. Through the closed door, his cook asked, "Mr. Axelrod, another cup of coffee; a brandy?" He didn't answer.

For perhaps a half hour, he sat silently in his favorite

chair, his mind a dark, swirling place of contradictory thoughts. Earlier that week, he had taken a step that he had never thought he would.

Fiercely independent and naturally acquisitive, he had developed a company with sales of several hundred million dollars through skillful management and the seizing of some unexpected opportunities. Less than a year before, he had bought a large company at a low price. Even though it had involved some problems that he hadn't anticipated, his finely sensitive instincts told him that it had great potential. Its current irritations were therefore quite minor. He had learned that it was vital always to look at the long-term prospect.

But now the buyer of many other companies was on the verge of selling his own. He had succumbed to the blandishments of one of the country's most dynamic "conglomerators." The young, foreign-born entrepreneur had convinced him, as he had many others, that he was better off selling now and obtaining his equity than to wait. But Axelrod knew better. He knew why he was selling the business.

Since his wife's death six months before, he seemed to have fallen into a depression that he couldn't shake. It surprised him (thinking outwardly of himself, as he often tried to do) that the passing of the small, pale, reserved woman would hit him as hard as it had.

The void had grown in past weeks. His one married daughter was increasingly occupied with her growing family. And Joe, his quiet, restrained son who was so like his mother, had dealt him quite a blow only a week ago.

The thirty-year-old Harvard Business School graduate had phoned from his own office down the hall in the Axelrod suite and asked if he could drop by for a moment. And then calmly, as though he were talking about going on a cruise, he told his father that he was quitting the company. With another Harvard man, he would start his own financial consulting firm.

WHY? Sam Axelrod had demanded, in a loud, uncharacteristic expletive that had boomed across the staid office.

Joe, who looked more rail-thin than ever, was perspiring and his big adam's apple bobbed jerkily as he replied, "I've got to do this, Dad. My psychiatrist says I've got to cut the parental apron strings cleanly and forever. He says that's why my marriages to Dotty and Bernice fell apart. He says that's why I can't get fulfillment in my work with the company. He helped me to prove to myself that I have a wish for impotency and it's true. You dominate people so much that they can't function. Especially me. If I can just get away . . ."

Axelrod swung his chair in a half-circle, his back now to his son, staring at a favorite tapestry on the wall. He often did this, almost unconsciously, to avert an immediate sign of reaction to an irksome confrontation. The artifact, the painting, or the view from the Axelrod penthouse, whichever his gaze fell upon, invariably pulled him in and allowed his subconscious to fix his response. How had he first come on this little trick? he wondered. He slowly swung around, saying, "You never told me you were under analysis. . . ." But his son had left, without waiting. This in itself showed that things had changed and not particularly pleasantly.

He had sat there a bit longer, not so much stunned as hurt. It went to his core that his only son could walk out on his unquestioned succession to a company with sales of close to $500 million. Couldn't he understand that a man had to guide, even nurture a son, so that the turning over of the family business could be safeguarded?

Now, Axelrod sat in his study, a week later, confused and unhappy. He felt alone and, for one of the few times in his life, defeated. Then he remembered something. He opened a drawer in his desk and removed a letter. His wife had written to him five years before when she had been away at a resort recovering from an earlier, serious illness. He read portions of it, his vision misting over instantly.

"Sam, I never asked much of you, but you gave me more than any woman could ever expect. But one thing you didn't give me. Peace of mind about Yussie. He is our only son, but you never treated him right. You were always so dignified, like God to him, and he was your slave. He looks up to you and you only look down on him. You told him what schools to go to, what courses he should take, the friends he should have. You even discussed his girl friends with him, like it was a classroom project. His love for you is like a trap for him. You must stop all this, Sam. If you don't, someday he'll break with you and that would mean that my life just wasn't worth anything. . . ."

He put the letter down on the desk top. Then, without any hesitation, he dialed the telephone quickly and spoke, with respect and yet with growing conviction. "The deal is off. Completely and irrevocably. Thank God we didn't put anything on paper yet."

He listened but not attentively to the stream of complaints and to the beginnings of invective. Then, he hung up and dialed his son. "Hello, Yussie?" he asked, his tears falling like rain on the desk blotter. "I have a letter here that I would like to read to you before you go. May I begin?"

Across the city, on the second floor of an imposing townhouse, a short, intense man hurled an elaborate telephone across the room. Turning angrily to his companion, he said, "That old bastard changed his mind! I wouldn't be surprised if it wasn't that son of his—that palefaced fairy that always hid behind his mother. I'll bet they made up."

"What's the next move?" the other asked. Without waiting for an answer, he went to the telephone, picked it up and brought it back.

The burly, little man was calmer now, as if the act of throwing the telephone had absorbed much of his venom. He sat carefully down at his desk and spoke with deliberation. "We have invested too much time and motion into this deal, not to mention money, to drop it. Besides, now that it is a fact, I'm not so sure that what happened is so bad. We already own ten per cent of the stock. It gives us a base to make a tender offer. If the old man's changing his mind means he patched things up with the son. Axelrod will have his back up trying to keep the company for Yussie. That means we will have to fight him through the shareholders by offering to buy their stock. Logical?"

"Logical."

"All right. We'll offer three or four points above the market price and hammer away at the fact that Axelrod's profit margin has crept down in the last three years. That means bad management. And we'll say that's why the dividend hasn't been increased. Possible?"

"Possible."

"Get the old man and Yussie on the phone and tell them that tomorrow we'll initiate a tender offer. Maybe we can scare them. Throw them off guard. Then they do stupid things."

The assistant, once again, paused to marvel. The little man had started out to be a dentist, had become intrigued with the stock market, had bought into his first company and then into others. Today, he sat on top of a $1 billion corporate edifice, employing some fifty thousand persons. And despite his constant financial activities and maneuverings, he had never violated any laws, even, if, on occasion, his moves worried certain federal agency officials. It was said of him by those who professed to know that "money talks to him."

A few moments later, the assistant said, "Both lines are busy. Maybe they're talking to each other."

"No question about that. Keep trying. But, first let's get started. Get the lawyers on the phone and tell them I want them here as soon as possible. Then get Katherine and tell her to get hold of one or two of the best typists and to come over with them. There will be a lot of dictation and transcrib-

ing. Then phone Howie and tell him to get any of the records
he needs from the office and to come right over. Do that first.
We'll work through until we're finished. Sensible?"

"Always."

In an hour, the handsome library was filled with people.
Excitement and tension grew as the work progressed, as the
material accumulated for the attack that would seek to force
the Axelrod family to yield ownership of the controlling stock
in the company it had founded. Down in the lavish kitchen,
after she had made coffee for them all, the cuddly blonde
wife of the "conglomerator" sat alone, chewing on a chicken
leg and watching the picture on a tiny television screen,
until she fell asleep in her chair.

Upstairs, they worked all night long. By dawn, they were
ready.

2. THE SUCCESS . . .

NICHOLAS Murray Butler, the late president of Columbia University and of the American Academy of Arts and Letters,
once observed that there were three types of men in the
world:

Those who make things happen
Those who watch what is happening
And those who do not know what is happening

"Most successful entrepreneurs are products of three elements—opportunity, environment, and heritage—with a good
measure of luck thrown in," said Lawrence A. Appley, retired chairman of the board of the American Management
Association. "People who take advantage of these factors are
what I call 'do-do' guys."

"There are three kinds of self-made man," noted Harold
J. Szold, a man who ought to know. As a partner in Lehman
Brothers, one of America's leading investment banking

houses, Szold has had many an opportunity to spot an authentic human dynamo in the making or to sense a dud.

"The types," this Wall Street banker said, "are those who started at a fairly low level in a corporation and ultimately filled a top management slot, those who started a business and built it up, and those who 'entrepreneured it up.'"

Putting these three views together, what is the self-made man? Most simply, he is a man with an idea and a drive to make money and become important. A man with the personal characteristics to do this and able to find the right vehicle for it. And a man who, having achieved his immediate goal, can repeat the cycle in widening curves, making more money and building a power structure with himself sitting happily, if nervously, at its apex.

He perches gingerly on that peak, its tip frequently jabbing his buttocks as the wolves and the goats chasing underneath or on other mountain tops emit warning howls and bleats. Looking down from his vertex partly obscured by rosy clouds, the self-made man is keenly sensitive to the confusion and alarm below. He knows that an explosion there or from other nearby pinnacles await only a sign of uncertainty or fear from him.

So he swallows his tensions, the self-doubt, the conviction that all associates are inadequate if not potentially disloyal, the feeling that persecution is at the core of his opposition.

Thus, the self-made man, the successful entrepreneur, the tycoon, finds his life stressful, but he must be able to take it even if his insides are churning.

But he has been living a charmed life. His triumphs have been greater than ever. In the sixties, which turned out to be quite fabulous, after all, the cynics who observe business through veiled eyes had something of a rough time. The imminent demise of the self-made man that they had been forecasting for years just didn't happen.

Instead, a decade and a half after World War II, the

American system of enterprise hit its greatest stride. A new decade unfolded in which more men pulled themselves up by their shoestrings than in any like earlier period, youth became an earmark of the enterpreneurial profile, innovators created new industries with new methodology from old products and old systems, and more giant companies than ever before emerged from small, shaky enterprises. It was a golden decade for entrepreneurship—and enough to cause the cynic's bile to rise.

But he had a great deal going for him. His dogmatic reasoning had certain kernels of reality. And, what was more, he had his advocates, too.

The age of the individual was over, he insisted. (Automation, electronic data processing, robot factories, not to mention widening fissures in society would seem to indicate some truth to this.) The consumer was no longer the fulcrum on which business teeters (John K. Galbraith said it arrogantly and with finality in his *The New Industrial State* in describing the new business "technostructure," while Betty Furness, President Johnson's consumer affairs assistant, criss-crossed the country trying to make certain business had no such idea). The all-embracing business oligarchy maneuvers the public according to its will, the cynic insisted, while cajoling it with spurious social reforms. (Out-of-power politicians adopted the theme as a moose call to dissidents from all points.) Government may be omnipotent but it was yet suspiciously subservient to powerful special interests. (This, from other, opposing politicians.) And labor had become at least as important a pressure force as management. (Anti-labor forces, and some others, said it.)

To sum up their baneful views, the doubting ones insisted that current and future enterprise would lock out the ambitious, the hopeful, and the self-driven. Why? Because of the business community's headlong drive toward giantism, complexity, and nonpersonalization of the individual.

Like any hard, arbitrary position, this was a case of over-compensation. A few kernels of truth, related to the premise, were hardly enough on which to mount a full conviction. What was lacking in the process of observation were two special ingredients in the makeup of the sixties, both of a more intensive nature than in the two previous decades. They were the entrepreneurial instinct that lies deep in man's viscera and the dynamic forces that were shaping the country's economy.

The cynic failed to realize that together these represented synergism, success, power, and yet perhaps a reason for persistent idealism in a troubled time.

Of the two factors, the most vital and perhaps the hardest one for the cynic to accept was the explosion of entrepreneurship.

Conglomerates with annual sales from $200 million to $2 billion grew quickly from a tiny base established by feverish young men, and some not so young.

New companies to service the burgeoning food, clothing, shelter, and entertainment and other not such basic needs were started and mushroomed to substantial proportions on sheer energy and enterprising sense.

Financial services to sell securities, mutual funds, insurance, or just plain advice were founded by fast-talking, peripatetic young men who less than a generation before could have been only clerks or messengers on Wall Street.

Perhaps it is the seeming contrast of today's more controlled business environment with that of the post-Civil War period when the great American tycoons cut their swath across the adolescent economy that caused some to predict a narrowing opportunity. There is no question that today's business climate is more restricted insofar as industrywide penetration is concerned (now all one can aspire to are market segments); that personal and corporate taxes exert a great, restraining influence (the capital gains tax and the

tax-loss carry-forward notwithstanding); and that business
ethics while far from admirable today are much more severely
scrutinized and laws aimed at curbing business excesses are
being frequently enacted.

But, with all this, it is hard to shrug off the many remarkable successes of the post-World War II period, and especially, giving the due to the protracted shift from a wartime to
a hungry civilian economy, those of the midfifties and the
sixties. There can be only one conclusion: Vast opportunity
was seized by those with fine entrepreneurial "tuning."

The saga of a boy who emerged from impoverished circumstances, left school early, but ran all his life as though his
heels were on fire to catch up with a dream and did it by
making millions is as true today as it was in the days of the
nineteenth-century tycoons. The game is essentially the same
one that Horatio Alger wrote about so piously and platitudi-
nously in the late 1800's. The rules are different, making the
achievement more difficult than it used to be, but with the
proper motivation, one learns the rules.

In such an environment of challenge and opportunity, the
ranks of the millionaires and the near-millionaires naturally
swell. Even the list of the multi-millionaires grows longer
every few months. The seesaw of motivation and achievement
teeters in the early years and then balances delicately in the
years of success. Soon, the drive for security shifts to a drive
for business and social position, as the efforts of the zealous
and the undeterred men produce a cascade of money and
solidity for themselves, their children, and ultimately perhaps for their grandchildren and even great grandchildren.

So, the initial goal is money. The later goal is possessions.
And the final goal is position and, in many cases, perpetuation. And with it all there is the stress and the pace of the
long, hard track.

How is success being grasped today? About as it always
was. Starting with a tiny base and expanding it, holding on to

the reins of the business or to the stock. And constantly moving ahead because standing still means falling behind. Always making sure that the controls of the business and of its direction remain where they belong—in the fertile fingers of the entrepreneur.

Some of the new millionaires are already among the wealthiest men in the land.

Edwin H. Land, founder of the Polaroid Corporation, started with a little company and within twenty years amassed an incredible fortune.

After some lean years in the forties when Land, an engineer and inventor, imperiled his company by investing considerable time and money into developing a radical sixty-second camera, he finally put the Polaroid camera on the market in 1948. It took hold and sales shot up awesomely. The controlling stock in the company which he and his family own and had seen plummeting during those rough years to only $1.5 million shot up in 1968 to a worth of about $500 million. And, with that, the self-made Dr. Land became one of the ten wealthiest Americans.

W. Clement Stone had a talent for salesmanship but precious little money. Starting in the insurance business while still in his teens, he launched his own insurance firm in the twenties. Together with his wife, Stone built up one of the country's major new insurance companies, the Combined Insurance Company of America, a Chicago concern with assets of $142 million. Stone is understandably an advocate of "self-help" and "self-motivation." Today, he and his wife have holdings totaling more than $130 million.

E. Claiborne Robins graduated from pharmacy school in the bottom of the Depression, 1933. He then assumed the management of the family business, the A. H. Robins drug firm, which had been barely surviving.

Research and diversification-minded, young Robins guided the company into a testing program and into a diversity of products, including cosmetics and pet foods. By 1967, the firm's sales had reached $100 million. They were only $4,800 when the young pharmacist had taken over the business from his widowed mother. The Robins family now owns over $200 million worth of the company's stock.

Today's opportunities, like those that favored Land, Stone, and Robins and many others, are being exploded not merely by a record population's demands but by a collection of happy circumstances.

New financial criteria and a money market that seems eager to back the entrepreneurially-minded (even if it is often critical of their methods), tight money notwithstanding, are more amenable today than ever before.

The trend of franchising consumer services cuts the time lag by offering know-how and the physical essentials to start one's own business.

Government subsidies in the form of loans at favorable business interest rates make entry and expansion for the small businessman easier than in the past.

3. THE CONGLOMERATORS

BUT the most striking examples of the self-made man, circa 1945–69, are not small businessmen at all. They are the "conglomerators," the financially oriented, early risers who erected structures of unrelated companies by using the assets or the securities of one to buy another. No other type in the business-financial community has been so widely criticized, praised, and studied.

Bankers prefer a corporate organization based on a foundation of product or related products, or a fundamental management idea, which can blossom from internal entrepreneurship and emerging administrative skills.

Harold Szold of Lehman Brothers, for example, says of the conglomerate builders, "I look with a degree of skepticism on them because they are merely wheeler-dealers. Their pyramiding tactics are like all deals—risky and not very promising. I prefer a basic management concept that can grow from internal effort."

Bankers, as a matter of fact, disavow the pyramiding device as one that is not ingrained in the money market. The late Murray D. Safanie, honorary chairman of Shearson, Hammill & Co., another leading investment banker, told this writer:

"The device of pyramiding of equity capital with a heavy flow of senior securities (bonds, preferred stocks, loans, anything other than common stocks) has made it possible for the users of the device to get exaggerated advantages and results in acquisitions.

"It is hardly a new technique, for it was used dramatically in the twenties. Many men built fortunes by this device of erecting one structure on top of another on a base of common stock and with each of their accumulated companies issuing new debt. Now this technique has returned, with all its illusory characteristics," Safanie said.

The ploy, he added, is largely designed to bring down to the basic holding company the maximum earnings per share. The banker, an esteemed security analyst for forty-three years who died late in 1967, said, "I feel that while the peak of the capital leverage trend may not yet have been reached, it is approaching an excess. It is getting close to a mishap. This economic phenomenon of our time holds, I believe, some serious consequences."

Such warnings have been issued by others over the past decade. Yet, the energetic James Ling, Charles Bluhdorn, and Meshulam Riklis, all of whose frenetic activities are examined in detail in the ensuing pages, have created vast corporate structures by processes generally of the "leverage" type. More important, these "conglomerators" have permitted and spurred the great majority of their subsidiary companies to thrive, to increase their earnings, and to benefit the general economy.

What the future holds for them and their shareholders is, of course, impossible to predict with accuracy, but the likelihood is that the conglomerates will grow as will the opportunity for improved earnings.

James Joseph Ling is a cold-eyed, brooding, endlessly calculating "conglomerator" who did what millions of Americans yearn for but never achieve beyond the dreaming stage.

He sold his house in Dallas, after his discharge as an electrician's mate from the U.S. Navy in 1946, and invested the $3,000 in an electrical contracting business. His home became a room behind the shop. A little more than two decades later, his Ling–Temco–Vought, Inc., had established itself as one of the largest companies in the United States, with annual sales topping $1.8 billion and net income of $34 million. That year, 1967, he was forty-four years old.

Ling, a school drop-out at fourteen, was born with a deeply wayward and competitive streak. School was too slow, too drawn-out a process for him. He ran away from home in Shreveport, La., and went on the bum for a while. Five years later, he came to Dallas and took a job as an electrician. Before enlisting in the Navy, he passed muster in the trade as a journeyman electrician and then as a master contractor.

As a peacetime contractor, he built his company by 1955 to a volume of $1.5 million. That year, he became enamored with finance and tried to convert his firm into a publicly owned company. But he found something less than enthusiasm for underwriting the shares of a small contracting concern among the local brokers. Ling decided to handle the offering himself. He and his friends started selling shares around the city and even took a booth at the Texas State Fair to hand out prospectuses.

This type of flamboyance and courage appealed to Texans. Ling issued 800,000 shares, kept half and sold the rest at

$2.25 each. But this was only a first step. When a West Coast electronic-vibration testing company became available for sale, he bought it by offering $19,000 in cash to give the California workers back pay and by assuming $66,000 in debt.

Then came a series of small acquisitions, helped by two issues of convertible debentures and bonds. Fired by his success, he moved ahead now, trying to scale the heights, acquiring between 1959 and 1965 the Altec companies, Temco Electronic & Missiles, Chance–Vought, and the Okonite Company. In January, 1967, the company obtained a 53 per cent interest in Wilson & Co., a sporting-goods and meat packing giant whose sales were double those of Ling's conglomerate and absorbed the $990 million company into the L–T–V fold. The trick: a tender offer to Wilson shareholders of 25 per cent a share over the market price.

Ling bought first small and then large companies by assuming short- and long-term debt with an amazing insouciance. All this evolved into what seemed to be an endless series of acquisitions, spin-offs, and mergers, using every possible type of stock and security. It was a dazzling performance.

But his greatest coup was to turn his subsidiaries into public companies, the corporate shell always retaining the bulk of each stock offering. This not only built a market value for L–T–V's holdings, but allowed the subsidiaries to function in all ways as independent companies (making all their own bank loans, for example) except that they were not really independent. L–T–V still owned them, but anyone could buy in.

Ling's goal was to have a complex with sales of $5 billion, making it one of the top twenty-five industrial empires in the world. Already, he has a fully diversified and comprehensive electronics-aerospace group that is a formidable contender for the most important military and civilian contracts in its fields.

Sheer size and assets have been his goals, followed closely by power. "Money," he told an European banker, "is how we Americans are measured."

The alternately shy and garrulous empire-builder gets some of his best ideas when he awakes at about 3:30 A.M. in the cavernous bedroom of his $750,000 home, one of the show-places in Dallas. In his case, apparently, his subconscious works overtime.

Despite the immense size and complexity of his business, Ling nevertheless told *Fortune* magazine that "all forms and devices in modern management will never become a substitute for the entrepreneurship of man."

His statement is not far removed from the definition of the "real self-made man" by Lawrence Appley formerly of the American Management Association. Says Appley, a veteran corporate executive and trade association chief, "The real self-made man may be the one who makes opportunities which would otherwise not have existed."

Such a man might well be Charles B. Thornton. At least, that was how he evaluated himself and two other ex-Hughes Aircraft executives in 1953. It occurred when they dropped in on Lehman Brothers to ask for $1.5 million in backing to invest in a profitable but tiny San Carlos, Cal., producer of microwave tubes. Its name was Litton Industries.

Recalling the incident, Lehman's Harold Szold said, "We have always tried to look for the man pushing the idea, and, of course, for the idea itself.

"We were impressed with both in Thornton's case. His credentials were good and his idea was sound, if unusual. He told us that there were a lot of scientists floating around in business. Many had entrepreneurial instincts and imagination, but were hampered by individual situations that wouldn't allow them to capitalize on their instinct. He proposed that a diversified company be built around such people, allowing

them to engage in research toward practical ends, and spur-
ring their efforts by capital gains, stock options, and other
incentives, rather than by salaries."

Thornton made tiny Litton's the basic block of a great
business edifice. Then forty years old, a business administration graduate who had been at Ford Motor Company before
coming to Hughes Aircraft where he was a vice president and
assistant general manager, Thornton plumbed the use of
Litton's laboratories to expand in inertial guidance, radar, and
computers. Then, in the next four years, he acquired ten other
electronics companies.

Thornton was enthralled with the new technologies. From
then on, his new acquisitions involved business machines
(Monroe Calculating Machine and later Royal-McBee),
medical electronics (a German company), and other technical entities. For $8 million in stock and the assumption of
$9 million in debt, Litton in 1961 acquired the third largest
American private shipyard, Ingalls.

Why an old, debt-ridden company then locked in a fight
with its founder's heirs? Thornton, whose moves are intuitive
as much as they are rooted in economics and science, wanted
Ingalls partly for its attack submarines, which, he believed,
would come into importance as a defense against Russia's
underseas forces. But Thornton's reasoning went deeper.
Oceanography, in which Ingalls has diversified activities, is
potentially as significant as outer space, he was convinced.
Space will be important in exploration, communications, and
military use, but the oceans have food, minerals, and chemical
elements much more basic to a hungry, congested humanity.

However, initially the more practical side of Ingalls' work
proved a boon to Litton's, with sales rising substantially, a
resumption of profits, and a retirement of the debt obligations.

Since then, Litton has made a name for itself as a source

of s stems management and technical assistance for the U.S. anc other governments. It is also providing plans and technical assistance to alleviate urban congestion.

With annual sales having risen within fourteen years to well over $1 billion and with high per-share earnings, Litton under Thornton successfully wedded corporate growth with the exercise of entrepreneurial drive. Each of Litton's division managers is a highly motivated entrepreneur, who thinks and acts as if he is in business for himself. And, living in such an environment, at least twenty times that many of the company's executives approach their work as though they, too, were owners.

Another intense conglomerator, Dr. Armand Hammer, the president of Occidental Petroleum Corporation, called the $1 billion company a "natural resources" concern. But Occidental, which made many speculators rich in the midsixties by the amazing climb in value of its common stock, is very clearly a conglomerate. It has sulphur, fertilizer, and agricultural chemical subsidiaries and real estate holdings in Los Angeles. And an obvious quest has been under way to seek diversity in depth.

Hammer has emerged as one of the oddest and most interesting figures on the American business scene. A physician who never practiced, Hammer has undertaken varied activities in a life which contains more surprises than a play in the theater of the absurd.

The son of a Bronx physician, Hammer attended Columbia College of Physicians and Surgeons where he and an older brother bought a large supply of surplus World War I pharmaceuticals and sold them in a rising market. This made them millionaires in their early twenties.

As he awaited his interneship assignment, Armand decided to buy a U.S. surplus field hospital and took it to Russia to help the famine-stricken peasants. There, seeing the opportunity, he made deals involving the bartering of surplus U.S. wheat for Russian products. He became a U.S. sales representative in Russia for thirty-eight American companies. Nine years later, he returned to America, having made $9 million from his barter arrangements.

"One thing leads to another in business," he once observed, and then demonstrated what he meant. When, in 1944, he heard that the American Distilling Company was planning to declare a dividend of one barrel of whiskey for each share owned by a shareholder, he bought five thousand shares on margin. To stretch the "dividend," he had the whiskey mixed with alcohol made from government surplus potatoes and sold the blend to the war-dry public and other distillers. But to make the alcohol, he acquired several distilleries, wound up with eleven, and then disposed of them in 1956 for $10 million.

One thing leads to another, as he had said. Because his distilleries made a cattle-feed mash, he became interested in cattle and bought prize Angus to raise in New Jersey. One bull, Prince Eric, was highly productive. He sired two thousand calves in the last three years of his life and earned $2 million for Dr. Hammer.

Hammer decided to retire in 1956 and moved to California. But he soon became bored and responded with interest when a friend suggested some speculation in oil. The result was an investment of $60,000 in Occidental, a failing refiner, which he took over in 1957, becoming its president, with astonishing results. By installing professional oil engineers, diversifying, and obtaining lucrative oil concessions in Libya, he raised Occidental's revenues from about $1 million in 1957 to more than $1 billion a decade later.

Now in his seventies, the entrepreneur may be engaged in his boldest maneuver. On a busy, commercial street not far from downtown Los Angeles, he has set up a drilling rig for oil to prepare for the first of twenty-nine wells with which he expects to tap "the world's largest pool of oil which lies under Los Angeles."

To remove the usual unsightliness of the oil-drilling scene, the rig will be covered by a shell that resembles a typical sky-scraper office building. And, as the rig moves from well to well on the 513-acre property, its office building superstructure will go along with it.

4. WILDCATTERS TO WALL STREETERS

THE roster of the twentieth-century self-made men could easily be divided into two columns. One would include those who were born in the previous century and made it big in the new one. The other would list those who were born between the two world wars and achieved their success in the fifties and sixties.

Let's examine one of the oldest and one of the newest successes.

Sid Richardson is a legendary figure in the oil industry. He was a wildcatter, whose failures and successes in Texas left him broke many times in his life but at the end gave him an estimated worth of about $500 million. He was born in 1891, the seventh son of a farmer and rancher and he was making shrewd cattle trades by the time he was seventeen.

In his early career, Richardson alternated between ranching and trading in oil leases, but did much better in oil. He made a million by 1921, went broke when oil prices tumbled, made another fortune, and lost it again in the Depression. In the late thirties, when oil prices rose, his confidence returned and so did his luck. Borrowing money for labor and equipment, he brought in one of West Texas's greatest oil finds.

He became an oil adviser to President Franklin Roosevelt and later helped persuade General Dwight D. Eisenhower to run for the Republican presidential nomination. Massive, folksy, and shy, with a deadpan country sense of humor, he enjoyed his wealth and dabbled in many fields besides oil until his death in 1959 on his vast, island retreat in the Gulf of Mexico.

Ken T. Jones does not precisely fit into the new category of entrepreneurs since he was born in 1917. But he accomplished what many World War II veterans who served in the Pacific yearned for but never realized. He returned to the tropical island where he had been a Seabee and settled down to live— in great style.

After the fighting subsided on Guam, the North Carolina farm boy decided not to go back to the plow. The island's central location in the Pacific and the challenge of building an enterprise of his own there intrigued him. He saved up a kitty of $3,000 but saw half of it dribble away in a poker game on the way back to the States. Then, at home, he used the rest of his funds to buy inexpensive jewelry and watches which he mailed to a friend on Guam to sell.

Returning to the island as a civilian (he had to join the U.S. civil service for a year to do so), he made a good deal with 140 surplus war jeeps and used the receipts as a base to start several supermarkets and a department store. Since then, Jones has become a millionaire operator of a diversified business complex, which includes the Royal Toga, the first luxury hotel in the U.S. Trust Territory of the Pacific, another hotel, a shopping center, an American Motors agency, a restaurant, and other enterprises with total sales of $20 million.

Late in 1967, he leased 7,500 acres of government land, almost one-third of the island's land area, to build the Bar-K ranch. There, in the midst of the vast Pacific, where a quarter century ago American forces hit the beaches under intensive fire, he is raising Black Angus-Hereford cattle from New Zealand and race horses from Australia.

"Luck is around for anyone willing to flag himself for performance," said Albert M. Greenfield, of Philadelphia. Greenfield, who, at his death at seventy-nine in 1967, was one of the wealthiest Americans, explained, "A man doesn't need brilliance or genius. All he needs is energy. Luck, what is it? Luck is an accident that happens to the competent."

Greenfield seemed to have those qualities, energy, competence—and all the luck. Born in the Ukraine in 1887, he came to Philadelphia in 1892 where his father opened a grocery store. The boy left school at fourteen and held a number of jobs. In 1905, he borrowed $500 from his mother and opened a real estate office. Five years later, at twenty-three, he was earning $60,000 a year.

He was shrewd, daring, relentlessly on the prowl. At thirty, when he was the owner of a fortune of $15 million, he was known across the country as one of its most powerful real estate operators despite his youth. Through Albert M. Greenfield & Co., and other corporations, he acquired five of Philadelphia's largest hotels and one of its major department stores.

Greenfield loved to buy a bargain, a struggling business or depreciating real estate whose owners were anxious to sell, and then build it up with expense-conscious executives who would raise its profits. From 1945 until he retired in 1959, he was one of the most active "wheeler-dealers," winding up in control of City Stores Company, a chain of 112 stores, the Bankers Securities Corporation, the Loft Candy Corporation, and the Bankers Bond & Mortgage Company of Pennsylvania and New Jersey. At his retirement, the total complex had sales of $850 million.

Short, heavy, dapper, with a shiny, round, bald head and a clear gaze, Greenfield was disarming. He could ooze charm, especially toward women, and cow competition in an acquisition or real estate deal with hard, vicious bargaining.

Oddly enough, he was fiercely vindictive against subordinates for their disloyalty but not nearly as much for their incompetence. His compassion for some bumbling executives was at odds with his demands on himself and on others, including his sons. He was, however, hypersensitive to criticism. Reporters particularly annoyed him, especially when they queried him on rumored deals. Once, he coldly told this writer, "You newspapermen. I was one myself for a short time. You're all whores. Why don't you find yourself some decent work?"

Yet, when he learned that a secretary of one of his division heads had defrauded the company of several thousand dollars, he was more amused than angry. "I don't understand the guy," he told another executive. "Why did he let her get away with it? He wasn't even sleeping with her."

Then there is the new breed of Wall Street millionaires, most of whom are only in their thirties. Almost all had worked at large brokerage houses but decided to venture out on their own as brokers, mutual fund managers, private investment partnerships (hedge funds), or as securities researchers. Individual entrepreneurship in the chaotic financial world is about as risky a gamble as one can take. But many of the young men who took the step were already professionals in a speculative market and were attuned to taking risks.

Donaldson, Lufkin & Jenrette, Inc., is one of the most successful new firms whose record of achievement in a few years has compelled the old-established houses to sit up, take notice, and even imitate. DLJ was formed in 1959 by three graduates of Harvard Business School to specialize in securities research for institutional clients as opposed to research for the ordinary investor. The popularity and growth of mutual funds and the burgeoning securities investments of banks, unions, and pension funds created an important market for the partners. And some highly accurate judgments on their part didn't hurt, either.

Tousle-haired Fred Alger received a good education at the University of Michigan and Yale and had held several jobs in the securities field when, in 1964, at twenty-nine, he decided to start his own investment advisory firm. He was an unknown fledgling in a world of giants and it was a struggle. When he was virtually down to his last gasp as an entrepreneur, the young man was suddenly recommended by Donaldson, Lufkin & Jenrette for his first major investment management account. Since then, Alger has taken on the supervision of more than $200 million of client investments and at excellent fees: 10 per cent of the total appreciation of the stock involved, or at least 1 per cent of the client's portfolio.

Abbey Butler, in 1959, was earning $50 a week as a twenty-two-year-old trainee. By the end of 1967, when he was thirty, he was worth well over $2.5 million. Young as he was, he found it no burden, after having arrived, to borrow $600,000 to buy memberships on the two big New York stock exchanges.

Operating on the basis that the best stocks to buy were those that appreciated rapidly, he did well by himself as he served his customers. He bought fifty thousand shares of a then obscure phonograph record company, Cameo-Parkway Records, at $2 a share, and then gleefully saw them run up to $50 each the following winter.

The new Wall Street tycoons are not so different in achieving success from those of previous generations except that the newer vintage got there at an earlier age. Money managers all, one way or another, they work long hours (the market's closing is only in the early part of their day), are egotistically involved in their pursuit of wealth and fame, have great stores of energy, are highly imaginative, and have an ability to communicate with others at all levels.

5. . . . AND THE STRESS

"THE businessman's greatest asset is motivation but his main vice can be money," observes Sidney J. Weinberg, a gnome-like man who has probably had a greater influence on American business through his sixty years on Wall Street than ten

contemporary tycoons of large, physical proportions. Weinberg is senior partner of Goldman, Sachs & Co., one of the
country's largest investment-banking houses.

The danger of money lies in a father's giving too much or
leaving too much to the children—"the sons frequently become alcoholics, because their motivation is gone and they
don't know where to turn, except to the bottle, and even the
married daughters are unhappy, unless they are unusually
fortunate in their choice of husband," Weinberg said.

That problem, of course, relates only to the self-made man's
children. But it is safe to say that almost at no point in his
career is the entrepreneur without pressures and tension.
Much of it is self-generated. Virtually all of it, in fact, comes
from his success traits, except perhaps when a portion of it
represents his contra-reaction to the effect, usually abrasive,
that he causes on other people.

The self-made man is not necessarily an unpleasant personality. Many are. Some have both their genial and uncongenial
sides. Others are downright nasty. But the mountain of de-
termination-ego-devotion that most carry on their backs
throughout their business lives places them almost constantly
under stress. And that stress, varying in symptom and degree
during different stages of his career, is something he cannot
shrug off. He carries it on him everywhere, like his wallet (in
superb leather, of course, with separate money clip) or his
wrist-watch (in eighteen carat gold).

Does that make him unhappy, neurotic, even possibly psychotic? That is the psychiatrist's realm and it is covered in
some detail in Chapters Five and Six. But there is an observer's realm, too. It doesn't take much psychiatric ability
to note that in the dynamic sixties, more than in the two
preceding decades, the push-pull drive of the self-mader exacted considerable emotional distress and sent him often to
his bottle of tranquilizers.

Caught in his own slipstream of restlessness and anxiety to

succeed, the enterpriser of the last decade also found himself faced by a sometimes crushing number of external pressures. These included ever-increasing competition, intractable or inadequate colleagues and employees, government that was alternately restrictive and permissive (the former directed toward himself and the latter toward his competition), and socio-cultural changes that invaded into his very home.

The result of the internal and the external pressures varied according to the individual. But there seem to be at least nine types of self-made men who, because of their own particular temperament, feel the greatest ping-pang effect of stress on their nervous systems:

THE PERFECTIONIST. Many men who built companies are endless seekers of perfection but the effort to achieve it or a state near it produces pressures and tensions that are both inner- and outer-directed. The boss's frown is constant. The resulting harassment of both executives and workers scarcely seems to let off.

Viewing the spectrum of his operations, the head man keeps asking himself why so many of his employees are letting him down, even fooling him. An administrative vice president is never quite efficient enough; the sales manager and his staff never "learn" the best techniques. And the employees appear to be more interested in coffee breaks, days off, and vacations than in helping him, and thus, indirectly, helping themselves. For a boss such as this, life is indeed frustrating. Although he tends to get more of a performance from his staff than if he were less demanding, he always bears the disappointment and disillusionment in his fellow man. He usually carries this conviction to the grave.

THE DO-IT-YOURSELFER. A similar, if more repressed type. Not only does this one demand a high degree of effort but he is convinced that the results of others will never meet his hopes. So, he gets into everything, from the data communications room to the file room, frequently fouling things up, satisfying, for the moment, his own lack of confidence in others. But it all wears him down—he's in the earliest and out the last. And his rather foolish involvement in the nitty-gritty of the business dooms him to lesser attainment and unending frustration.

THE SHORT-DISTANCE RUNNER. This is the man who puts all into an immediate project and then finds himself bereft of stamina, ideas, and mental power to move ahead, even though his instinct is always to seek new triumphs. Eventually, he finds the reserve that he needs, but usually he, too, remains a small entrepreneur, although his appetite is great. Comparing himself to more successful operators, he continually grapples with an inferiority complex. Inevitably, he settles for less than he wants to and it leaves him an unhappy man.

THE HIT-AND-RUN DRIVER. Just the reverse type. He goes from one successful attack to another, scarcely pausing to put the pieces together. This chore he leaves to colleagues whom he pays well to dust off and cement the blocks that he is building into a business pyramid. But, while he is gratified by the swift rise of that structure and the power it brings him, he is subject to much criticism both inside and outside his business. However, since he cannot change his personality and temperament, he keeps running to new projects, seemingly running, too, from impending disaster. Like the auto hit-and-run driver, he suffers from a guilty conscience.

THE WHEELER-DEALER. A similar type, but different in that in his credo there need be no common denominator to his exploits but the attainment of more assets and more power. He goes blithely from one deal to another freely manipulating people, money, and events, unconcerned by the lack of any continuity or homogeneity in what he puts together.

But, occasionally, like the hit-and-run driver (entrepreneurial type), he keeps looking back over his shoulder, seeing his jerry-built structure swaying in the wind. He despises the name "wheeler-dealer," and he only somewhat less resents that of "conglomerator." Nervously, he knows, too, that some notable American examples of his type came under such severe scrutiny that they either barely missed imprisonment or were jailed, or faded from view, fled the country, or committed suicide.

THE FIRE-BREATHING COMPETITOR. Fiercely avaricious, this self-made man never quite loses his natural state of insecurity. He battles endlessly with his rivals, despite the quite evident fact that there is a big enough pie for all to eat. He lashes his staff almost as much as himself—every minor coup or edge achieved by his most direct competitor becoming a source of momentary hysteria for him.

He often misses the big picture, the potential that can be seen only by indulging in some creative thinking, and sooner or later this discovery comes to him, adding to his basic inferiority. But, for others with a broader view, the competitive streak provides a direction for success, especially if they have the capacity to grow.

THE MAGNIFICENT PATRIARCH. The father who has sons who come into the business faces an especially delicate matter. Is he big enough to admit to himself that his son's accomplishments may someday exceed his own? Those fathers who are naturally unable to countenance that consciously or subconsciously spend much effort proving that they are correct as to their own superiority. But, in addition to the punishment thereby inflicted on the son, the father begins to learn (usually from outside sources) that what he is doing is cruel, devoid of the parental instinct, and even inhuman. Yet, he finds it difficult to change for the indomitability and the egotism that prevent it are the very reasons why he himself has succeeded.

THE ONE WITH THE DORIAN GRAY COMPLEX. A closely related type. Oscar Wilde's portraiture of the man who keeps viewing a painting of himself only to find it growing old and ugly is not unknown to the self-made man. "Can that be me?" he asks himself, as he stares painfully in the mirror. Advancing age is a threat to his business-making skills, to his virility, to his confidence and that which he hopes to inspire in others. How can it be that age, with all its accompanying discomforts and problems, catches up with him? he wonders. Couldn't he have avoided it as he solved all the other problems that beset him? The answer to these is, of course, the awful truth. He is just as mortal as anyone else.

THE HYPER-SENSITIVE. Of all types, this one seems most prevalent. Perhaps it is the constant exposure to the flank caused by their risk instinct that makes so many self-maders highly sensitive to possibly disloyal executives, ridicule, the press, the academic world, the government, youth, ideological extremism, and social change. To the casual observer, the self-made man's combination of sheer guts and thin skin is difficult to comprehend. But to the long-time observer of the species, it is evident that they are closely related.

Some of these types of men under stress are often combined in the same man and, as a result, the tensions may be compounded. But it must be left to the psychiatrists to define much more exact causes and effects. More of them today, it seems, are being pressed to help the businessman gripped by anxiety.

Does today's man of enterprise undergo greater stress than

his progenitor of fifty and one hundred years ago? We can safely assume so, even though it is, of course, difficult to be certain. But, lacking that, how did the entrepreneurial climate unfold for those who swagger across today's business arena?

Two

---·•·---

BUSINESS DOWN
THROUGH HISTORY

1. THE FIRST 50,000 YEARS

CAIN, Calvin, Franklin. Rarely has a more unlikely trio been cast in the same frame of reference.

Yet, it may be that Cain, the banished son of Adam and Eve, John Calvin, the fiery French theological reformer, and Benjamin Franklin, the first of a native strain of American self-starters, are at least to a marked degree responsible for the concept, the shape, and even the ideals of modern business.

At least, the framework of their lives—the workman-builder, the pragmatic-minded ecclesiastic, and the entrepreneur of diverse interests—produced a mold into which many later models were cast.

The rejected Cain, for example, was not only history's first tiller of the soil but he also built history's first city, Enoch, in Nod.

Calvin, the disputatious church orator and scholar, established a more humanistic aspect of religion, stepping with bold, giant footsteps through the murky Middle Ages as they emerged from an agrarian, medieval economy into a commercial and industrial era.

While Martin Luther preached for a return to primitive simplicity, the toughminded, warmhearted Calvin welcomed the newly emerging capitalism. He encouraged trade and production but he made sure that its managers would behave themselves by insisting on curbs on oppressive greed and exploitation. A much freer attitude about the morals of earning a profit emerged from his reform movement.

Franklin was the chubby, effervescent beginner of many things in a country that was itself just beginning. He was ultimately practical yet inventive; a dreamer, a diplomat, and yet a most candid communicator of his own thoughts. More than any other man—even Washington and Jefferson—he set the country's economic tone: ambitious, acquisitive, hard-working, frugal, God-fearing.

That he freely admitted in his unfinished autobiography amorous dalliances, a difference between his public and his private faces, and a hard core of calculation only adds that extra human dimension that has made him appealing and recognizable.

One may, certainly, debate the choice of these three as progenitors of today's business tycoons. Candidates there are many for the role. One may choose freely, and perhaps more justifiably, from the long and diverse list.

The history of business, after all, like history itself, is really nothing other than the confrontation of people and situations, the interplay of protagonists and antagonists on a stage of events and environment. Often, the turns and trends in business involves an individual who was too ignorant to know that what he wanted to do couldn't be done—and then went ahead and did it. More often, the changes that repre-

sented progress boiled up from the pressures of many people, their needs and yearnings on the shifting conditions of
the time.

And business history, like human nature, is full of nagging
paradoxes. Especially so is the romance of that dynamic instinct, the dark, almost savage strain that creates important
entrepreneurs out of perspiring but dogged amateurs. That
saga is curiously composed of the beliefs of church, state,
and the ethics of the time—that the profit motive is evil and
immoral—and of many instances of commercial success that
were even then deemed good, moral, and socially beneficial.

Centuries before the birth of Christ, Demosthenes, the
greatest of Greek orators, operated his own furniture and
armor factories. Pericles, one of the Greeks' most illustrious
statesmen, owned a factory, too, as did his ward and fellow
statesman, Alcibiades.

In the Roman Empire of the first century, it was simple
for the rich and the powerful to share handsomely in the
high state of industrialization of that age. Three Roman emperors did it, in fact. Marcus Trajanus, Hadrian, and Marcus
Aurelius owned potteries, which they found to be an excellent source of extra income.

Many centuries later, during the Middle Ages, however,
the Church insisted that "No Christian ought to be a merchant."

And, for many years, the Roman Church continued to
frown upon the concept of earning a profit. It wasn't until
the Renaissance and then Calvinism, when the more romantic ways of life, with their concomitant comforts, brought
profound changes in attitudes that the trader or merchant
became more generally looked upon as more of a necessity
and more of an honorable human being.

Even later, in the seventeenth and eighteenth centuries,

the Pilgrims were horrified by the concept of gain as a life's goal, considering it the very devil's work.

Although trade began to flourish in the Middle Ages, the era had a dichotomous attitude toward the merchant, the trader, and the entrepreneur who sought to expand their activities. There was, for example, a grudging realization that trade brought the means of ending poverty, serfdom, and lack of national economic power. But there was an over-riding, greater fear of it built on centuries of tradition and such poor moral or ethical conduct in the marketplace that many traders and merchants were considered nothing more than common thieves.

When the inexorable change developed, officialdom often reacted violently. The first English weaving factories in the 1600's were outlawed by the king. In France, imports of printed calico which threatened the domestic industry drew drastic measures, resulting in many deaths.

Steeped in opulence for the few and poverty for the many, fears of newness and of domestic ambitions, the Middle Ages were scarcely ready for the striving for profit or for the spirit of commercial venture. But that movement was already astir.

Was that era, the fulcrum centuries between ancient and modern times, less moral than others? One would certainly think so on reading Boccaccio and Chaucer, even Shakespeare. But Will Durant, in his monumental *Story of Civilization*, offers this picture of the business morality of the time:

> Despite a thousand guild and municipal statutes and penalties, medieval craftsmen often deceived purchasers with shoddy products, false measures and craft substitutes. Some bakers stole small portions of dough under their customers' eyes by means of a trap door in the kneading board; cheap cloths were secretly put in the place of better cloths promised and paid for; inferior leather was "doctored" to look like the best; stones were concealed in sacks of hay or wool sold by weight; the meat packers

of Norwich were accused of "buying measly pigs and making from them sausages and puddings unfit for human bodies." Bertholds of Regensburg (*c.* 1220) described the different forms of cheating used in the various trades and the tricks played upon country folk by merchants at the fairs. Writers and preachers condemned the pursuit of wealth, but a medieval German proverb said, "All things obey money"; and some medieval moralists judged the lust for gain stronger than the urge of sex. Knightly honor was often real in feudalism, but the thirteenth century was apparently as materialistic as any epoch in history. These examples of chicanery are drawn from a great area and time; though such instances were numerous they were presumably exceptional; they do not warrant any larger conclusion than that men were no better in the Age of Faith than in our age of doubt, and that in all ages law and morality have barely succeeded in maintaining social order against the innate individualism of men never intended by nature to be law-abiding citizens.

Within the next four centuries, the accomplishments of men and the thrust of events, Calvin, the great English, French, Spanish, and Portuguese explorers, Franklin and the first group of American merchant bankers and traders, as well as the Industrial Revolution, wrought sweeping changes that created the environment for modern business and commercial practices.

But it would be an oversimplification, a presumption that accomplishments are full-born of themselves, if one were to conclude that this foundation was laid in just three or four centuries.

The fact is that human achievements are built on a series of previous steps taken by people who strove, stumbled, fell, and started all over again to repeat the process, ad infinitum, throughout history. Each turn of the cycle, however, added some new knowledge, a bit of experience, a touch of skill to the fund of achievement.

It may strike deeply at modern man's vanity, but there

are historians and sociologists who are convinced that numerous of man's early accomplishments, charted against the then current degree of knowledge, were equal in achievement to any of our own era.

Perhaps it is a far cry from the Paleolithic hunter's flint weapons, with which he foraged for living food, to today's sophisticated management techniques or the financial devices of the "conglomerators," but their only difference is fifty thousand years of economic and social experience.

Man learned from the progress of his predecessors but the strange thing is that the principle is hardly one guaranteed to all men, any more than it is that all men will learn equally. As historians like to point out, different peoples living at the same time develop at different tempos, depending on their customs, environment, and opportunities. Even today, there are in the world examples of peoples existing at virtually every level of civilization.

The culture, subsistence level, and behavior patterns of natives in the remote areas of Brazil are vastly different from that of the sophisticates of Rio de Janeiro. An example more close at home is the condition of the American Indians on their reservations in the United States today compared with the daily environment of even the middle-class family in Dallas, San Francisco, or New York.

Facing a hostile world and having only a limited means of surviving in it, prehistoric man was forced to put all his efforts on survival. From the Paleolithic Age (which ranged from man's earliest years to about ten thousand years ago), through the Neolithic Age (from 8,000 B.C. to about the fifth millenium B.C.), to the Age of Copper (from the fifth to the fourth millenium), man's daily existence was dedicated to combating the elements, the wild life, and to having a cave over his head.

During those millenia, he learned to control fire and to

produce it when he wanted to. He added bones and ivory to his hard, stone tools. He learned not just to subsist on his own fat through the cruel seasons but to store food away in horns and skins. Eventually, he fell upon using hooks and lines for catching fish. He domesticated the dog to help him hunt.

He learned the principle of the lever and the fulcrum to move heavy weights. He devised ways of transporting his goods on land by dragging them on poles, or pulling them on sledges and he developed a crude form of boat to move on water. Then as the last glaciers receded and oases were created with river basins and forests more temperate than anything he had known, man entered into the agricultural era. He grew grain and tamed animals to serve as beasts of burden and to be his food.

With his survival efforts less desperate, early man turned to measures of security. Tools were improved; earthen pots were shaped for storage; new forms of clothes were developed to replace the scarce and uncomfortable animal hides.

It is probable that prehistoric man took the biggest strides toward his survival and security during the Age of Copper. Men in the Age of Copper "were to witness still further changes which were to revolutionize man's economic existence," points out Shepard B. Clough, in *The Economic Development of Western Civilization*.

The most important of these innovations were the development of a technology of smelting and of working copper and later tin and lead; the growth of trade and the perfecting of instruments of exchange, the most important of which was money; the effecting of a greater division of labor than had ever been realized before; and the founding of more and larger settlements. Emerging in the Eastern lands, these economic developments opened up a vast, new horizon for a civilized, self-sufficient man.

2. MONEY, THE ROOT OF CHANGE

DURING the Bronze Age (approximately 4000 to 2000 B.C.), a great and tangible lure was created by the invention of money.

"Money . . ." says Professor Clough, "was one of the most important inventions of all time in that it greatly facilitated the exchange of goods and thus a division of labor . . ."

Money—money—money. The word quickly became a magnet to many ("Gold is a wonderful thing," said Columbus) and anathema to others (thus, the phrase "filthy lucre"). Professor Clough was right, of course, in his projection of the impact of money on the economics of civilization but no such symbol of man's striving to uplift himself or, for that matter, of his greed, could possibly have escaped the scorn of moralists, doctrinaires, and social historians. The Welsh Utopian Socialist, Robert Owen, wanted it abolished. John Maynard Keynes, the economist most identified with the John F. Kennedy program of a welfare society, warned of the "fetish of gold."

Inevitably, after the successive use of cattle, stones, shells, ivory, wampum, beads, tobacco, furs, and dried fish, more manageable objects had to be adopted as mediums of exchange. Gold, silver, and copper were used because the metals were generally held to be valuable. They were also desirable because it was simple to handle them; they were portable and easily divisible. State coinage is said to have started in Lydia (now Turkey) in the seventh century. Paper money was first used about three hundred years ago, according to most authorities, but this is disputed by some.

As the money-form came into greater use during the second and first millenia, the practice of banking and the charging of interest arose. In a particular sense, money was only the rough clay which was molded by the developing monetary system. Those who were either opportunistic enough or especially inclined toward the handling of money acted as guardians of others' funds. They were happy to pay for the privilege of lending it at a profit to others who used it to further their own ventures and business endeavors.

This practice is clearly one of those monumental occurrences that could only emerge from a painfully slow series of steps taken by man throughout history.

But, on it, the whole world turns today.

In the same millenia, 4000 to 2000 B.C., the Bronze Age, writing was developed. This took the successive forms of pictograms, hieroglyphs (conventional signs), ideograms (symbols for ideas), phonograms (audible values to objects and thoughts), and, ultimately, in 1900 B.C., the alphabet itself. As Professor Clough points out, all of these seem, from the archeological information available, to stem from economic activity. The earliest forms of writing and of numbers came from the keeping of records of business transactions.

The Bronze Age man, his brain flexing from a curious blend of expanding knowledge and a developing instinct, sensed that certain conditions were necessary to achieve the desired results even though he did not understand what these conditions were. He began a protracted search and the answers came, hard-earned and yet not fully learned.

For one thing, lines, curves, angles were different from each other, but they had a mutual relationship. They were finite things, like the earth and the heavens. For another thing, five objects of any type always constituted five, ten always ten. He could always count by creating a groove on the surface of a rock or perhaps counting on his fingers. Thus, he reasoned, there was a constant world within a changing world.

The result of these deliberations and discoveries led to the amazing accuracy in the building of monuments in Egypt, to the discovery of astronomy and the measurement of time, the development of the calendar, to architecture, and to early forms of musical notation.

That age was not to end without one more significant discovery, that of iron-making. Up to that point, tools and weapons made of copper and bronze were available only to the rich and they grew richer and more powerful because of it. The subsistence and economic gap was wide between the very wealthy class and the very poor class of slaves and serfs.

But both groups, for different reasons, the rich for their indolence and hedonism and the poor because they had insufficient leisure or resources or incentive, failed to generate any unusual efforts toward economic growth.

The discovery of iron, however, changed all this. This relatively cheap metal, with all its manifold applications, came into wide use by 1100 B.C. in Greece and Syria, and soon spread to other lands. Iron, unlike the two earlier metals, was available almost everywhere. Its usage extended into agriculture, crafts, and industry, providing greater speed of operation, more economy and flexibility. The first iron saw came in in 500 B.C. and augers and planes by 50 B.C.

3. PARALLELS: CIVILIZATION AND ECONOMICS

At this stage in the history of economics, or the story of man—the two are essentially the same—the pendulum of fate was swinging in the direction of Greece. For the next 1,200 years, this primarily agricultural economy, a land about the size of New York State, would absorb much of the learning and the skills of the Mideast, create a unique body of knowledge and moral doctrine, and reach a level of civilization that would serve the future such as no other would. That is, until 146 B.C., when the Romans conquered the land of olive oil, wine, and Aristotle.

Yet, Europe, even Greece, was late on the calendar of civilization. "Europeans were by no means the pioneers of human civilization," observe R. R. Palmer and Joel Cotton, in *A History of the Modern World*, adding:

> Half of man's recorded history had passed before anyone in Europe could read or write. The priests of Egypt began to keep written records between 4000 and 3000 B.C., but more than two thousand years later the poems of Homer were still being circulated in the Greek city-states by word of mouth. Shortly after 3000 B.C., while the pharaohs were building the first pyramids, Europeans were creating nothing more distinguished than huge garbage heaps. Ironically, like the pyramids, they still endure and are known to archeologists as "kitchen middens."
>
> At the time when the Babylonian king, Hammurabi, about 2000 B.C., caused the laws of a complex society to be carved on stone, the most advanced Europeans were peoples like the Swiss Lake Dwellers, simple agriculturalists who lived in shelters built over the water to protect themselves from beasts and men. . . .

From an agricultural country, Greece transformed herself into a producer of specialized industrial goods and the creator of perhaps history's greatest works of art. Her exports grew and her home market expanded. Among all her citizens there was a fair degree of equality and for a long period only a relatively small core of slaves. Some manufacturing enterprises employed sizable numbers of workers, ranging to one hundred.

The accumulation of wealth unfolded great opportunity for leisure, philosophical meditation, intellectual growth, and devotion to the arts. ". . . It is not without significance," writes Professor Clough, "that the height of Greek civilization came at the period of greatest economic growth, that is, between 600 and 400 B.C."

The logical relationship between a nation's economics and the state of its intellectual life is also stressed by Professor Durant in his massive study of civilization. Writing on "Work and Wealth in Athens" in *The Life of Greece,* he notes:

> At the base of this democracy and this culture lies the production and distribution of wealth. Some men can govern states, seek truth, make music, carve statues, paint pictures, write books, teach children, or serve the gods because others toil to grow food, weave clothing, build dwellings, mine the earth, make useful things, transport goods, exchange them, or finance their production or their movement. Everywhere this is the foundation. . . .

However, the future of Greece, as well as the Hellenistic East and the Roman civilization, was due to darken because the society and its economic concepts held the seeds of self-decay. Greece's industrial and agricultural techniques were adopted by other developing lands. The resulting decline in its own production, a lack of political integration which cut the size of its domestic market, and a series of invasions wiped away Greece's economic superiority for all time. The age of light had dimmed.

4. ROMAN GLORY, ROMAN DECAY

THE Romans' succession was partially due to their absorbing many techniques and skills that had originated in Greece or from earlier Etruscan culture. Rome enjoyed an economic surplus in the first millenium from expanded agriculture and from a varied manufacturing industry, including military and agricultural equipment, pottery, pots and pans. Later, when the Roman Empire swallowed up Syria, Greece, Egypt, Carthage, and Macedonia, its rulers used their political power to provide economic spoils. By receiving tribute in various ways and obtaining important raw materials that Romans did not have, the cities of Rome prospered.

As in the case of Greece, the zenith of Roman attainment in the arts and letters came at the end of Augustus Caesar's reign or about when the empire's economic health was most robust.

Roman business life was busy, colorful, pungent. Peddlers hawked all manner of wares in country and city. Auctioneers served as town criers and dealt in lost goods and runaway slaves. Small merchants of all kinds sold food, silks, gifts, and handicrafts, zealously bargaining and freely cheating the public. There were many shops that made their own goods and sold them direct to the public. Dockside wholesalers sold goods, either at retail or wholesale, from newly arrived ships. Daily markets and occasional fairs, which offered the populace the products of the world, were a vital element in commercial life.

Roman industry was marked by advances in market expansion and demand, rather than by any fundamental improvements in organization or technology. Producers were widely dispersed, because of the hardship and expense of transporting goods across the breadth and length of the empire.

Romans pursued money madly. The richest were businessmen, many favored by the emperors. There were many bankers, performing varied roles as money-changers, issuers of travelers' checks, lenders, and investors. The currency was reliable. Even a panic in 33 A.D., which came from a tightening of money after an excessive circulation, only temporarily stunted the greedy race.

The decay that crumbled Rome came from deeply fundamental sources, representing a rottenness at the very core. These were the concentration of land in vast estates known as the *latifundia*. Absent proprietors luxuriated in the cities while first their slaves toiled on the estates in abject misery and later their workers existed on a bare subsistence. Skills were exported to conquered territories, and this resulted in competition to Rome. Other causes were the all-too familiar reluctance to make economic investment; social unrest as disillusion set in and unemployment rose; unwise handling of territorial economies resulting in a decline of production and refusal to pay tribute; and attacks by frontier barbarians who had painstakingly scouted Roman know-how in industry and warfare.

History always reveals the same human traits, it seems, regardless of the age. In Rome, as in Greece, Egypt, and Alexandria, and in many later economic and cultural centers, the conscience of the citizens became the conscience of their government and of their society. In the ancient civilizations, despite all that they have contributed to our present, indolence, insufficient interest in future planning, hedonism, arrogance, and selfishness earmarked one downfall after another.

5. PROFIT RAISES THE BLINDS

IF that is the case—if people and their governments permitted self-destructive forces to undermine the economic base of their countries, and continuing social disdain for the profit motive made the trader an outcast—what changes transformed the Old World from a rule-by-dictum, rule-by-tradition society to the tense, creative, frenetically productive society of today?

The changes were massive, evolutionary, inexorable.

If today's wheeling-dealing "conglomerator" who buys and sells companies from a telephone in an office were to have been born in the year 1000, he probably would have been hung by an outraged society. Of course, had he been born then, he would never have had the opportunity to follow his natural bent in a manner even remotely like his present one. His type would not be allowed to exist within organized society.

In the early centuries of the Middle Ages, the greatest trading dynamism was evident mainly among those who lived on the fringes of society or who successfully flaunted their independence by traveling fast and lightly, greasing the right palms and skillfully seeming to be what they were not.

They were a varied crew: Salvagers of shipwrecks who traded on the spoils of the sea. Merchants at the fairs who bought cheaply and sold dearly, moving swiftly from one town to another. Usurers extracting illegal rates of interest. Factory masters who often fled from the wrath of guilds and governments. Peddlers living a grubby, desolate existence, dealing in a rag-tag of goods, some eking out only a livelihood while others became rich.

Through the twelfth century, the feudal system kept a balance between those who ruled and those who toiled. Obedience was absolute. Harsh punishment was meted out to those who misbehaved. The agrarian life and the urban tempo were relatively calm, as yet undisturbed by contrary philosophies, liberal-minded politicians, or economic zealots. If one arose, he was either quickly stilled or forced to maintain only a hazardous existence. Life, at least on the surface, was bucolically content—despite grinding poverty and deprivation just outside the manorial walls.

Yet, by the year 1000, a good deal of western Europe's economy was in a state of decay. A rigid land system, a lack of economic planning and order, and production of goods for immediate than for future use had darkened the outlook for both self-sustainment and growth.

Between 1100 and 1300, some of the convulsive changes were already at work, reviving the economic pulse and creating a brighter aspect for the future.

The greatest, single evolutionary movement was probably the emergence of a type of nationalism through centralized monarchies that resulted from feudal wars. Restraints on internal trade were removed. Customs were standardized or liberalized, permitting easier commerce within the borders of a monarchy. The nationalistic spirit spurred royal subsidies and patronage for industries that had won favor.

Rulers who gradually saw that their salvation lay in competing on a regional or continental basis with other, emerging nations took a paternal interest in fostering common laws, common currency, common measurement and weights. Bowing to the enthusiasm of explorers like da Gama, Drake, and Columbus, they encouraged foreign adventure, exploration, and the taking of valuable spoils from across the seas.

Shipbuilding and navigation had improved steadily since Roman days. The strong sense that the opening of the New World might mean a new era spread strongly across Europe, despite the many scoffers and cynics who masked their fear of the unknown with ridicule.

As it gradually became unshackled, commerce began to bind Europe in a web of trade routes connecting with Africa and Asia.

But, as industry developed, transport seemed to progress least. Waterways remained popular and led in the movement of goods. Natural power was slowly being harnessed through the use of water mills. Pressure mounted for the production of better farm and industrial tools, textile equipment, and more utilitarian and sophisticated consumer goods. The development of these to meet the demand resulted in the Industrial Revolution.

The more liberal attitude toward commerce which was ushered in with the Italian Renaissance, the rise of Protestantism, and the concepts of Calvin probably had greater significance in the years that followed than can be properly measured. The extent of the change in the Church's dubious view of the merchant was clear, however.

The building of economic power, either by the individual, or by a community, was not considered to be necessarily selfish. One's life on earth could be full and replete with comforts, provided one honored God spiritually and materially, the ecclesiastics were now saying. In this way, the profit motive, hopefully pursued without gluttony or immorality, gradually became respectable.

Today, it may be added parenthetically, this attitude has blossomed forth into an ambitious entry into commercial endeavors by the Church itself. The Catholic Church in Europe and in the United States has large real estate and industrial holdings. Only a few years ago, reports were current that a midwestern diocese of the Catholic Church in America was attempting to acquire a concern named Cohen! Hebrew and Lutheran church organizations in the United States own property and make investments of their funds to build up their treasuries. In Salt Lake City, the Mormon Church has a large holding in the city's largest department store and has extensive other commercial interests in the area.

Irony often crops up in history. The Crusades, for example, which were then the Church's greatest expression of courage and adventure, helped to shift the attitude of European society away from the traditional disfavor of trade. As the horde of zealot-knights fanned across Europe into the East and met the wealth, the incenses and the lushness, and the urbanity of Byzantium, their parched and ascetic senses became inflamed.

Alternately fleecing and being fleeced, the Crusaders brought back not only spoils but new ideas, and a vivid sense of the more brilliant, if not the more civilized life. The Crusades' influence was to send a fresh, piquant breeze of zest for a fuller existence across the still rural enclaves of Europe.

6. THE GUILDS COME AND GO

AN economic phenomenon that lasted for almost two hundred years was the *hanse,* which is German for union or guild. The Hanseatic League was the most important economic alliance founded in the twelfth to fourteenth centuries. This particular guild was formed by twenty-four commercial towns of northern Europe to protect themselves from highwaymen, pirates, changes in currencies, tax collectors, varying tolls, and lagging debtors. Their objective was also to hold an international fort against external economic competition and to offer social friendship for visiting merchants. In the fourteenth century, the league had fifty-two town members and controlled the mouths of all the great European rivers that connected Central Europe to the North and Baltic seas.

It established courts to settle disputes among its members; enacted laws regulating the commerce and moral conduct of its cities and residents; protected merchants from unfavorable laws, taxes, and fines; established factories or trading posts in each member city. It even waged wars as an independent power.

But the Hanseatic League became tyrannical, an oppressor, forcing new memberships by boycotting, hiring pirates to hurt a rival's efforts, organizing itself as a state within a state. It became a monopoly feared by the artisans who supplied its wares but found that they were being oppressed instead.

As a result, the league was doomed by its own tactics and by new leagues that arose in competition.

New guilds emerged from a tide of human traffic trudging along those roads that stretched across the Continent and to the south and far east. Where these itinerant merchants, these merchant adventurers, these leather faced, red-eyed thin-lipped precursors of today's road salesmen came to rest were ultimately developed new trading places. As these areas evolved into new towns, they, along with the growth of medieval cities under the spur of expanding commerce, became integral parts of the urbanization of the time.

A slow process this was, the birth of new towns. It was delayed by the surrendering of fealty and power by the vested rulers of the time. While often near the walls of the manor, the trading posts existed outside them, not merely in physical terms but in relation to their independence as economic units, local political blocs and enclaves with their own laws. Gradually, as these towns grew unchecked, by necessity, the more affluent of the merchants assumed the power virtually by default on the part of the lords. Those inside the manors were convinced that the world of power and obedience would revolve inside their walls.

Evidence of this unrealistic attitude prevails in many European cities today, in Scandinavia, and in Russia, where the tourist can easily see it. Many a castle, a fortress, a manor stands forlornly, darkly enclosed within a sprawling metropolis that grew up around it on all sides.

Within the budding towns, the guilds flourished. First, there were the merchant guilds, a throwback to the old Roman *collegia,* and then the craft guilds, formed to counteract the monopolistic tendencies of the others.

So, by the twelfth century, local groups in Germany that had arisen to provide mutual help, religious activity, and holiday observance emerged as either trade or craft guilds. In Italy, cities such as Florence had guilds of clothiers, bankers, physicians, silk dealers, furriers, and armorers. By the thirteenth century, almost every sizable English town had one or more guilds.

More specialized but geared to the same protective objectives as the town guild or league, such as the Hanseatic, the merchant guilds were composed of only independent merchants or master workmen. All those not self-dependent were not admitted. These guilds exerted political influence, managed to restrict entry of outside goods by high tariffs, or set prices on such goods that was allowed to enter. Trade monopolies were obtained from a monarch or a lord. The guild

masters set their own prices and adjusted them at will. They
bought raw material wholesale, insured themselves against
losses, regulated wages, hours, working conditions, and apprenticeship rules. By common consent in the interest of accumulating power, they also held strong sway over the personal lives of their members and of their workmen.

The pressures the merchant guilds exerted resulted, in
great measure, in the rise of craftsmen's guilds, beginning
in the twelfth century. Fullers, goldsmiths, tanners, and weav-
ers formed their own guilds in the English cities. Soon, they
seemed to be everywhere—one hundred in Paris, fifty-eight
in Venice, thirty-three in Genoa. Each craftsman sought to
align in protective association with the specific artisans of
his own kind—in carpentry, there were at least six different
specialist's categories, each with his own guild, and there
were at least that many in the leather crafts.

The craft guilds, too, became overly restrictive and tyrannical. They limited master's permits to sons of masters. They
continually raised barriers to membership. And they pro-
hibitively underpaid journeymen, who insisted on revolting.

Those alliances were products of their times, yet of immense influence on the stability of that emerging industrial
age. They were, however, still medieval in their thinking and
practices. They permitted no freedom of enterprise, no new
technical gains or competition of price or product. When the
financial and banking communities caught up with the commercial opportunities in the fourteenth and fifteenth centuries, the guild masters found the power of their dicta and the
control of the market conditions slipping from their grasp.

7. THE RISE OF THE MONEY-LENDERS

MONEY was gradually becoming a stable commodity in this
age of commercial and industrial expansion. But it was hardly
a smooth transition. In the twelfth century, the English king,

Henry, ruled that all counterfeiters ("mint-men") should lose their right hands and their testicles. And, although numerous monarchs ordered harsh treatment, even boiling alive, for counterfeiters and those who saved coins for the metals, the kings themselves often debased their national moneys.

Even at the end of the Middle Ages, Europe's economy was in a turmoil because of widely different currencies. But, in the thirteenth century, first Italy and then other European countries minted gold coins. By the century's end, all major European countries except England had stable gold coinage. England achieved that state in 1343.

The Church was the largest single source of money. But loans by Church bodies were mostly to persons, monarchs, or institutions having financial problems. Farmers, for example, were aided so that they could modernize their farms. Monasteries gave mortgage loans to lords and obtained a share in the money that the properties earned.

Commercial credit began, however, when a family or an affluent person "entrusted" money to a trader or a merchant for a special project and got a portion of the profits.

This sort of "partnership" flourished in Italy. As Professor Durant notes, "So useful a way of sharing in profits without directly contravening the ecclesiastical prohibition of interest was bound to spread; and the company (*com-panis*, bread-sharer) or family investment became a *societas*, a partnership in which several persons, not necessarily kin, financed a group or series of ventures rather than one."

So, it was not the Church, but the financier—the professional and the banking family—who supplied the basic financial wherewithal for a new venture or a new company. From a moneychanger, the professional had evolved into a money-lender and then into an investment banker. In Italy, powerful banking families developed their investment banking activities to heights and skills not previously known.

These families, known as the "Lombards," became immensely powerful during the middle of the thirteenth century and were widely hated and feared. They made exorbitant profits, but rendered at least two important services. They extended a financial lifeline that businessmen needed in a difficult time. And these wealthy Italians developed and refined their operations so that these became the forerunners of the banking system of today.

Much of today's financial lexicography contains terms that emanates from the Italians, such as *credito* and *debito, disconto, netto,* and *banco rotta* (bankruptcy).

Two other financial practices, due to become important props in today's money society, also began in the Middle Age's declining years. In 1157, the Venetian government issued the first government bonds. Also, in the thirteenth century, insurance came into use.

For all this, however, there remained one big obstacle in the financing of commercial growth. Interest—the lender's spur—was forbidden by Church doctrine. Even though the laws of Rome had legalized interest, the councils of the Catholic Church and almost all its popes threatened excommunication to usurers.

Nonetheless, despite the prohibitive laws of governments backing the Church's position, the natural thrust of trade expansion and the growing availability of money resulted in a marriage that could not be denied. Under the blinking eyes of Church and State, the use of interest-bearing loans began to flourish. Political units engaged in war or other stringent situations simply decided it was wiser to borrow and pay interest than to tax an already overtaxed populace.

Nor were there apparently any restrictions on the amount of interest the trader, merchant, and industrialist paid at the close of the Middle Ages. In Italy, where the economy was prosperous and powerful, the rate was the lowest in Europe, 12½ per cent to somewhat higher. In England and France, the interest rate started at 33⅓ per cent and rose as high as 85 per cent. It was all due to the great risks, which were often not protected against by law. In later centuries, the usury and interest dropped as loans became safer and competition arose in the money markets.

The evolution of these financial doings required changes in the keeping of business accounts. The double-entry system of bookkeeping was probably adopted about the thirteenth century. It was soon followed by the bank check, which ultimately became society's second paper currency.

But the most dynamic new force was looming as the fifteenth century dawned—exploration and colonization. This outward movement, which opened the door on modern times, was stimulated by a missionary impulse, a search for greater trade and gold, and burgeoning nationalism.

8. LURE OF THE NEW WORLD

For three hundred years, the major exploring countries competed for commercial and political supremacy in America, first fiercely independent, then allying with one another, and then turning on each other.

The French fought the British. The Americans joined the British. Then the British and the Americans clashed swords and traded gun volleys in the bitter Revolutionary War. Others, such as the Portuguese, Spaniards, and Dutch proved much less capable of supporting and exploiting a large, overseas colonization. They surrendered a continent.

The victors, the British, however, had only slightly more than 150 years in which to call the American colonies their own. Almost from the time the first settlers touched ground on the new continent, many felt deep stirrings for personal and political freedom. This was heavily influenced by a yearning to be self-sustaining by freely partaking in the fruits and opportunities of the new land.

Their masters were more responsible for this than they realized. One doesn't deposit poor relatives in a verdant, ripe land, full of natural assets crying out for use and impose restrictions on their progress and freedom and make it stick. It couldn't work then anymore than it could today.

Had it been otherwise . . .

Three

---•---

SELF-MADE
IN AMERICA

1. WHENCE SUCH AS THESE?

THEY said he "had the soul of a bookkeeper." Yet, John D. Rockefeller, Sr., accumulated a personal fortune of $1 billion, the largest ever amassed by an American up to the time of his death.

When he expired in 1937, at ninety-seven, outliving both associates and opponents, the cadaverous, little man had been widely revered and widely despised, a subject of debate that endures to today.

A strange blend of religion, parsimony, and avarice, who plundered and yet gave away $600 million in philanthropy, he began life in an upstate New York rural area as one of five children born to an itinerant peddler of quack medicine and a pious evangelist mother.

Commodore Cornelius Vanderbilt, who breathed his last in bed in 1877 with his family gathered around him singing a hymn, had preceded Rockefeller as the wealthiest man who had ever lived in America.

He was born on a farm in Staten Island and died eighty-three years later just across the Hudson in Manhattan. In between, the tycoon of ferries and railroads accumulated more than $100 million, in a career marked by immoral conduct, greed, and swashbuckling initiative. He was perhaps more villified than any American entrepreneur up to that time.

Like Bernard Baruch decades later, Andrew Carnegie, a wizened, tiny Scotchman who "liked to manufacture steel, not securities," would sit in Central Park a few years before he died at eighty-four in 1919, conversing with whomever came along.

This complex, controversial figure, attacked on one hand as an exploiter of labor and on the other as an unscrupulous business competitor, was at the end of a career as perhaps America's greatest business innovator.

The son of a Scottish handloom weaver who emigrated here with his family to escape a depression and the introduction of the onerous power loom, young Carnegie came to America in 1848 to begin a career which was to establish the new country as the world leader in steel and which was to bequeath immense sums to education and charity.

Whence such as these?

Nowadays, when the likelihood of an American gross national product of perhaps $1,500 billion does not seem so far off, the country's early economic outlines seem remote indeed. It is only ten or eleven generations ago that the American colonies were a group of tiny, squalling, agrarian entities, sternly conscious of each other's boundaries and yet entirely dependent on British largess and foreign markets.

Between 1606 and 1790, when the colonists' dependency shifted from an external to an internal one with the rout of the British rule, the resulting opportunity for the individual invited the emergence of the prototype American traders and merchants.

The environment, the placenta, for the birth of such men was implicit in the very founding of colonial America. A yearning for religious, economic, and social freedom drove successive waves of colonists to the new shores, but, human nature being what it is, the stimulus was not wholly idealistic.

"Colonial culture reveals at the briefest glance a highly complex fusion of religious faith, political conviction, economic interest and social idealism," writes Professor Peter d'A. Jones, in *The Consumer Society, a History of American Capitalism.* "Yet, there may be some truth in the often-made claim that the nation was 'founded as a business enterprise' and that the early history of American society can be explained in terms of the given relationship among the economist's 'factors of production' (physical resources, labor and capital)."

Private business enterprise was instrumental in the settlement of the Atlantic Coast of the new land, he notes. Virginia's colonization was a business concept. It was planned and executed by a joint-stock company, an economic enterprise for profit, and a capital investment effort by a private corporation.

"Of the two expeditions authorized by royal charter in 1606," Professor d'A. Jones writes, "the men who went to Jamestown succeeded where the men who tried the Maine Coast failed largely because the former had superior economic organization and the backing of the City of London capitalists."

Just prior to the Jamestown expedition, the Stuart era in England was one of great ferment. The violent, totalitarian characteristics of seventeenth-century political life in England, exemplified by the beheading of many of the greatest public and royal figures of the time, struck down much

of man's faith in man. Sir Walter Raleigh and Charles I
had followed Sir Thomas More to the scaffold, after which
Oliver Cromwell's body was disinterred and also hung. The
persecuted began to run and some fled to Massachusetts.

"Society [at the beginning of the Stuart era] was in the
throes of a deep-seated transformation in agriculture, manufacturing, commerce . . . and religion," says Jonathan Hughes,
in his book, *The Vital Few.*

"Economic change was a political phenomenon since everywhere it contended with the creaking apparatus of economic
controls," he writes. "Economic change also had religious consequences because the non-conforming Puritans found ready
adherents in those sectors of the economy, especially in the
rising manufacturing towns and districts, where economic
self-interest was not in accord with Crown laws and the
Crown's devoted supporter, the Anglican Church."

The results of these conflicts were far-reaching for the
American settlements established in the seventeenth century,
notes Professor Hughes. He cites George Macaulay Trevelyan's contention that the medieval serfs of France or Spain
could never have built a dynamic empire capable of self-
government. But the early English settlers in America were
something else again: ". . . the English colonial movement
was the migration of a modern society, self-governing, half
industrial, awake to economic and intellectual change," said
Trevelyan, an outstanding historian.

Adds Professor Hughes: "The Pilgrim fathers, for example,
came primarily from English villages long freed from feudal
backwardness. Penn's Quakers, tradesmen and craftsmen, men
of commerce and industry, as well as independent farmers
needed only a free soil in which to flourish. England had
already prepared them for self-government, even the convicts
sent in irons."

The expanding social and religious horizons combined
with the unfolding physical aspect of the New World to fan

the hopes of the early colonists. Professor d'A. Jones points out that the economic motivation and organization cannot be claimed as a full and ample "explanation" or "even most of what there is to say about the early settlement of North America. . . .

"Venture capital and the technique of joint-stock business enterprise take the historian only so far. What about the inspiration of Sir Thomas More's Utopia, for example, and the beauty of John Donne's sermons, in which England becomes a bridge or gallery joining the New and the Old World to each other and to the everlasting Kingdom of Heaven? . . ."

The colonies were shy of people, currency, equipment, and much other than necessities. But the worst shortages were in labor and capital goods. And there was too much land, too much distance, and too many resources for the colonists to absorb and to develop properly.

Most of their tools came from abroad. Specialized skills were few and far between. And markets were missing. Canada took even longer to mature for many of the same reasons.

As the colonies received the influx of new and varied nationalities, now the Dutch and now the Germans, and the ethnic mix showed signs of what was to come, inter-colony trade began to flourish, often reflecting the national strains and the homogeneity of product. Exports of basic goods went to England in return for manufactured goods. Foodstuffs were shipped to the West Indies. Two-masted vessels made daring forays to southern Europe, testing the anger of the British authorities. These burgeoning efforts of colonial trade denoted a feeling of growing economic strength, but beneath the surface, they indicated also a desire to be freed from the restrictive dependence on the mother country.

Discords that split the colonists only aggravated this sense of frustration. The dissension involved disputes on boundaries, hostility between the money-lenders and the money-hungry rural settlers, and the beginnings of a class consciousness that stirred feelings between economic groups.

A class apart as yet was the indigenous trader or merchant, who exerted a cohesive influence on the shifting socioeconomic climate. A visionary but with his eye fixed on the profit motive, he presaged the investment banker and the merchant-entrepreneur of a century and two later, dealing in real estate, banking, insurance, shipping, bartering, and even international finance.

"The creation of the great landed estates was accompanied by the slow trader and merchant. Necessarily, they first established themselves in the sea ports where business was concentrated," writes Gustavus Myers, in his *History of the Great American Fortunes.*

"Many obstacles long held them down to a narrow sphere," Myers says. "The great chartered companies monopolized the profitable resources. The land magnates exacted tribute for the slightest privilege granted. Drastic laws forebade competition with the companies, and the power of law and the severities of class government were severely felt by the merchants. . . ."

In a straining atmosphere of an instinct for self-reliance pushing against a framework of severe dependence on an often indifferent, often bemused England, revolution stirred.

Severe navigation laws, royal civil servants who were dishonest and greedy, summary legislation, and discriminatory trading edicts brought the seething discontent to a boil. The eight-year war thrust the new federation of states into an era of virtually complete self-dependence long before it was ready for it.

If the War of the Revolution hurt the principal merchants on the Atlantic seaboard but stimulated manufacturers who were remote from the areas of fray, it soon brought severe inequities to the class structure. In his massive tract to describe the tactics and mores of the founders of "The Great American Fortunes," Myers said:

> Despite the lofty sentiments of the Declaration of Independence—sentiments which were submerged by the propertied class when the cause was won—the gravity of the law bore wholly in favor of the propertied interests. . . . The common man was good enough to shoulder a musket in the stress of war, but that he should have rights after the war, was deemed absurd. . . . The Revolution brought no immediate betterment to his (the worker's) conditions; such slight amelioration as came later was the result of years of agitation. No sooner was the Revolution over than in stepped the propertied interests and assumed control of government functions. They were intelligent enough to know the value of class government—a lesson learned from the tactics of the British trading class. . . .

The point is not much disputed by historians. The new democracy was in a terrible period of flux and danger. Charles Beard noted that the Constitution guarded the rights of a wealthy minority who formed pressure groups in every state. Slavery was encouraged, if not perpetuated, but other forms of property rights were protected.

Problems mounted. Tariffs between colonies were removed but the war debt remained immense and unpaid. A flood of currency emanated from the states to derive revenue and a rapid devaluation followed. Federal debt foreclosures brought Shays' Rebellion in 1786, an abortive attempt to close the courthouses by force. Unity was deterred by a weak form of federal executive structure.

But, through the turmoil of peace emerged some measure of economic freedom. A national economy, at least the framework of one, began to take some shape. Class-protective inheritance laws were wiped out, as were the feudal form of payments to landed proprietors. The church and state relationship, British model, was severed.

And, in the midst of it all, rose the men who were to be the nation's traders and financiers, big and small, many protected by the remaining vestiges of British class tradition. Others, rustic, shabby, with fever in their eyes, thrust themselves up through the wide rents in the old socio-economic fabric.

As early as 1835, De Tocqueville was to write in *Democracy in America:*

> The United States of America have only been emancipated for half a century from the state of colonial dependence in which they stood to Britain: the number of large fortunes there is small and capital is still scarce. Yet no people in the world have made such rapid progress in trade and manufacture as the Americans; they constitute at the present day the second maritime nation in the world; and although their manufactures have to struggle with almost insurmountable natural impediments, they are not prevented from making great and daily advances. . . .

After the victorious War of Independence, some 4 million artisans, farmers, workmen, and small traders were suddenly treading shoulder-high in the glorious future of freedom that they had yearned for and won. For more than one hundred years, they were to stumble over themselves, coping with a country and a destiny that in resources and scope were vastly larger than they could possibly adapt to, much less master.

Few were equipped to become their own men, entrepreneurs, even small ones, or, for that matter, to employ others. Handicrafts were the rule, the weaving of cloth, making furniture or pottery in the home. In between the farms, here and there a tiny 'factory' turned its paltry machinery. Travel and transportation proceeded slowly and inexorably by horse-post, ox-cart, river boat.

Amidst the grinding poverty and the burdens of the new self-reliance, land ownership became the basis for the start of large fortunes, mainly in Pennsylvania, New York, and Virginia. Thus, the sons of William Penn, who had received his grants from the king, succeeded to vast wealth. But great land grants on the Atlantic seaboard also went for bribes. In the northern states, shipping accounted for other great fortunes. Such members of the Continental Congress as Samuel Adams, Robert Morris, and John Hancock were either ship merchants or the affluent descendants of shipowners.

Aristocrats who strove to be democrats talked in lofty terms in the new village of Washington or in the drawing rooms or verandas in palatial homes in Virginia and Boston. Harsh, autocratic rule, so long the nature of European monarchy, was to be eschewed in the Republic. And the new Americans, faced by the uncertainties of every-day life and by the greater unknowns of the future, listened eagerly to the words, though many could hardly envision their existence in a state so idealistically described.

But one ideal the poor could surely see, even touch. The great sweep of land, the sea of green, the rolling hills, and the endless forests excited the passions of the eternally indigent and the wandering who poured in from Europe. Hard work, ambition, frugality, devotion, courage—the new land seemed the proper place for the exercise of these simple but most admirable of human traits and they were demonstrated anew in the heady climate of political freedom and pragmatic idealism.

Ben Franklin captured the mood of the moment: "Without industry and frugality, nothing will do and with them, everything. . . ."

As the federation's efforts stumbled toward a national economic unity, benefitting from the removal of inter-state duties and tolls, its shipping and exports grew, too. France and particularly England, however, resented the increasing number of Yankee brigantines that sailed into their traditional trading ports. Rather than leaving the states free to trade with one or the other or both, the warring French and English independently restricted the export movements of American merchants. Embargoes against their trade inflicted a severe loss on the new economy.

The second victory against the British in 1815 ended two years of onerous blockade and warfare and created a new boom in export-import trade. It helped bring three new southern states into the union, enriching the Republic's land resources and national product.

Much that America was to become was already portended only a few years after the "Second War of Independence." With the growth of the domestic market, the opening of the West, the building of turnpike highways, the construction of the Erie Canal, and the arrival of the steamboat and the railroad, all within fifteen years after the war ended, opportunities for business and trading opened up virtually on every side.

2. THE FIRST TYCOONS

THE most alert men had not waited. They had watched briefly, hardly pausing in the midst of their own energetic activity and then they had leaped at the beckoning opportunities. Others, many others, were to follow.

A son of a clergyman, Robert Livingston, born in 1654, became one of the largest landgraves in the colonies and at one time owned a manor in New York State sixteen miles long and twenty-four miles wide. He was adept at sensing changes in the political winds and soon held even the governor of the state under his obligation. He loaned money at high rates. As a contractor to the Army, he earned enormous profits. Before he died in 1728, he became very pious but remained true to himself in all other ways. He left what was then a colossal fortune.

Robert Carter was the grandson of "King Carter," one of Virginia's most affluent landowners and planters. Living in the magnificent splendor of the very rich, young Carter combined a life of luxury with the management of sixty thousand acres, six hundred slaves, an iron-works, and a flour mill.

Although he mostly oversaw his domain from the finery and culture of his mansion, a structure seventy-six feet long and forty feet wide, he left a reputation as a humane man. Before he died in the early 1700's, he emancipated some of his slaves.

What was great wealth in the pre-Revolutionary era?

George Washington left one of the largest fortunes, totaling about $530,000, mostly in land. At the end of a long, productive life, Franklin was considered quite wealthy. His estate was estimated at about $150,000, also mostly in land. But, according to Gustavus Myers, an earlier lender and liquor merchant, Cornelius Steenwyck, died in 1686 leaving a total estate of £4,382 and a long list of unpaid claims which "disclosed that almost every man in New York City owed money to him, partly for rum, in part for loans."

Merchants who sent privateers around the world amassed some of the greatest fortunes. Israel Thorndike made his first one as a successful privateer and then invested the proceeds into a diverse group of enterprises, including fisheries, real estate, international trade, and manufacturing. He left in 1832 an estate worth about $4 million.

Eli Whitney justifiably should have realized a fortune from his invention of the cotton gin in 1793. It had a great beneficial effect on cotton growing in the South and in the export and shipping fields. But Whitney was besieged by patent infringements, unpaid claims, and excessive court costs to protect his patents. Finally, by becoming a contractor of fine arms, he realized comparative wealth.

3. GIRARD: MAN OF ANATHEMA

In his last year, Stephen Girard lived in the ruins of the blazing, cold resentment that he had created for himself over eight years.

Childless, a widower, immensely wealthy, yet hated for his

inhuman treatment of employees and his indifference toward his debtors and the Church, he remained a recluse in a shabby house on Philadelphia's Water Street. There, he threw himself into reading and rereading the classical tracts of Paine, Voltaire, and Rousseau and, from his window, spat out his defiance at a world he considered hypocritical and whining.

The great financier of the American cause in the War of 1812, the French-born, one-eyed shipowner and banker ran away from an unhappy home in Bordeaux when he was fourteen. He had a sour nature which came from an early loss of an eye and a conviction that his parents had sadly neglected him.

Escaping to the sea, he rose in nine years from cabin boy to mate and at twenty-two he was in command of a trading ship. At times, he profited by stocking and selling his own cargoes. When the War of the Revolution came, he found himself fogbound near the Atlantic Coast, sold his ship and opened a foodstuffs store in Philadephia.

Soon, he was secretly trading with the enemy and profiting while other merchants were suffering the war's effects. He rebounded from patriots' charges that he was aiding the British by reentering the shipping trade. After the war, vessels that he had named after such classicists as Diderot and Voltaire sailed between the states and the Caribbean. Each trip brought him substantial profits, mainly because of the daring ways in which he traded the cargo.

He invested $500,000 in the Bank of the United States, the financial institution that Alexander Hamilton had visualized and created on the model of the Bank of England. Girard became the bank's principal creditor when its charter ran out. He also purchased its building and acquired a controlling interest. In 1812, he renamed it the Girard Bank.

As his wealth grew, his power and sway over the wartime economy mounted. Retaining the officers of the old bank, his own institution became one of the most powerful in the nation. In 1814, he subscribed for almost 95 per cent of the war loan of $5 million. In the meantime, despite the embargo enforced by the British, his ships continued to trade successfully around the world.

Yet, as his influence and means swelled, he remained indomitably what he was at heart: a harsh creditor, a difficult and unrewarding employer, uncharitable and anti-Church, and eager only for the exploitation of new opportunities. The stumpy, thin-lipped tiny man, with his face contorted into a grimace to hide his sightless eye, became a figure of dread and awe everywhere.

Finally, the day after Christmas in 1831 after eighty-one years of a bitter battle with the world, it was over. No more was expected of him in death than in life. But he held on to the final initiative. Uncharitable and supremely egotistical all his life, he left his entire $10 million fortune to relatives, apprentices, servants, the city and the state, and mostly to found an orphan's college in Philadelphia which was named after him.

It did not take very long for the anathema in which he was universally held while he lived to turn posthumously to paeans of praise, respect, and admiration.

4. ASTOR: TRAPPER IN FURS AND REAL ESTATE

IN an eighty-four-year life span, John Jacob Astor's career went to unbelievable extremes. The German butcher's son, ensconsed in a large house at 223 Broadway in New York in the early 1800's, lived the sedate, affluent life of a great fur merchant and New York landholder. He ate dinner at 3 P.M. every day, then played several games of checkers, drank a glass of beer, and then trooped happily and heavily to bed.

But, across the continent, his name was reviled. There, the agents of his American Fur Company violated the laws with disdain and frightened military authorities by selling liquor to Indians not only at inflated prices but to swindle them of the furs they had trapped. Even complaints that reached all the way to the White House could not halt the practice.

In 1784, the short, stout, 21-year-old Astor arrived in New York and opened a store selling musical instruments. He gave that up and worked for a merchant, beating furs, but took time out to talk to trappers who came in to dispose of their furs. Two years later, he was in his own fur business. Soon, he traveled through the Mohawk Valley, buying skins directly from Indians. He made a contract with Canadian fur interests to ship furs direct to New York. In 1808, he obtained charters to establish the American Fur Company, setting up trading posts along the Missouri and Columbia rivers.

The trading gradually assumed wide, international proportions. All furs from the western interior and from coasting vessels were collected once a year and transported by an Astor ship to Canton, which then returned laden with Chinese goods. The Hawaiian islands and India were also made stops enroute.

As the Astor fortune mounted in tremendous leaps, he invested it in land, principally in New York City, and in Missouri, Iowa, and other western states. The revenues and values of his operations generated by 1847 a personal fortune of $20 million, by far the greatest of its time. Much of it was achieved through means that were highly criticized at the time. Astor would hold on to land that he bought and never sell it. The dynasty which he founded emulated his plan of allowing its properties to remain unimproved while surrounding buildings and plots rose in value. In time, the Astor tracts became immensely valuable because of the improvement of adjacent and nearby properties and then the family demanded its own terms and got them.

Three days after his death in 1848, the New York *Herald* said: "He added immensely to his riches by purchases of state stocks, bonds and mortgages in the financial crisis of 1836-1837. He was a willing purchaser of mortgages from needy holders at less than their face; and when they became due, he foreclosed on them, and purchased the mortgaged property at the ruinous prices which ranged at the time. . . ."

His son, William Backhouse Astor, received the bulk of Astor's fortune, becoming the head of the dynasty rather than an older, feeble-minded brother. A heavyset, unemotional man with small, watchful eyes, he was at fifty-six already the son of his father, possessing even before his assumption to the family fortune a personal wealth of $5 million. He was to follow in his father's footsteps as America's richest man and one of its largest landholders. At his death, the "landlord of New York," as he was known, left $100 million to his two sons.

5. VANDERBILT: THE COMMODORE OF SAIL AND RAIL

In the last fifteen years of his fantastic life, Cornelius Vanderbilt accumulated $90 million. This meant that starting in 1862, the second year of the Civil War, the sixty-eight-year-old "Commodore" began to earn $6 million a year, an astonishing sum for that time and not so paltry these days.

Already the possessor of a large fortune, the hulking, dour-faced Staten Islander had become one of the nation's most successful operators of steamboats, after running a fleet of schooners plying the Atlantic seaboard.

But, quite suddenly, perhaps because he saw the potential that the entrepreneur Daniel Drew had in his ability both to control and manipulate the stock of the Erie Railroad, Vanderbilt began using his fortune to gain control of the New York & Harlem Railroad. He paid $9 a share for as many shares as he could buy. His reputation as a "winner" and his inexpensive acquisition of a streetcar franchise along Broadway by bribing politicians caused the N.Y. & H. shares to jump to $50 in months and then to $90 in a year.

Within five years the old shipmaster acquired by methods widely condemned as dishonest and cruel two other railroads and merged them into the New York Central Railroad. Thus, he showed himself to be the railroad master of his time.

He was a brutally strong, uninhibited, and illiterate boy, who, according to Gustavus Myers, at twelve years "could scarcely write his own name . . . but he knew the ways of the water." His father, a plodding, unambitious, ferry-boat operator, exposed the boy to the ferry trade. Perhaps Cornelius obtained his love of money from his mother who carefully hoarded every penny she could in an old house clock.

At any rate, the young man saved devotedly and then built his own schooners. Soon, he sold his boats and became a captain of a steamboat working along the Atlantic Coast. The family income at that time was augmented by Cornelius's wife who ran a wayside tavern at New Brunswick. Besides this chore, she was to bear him nine children, live in terrible frugality amidst all his later wealth, and be eventually confined to an asylum.

Vanderbilt was the fiercest, most avaricious competitor of his era. Yet, he was admired for his courage and a sense of adventure in a country that raised those virtues to a mantle of national honor. But he was also reviled for his methods, his inhuman treatment of employees, stockholders, and fellow citizens.

Congress, which voted him a gold medal for his patriotism in the Civil War, heard a censure resolution against Vanderbilt when he was accused of chartering to the government unsafe ships at high fees. But the motion was defeated. Only his agent, J. J. Southard, was censured, although the evidence against the tycoon was indisputable.

Vanderbilt, who also sired one of America's great dynasties, was no less difficult and demanding on his own family than on opponents and strangers. He left the bulk of his $100 million fortune to a fawning older son; cut off a happy but profligate second son; married a gay divorcee of thirty when he was eighty; and departed the scene to leave a family dispute over his estate that raged for two years.

6. FISK: THE FIRST BUSINESSMAN-PLAYBOY

ONE of the lesser-known assassinations in American history occurred when a series of bullets was poured into the startled, corpulent body of James Fisk on the staircase of the Grand Central Hotel in New York on a December afternoon in 1872. The pistol was held by Edward S. Stokes, a former business associate. He was also, at that point, a blackmailer of Fisk's and a rival for the affections of Josie Mansfield, Fisk's mistress and a well-known actress of the time.

Fisk, a big, beefy, blond man with curling mustaches who liked to wear a velvet vest and several rings on his fingers, was the progenitor of a peculiarly American type. This is the flamboyant, fun-loving contact man, a deceptively loud, good-time guy who is natively shrewd and predominantly avaricious.

The son of a peddler, he became a peddler, too, in his native state of Vermont, using his experience with a traveling menagerie to give his arrival in a town with Yankee notions, silverware, and shawls a circus appearance. He had an interesting, diverse early career. It included such exploits as running contraband cotton for a northern concern, selling blankets to the U.S. Army at exorbitant prices, disposing of Confederate bonds in New England, and rendering himself by his maneuvers so dangerous to an early group of colleagues that they asked him to leave them for $60,000.

Both Daniel Drew, the railroad speculator, and Jay Gould, who was to become one of the great entrepreneurs of the era, took a fancy to the bluff, young man. It seemed to them that he would be able to inject an appealing geniality that could cover up the machinations of the desperate deals in which they were often involved as though it were all a friendly game.

Fisk was ensconsed in a brokerage firm that was an agent for large stock purchases for Drew. Then Gould brought both men into his maneuvers to buy the stock of the Erie Railroad. The trio soon outwitted even the cagey Vanderbilt in a complex, desperate battle for control of the Erie. Their illegal printing of an excessive amount of stock brought the Commodore to his knees and precipitated a crisis on Wall Street.

In 1869, Gould and Fisk drew up a scheme to corner the gold market by exaggerating their purchases. The result was Black Friday, September 24, a day of cascading prices and personal ruin for many.

Fisk indulged himself in other ways, too. He left his wife for Josie, and lavished great sums on her which she turned over to Stokes, her true love, causing a break in her relations with Fisk. He staged many of New York's big social events and became an impresario with his own opera house where he produced drama and light opera.

He was a popular, public figure. Gould, who by then had become the dominant aggressor in the fight with Vanderbilt over the Erie, decided that Fisk's problems with Josie, which the public delighted in, had made the big man a liability. So Gould asked Fisk to remove himself from the Erie board. The now unsuccessful rival, Stokes, helped Fisk to do so with considerable dispatch.

7. GOULD: THE DEVIL OF WALL STREET

CONTEMPORARIES were convinced that Jay Gould was a Jew. During the numerous periods of his great notoriety, his name and his small, dark, bearded appearance, as well as his exploits, presented a clearly Semitic aspect to his critics. They used it as one more reason to paint him in the blackest colors. Even Henry Adams, the philosopher, mistakenly described him as "the complex Jew."

He was hardly that. He was born to a farming family of Yankee heritage, in Roxbury, N.Y., in the poorest of circumstances. The chores of the farm were a hardship on the small, skinny boy and no less was the grinding poverty. Rather than be a farmer, he studied from the age of twelve to be a surveyor or engineer. A year later, he decided that he would devote himself to building a railroad across the country, a big ambition for anyone, especially a boy.

Gould never realized that ambition but he came as close to it as anyone did up to that time. By a combination of immense ambition, daring, and skill at circumventing the law, the tiny, furtive Gould developed a fine ability to turn apparent defeats into victories. It began with his milking profits from a tannery that had been entrusted to him in Pennsylvania (his second partner committed suicide when he found how badly Gould had duped him). But Gould successfully exhorted the local population to clash with the marshals who were sent against him.

His ability revealed itself again a year or two later when he married the daughter of a wealthy grocer, who helped him to buy control of a decrepit New England railroad for ten cents on the dollar. By various transactions, he turned what had begun to look like a bad deal into a $100,000 profit.

Then, together with Drew and Fisk, he acquired control of the Erie Railroad and bested Vanderbilt, who wanted the road as the last link of a chain of track-line that would run from New York to the West. The trio dumped 100,000 illegal shares on the market, causing the normally wily Commodore to buy $7 million worth of fraudulent stock. After the three plunderers just made it to Jersey City, moments ahead of the frustrated process servers, Gould bribed members of the New

York legislature to validate his "paper" and to forbid a marriage between the Erie and Vanderbilt's New York Central.

Even the infamous effort with Fisk to buy up the country's gold, boldly making use of President Grant's name and apparent blessing, so as to kite the value of their purchases far above their costs brought Gould no censure. The fact that it had all resulted in Black Friday, with tragic losses to the naive and the duped, proved no great spur for censure against him. The reason a congressional committee declined to do so was the fact that Gould had used the President's brother-in-law, Abel R. Corbin, as a minor but very willing partner in the scheme. As Henry Adams described the attitude of the legislative investigating group, "It dared not probe and refused to analyze."

Gould acquired control of several broken-down western railroads, then took over the Union Pacific line and its connection to midwestern and eastern lines. To add to this near transcontinental railways system, he staged raids on the Western Union Company and acquired the Pacific Mail Steamship Company, in cooperation with Collis Huntington.

In the 1880's, when Gould's many enemies massed for the attack, using some of his own neat devices, he seemed to be headed for defeat in the midst of his greatest triumphs. But, by cornering stocks in which his adversaries were short, he boxed them in and compelled them to buy or sell. They bought.

Like Girard, Astor, and Vanderbilt, Gould was hated by his contemporaries. Yet, the battleground on which he played out his vast game of conquest consisted of unregulated business rivalry, pioneering buccaneers of finance and trade, and widespread unethical and illegal business practices. These were characteristic of the era, and the exploits of those tycoons led to the reforms and the restrictions that came in the 1900's.

But, in the end, in death, he lost. His son, George Jay Gould, to whom he left the bulk of his $72 million estate, was drawn into an expansion scheme for the rail lines that brought him into competition with the Pennsylvania Railroad and with Edward H. Harriman, the brilliant western railroad tycoon. He overextended himself in the process, witnessed the bankruptcy of many of the lines in the 1907 panic, and lost most of them by 1912.

8. COOKE: FIRST OF THE MODERNS

A YOUNGISH, ruddy-faced, pious man in his early forties, whose bright blue eyes were often filled with the light of an inspired opportunism, lived in what was probably one of the most magnificent homes of the era. This was Jay Cooke, whose home in Ogontz, Pa., a suburb of Philadelphia, had fifty-two rooms, frescoed walls, and contained three hundred paintings and statuary. The $1 million mansion also included a theater, fountains, conservatories, and an Italian garden.

He was literally on top of the world. He had emerged from the Civil War as its greatest financier. Sensing the great need for financing to support the Union's needs, he had volunteered the services of his bank, Jay Cooke & Co., at low fees as the Treasury's aid to obtain loans from private bankers, most of whom were not convinced of the Union's cause, and to sell government bonds to the public.

To say that he succeeded would be a rank understatement. About $3 billion worth of bonds were sold through Cooke's ministrations. His methods were thoroughly twentieth century. They were a blend of skillful Washington lobbying, Wall Street's adept handling of investors, banking, and the press, and Madison Avenue's flair for promotional selling and the ability to put catch-words together.

"His methods had been a revelation to the banking community," reports Matthew Josephson, in *The Robber Barons*. "He had advertised in all the press, paid all the financial reporters he could reach 'with edibles and bibibles'; he had thrown agents all about the country, distributed circulars by the ton. Over his office, he had hung out a flag with the legend 'National Loan' emblazoned upon it; he 'kept the papers fired up daily'; he dunned each war contractor and military supplyer. Thenceforth, he became the sole fiscal agency of the government."

He had come a long way indeed when President Grant gratefully visited him in Ogontz and sat long into the night, smoking Cooke's special brand of cigars and staring into space. The squat, little, black-bearded general and the aristocratic, handsome, white-bearded financier enjoyed each other's company, even if they weren't the most compatible conversationalists.

But disaster hung in the air.

Cooke's eager restiveness, which had moved him quickly from his war triumphs to acquire control of the Northern Pacific Railroad, impelled him to float a bond issue for the line at great financial hazard to him. Even as he sat with the President, bad news lapped just outside the walls at Ogontz. The failure of the house of Cooke to provide a full measure of refunding operations for the government, a series of postwar unfavorable economic reactions which slowed down factories and caused Europeans to reject the American securities they had so eagerly bought before—all these potential crises pounded through the head of the country's most brilliant banker. But, to all appearances, the President hardly sensed the seriousness of the situation.

The morning following Grant's visit, Cooke hurried to his great bank in Philadelphia, summoned by reports of a financial crisis. By noon, his bank's doors closed, the ruins bringing down five thousand other banks, brokerages, and commercial concerns. Wall Street cracked. Railroads ground to a halt. The Panic of 1873 lasted for ten terrible days. Great as was the havoc on business, the suffering, starvation, and illness of the public that resulted from the Panic and lasted into that winter and into the next year were devastating. Cooke's bankruptcy was considered the precipitating factor for it all.

That was ironical. For, from his birth fifty-two years before, the Sandusky, Ohio, boy seemed to have a golden, pious aura about him. A store clerk at fifteen, he moved to St. Louis to work in a dry goods store where he saved $200. Then, journeying to Philadelphia, he became a clerk at Clark & Dodge, a reputable banking house, and soon delighted its owners with his personable, zestful behavior. At twenty-one, he became a junior partner; at twenty-six, he was involved in various financial enterprises, backing small railroads and canal works.

Within four years, he founded what was to be the nation's largest private bank, sensing the advantage of working with and using the friendship of state and Federal politicians. His brother, Henry, who had been an influential Ohio editor, became his Washington lobbyist and capitalized on his own friendship with Treasury Secretary Salmon P. Chase.

After the 1873 Panic, Cooke eventually regained his fortune, at least a good measure of it, and he even repaid his creditors. But he never resumed his role as the nation's great banker. Others, such as J. Pierpont Morgan, hardier, more indomitable and resilient, replaced him.

9. ROCKEFELLER: GREATEST OF PLANNERS AND CONSPIRATORS

As he gazed out at a broken, darkened landscape, with its makeshift derricks, shacks shaking in the wind, and the rank odor of crude oil, the end-of-the-world aspect that confronted him numbed his fastidious nature. He turned away, his stomach suddenly hot and sick. It was not merely the chaotic exploitation of the oil discovery in Pennsylvania in that year of 1860 that disturbed him. It was the insecurity of the return, the disastrous fires, the sudden rise and fall of prices, and the fluctuation of oil acreage values that upset him.

He returned to Cleveland, where, at twenty-one, he already had a successful wholesale produce business netting him $17,000 a year, to render a negative report to the businessmen who had dispatched him to study the potential of the new oil finds.

Five years later, John D. Rockefeller completely reversed himself. It was the most momentous decision of his life and it had a powerful bearing not only on his future but on the future pattern of American business.

What brought him to this move began with a minor investment he made after his first visit to the oil fields. He and his partner, an M. B. Clark, put up $5,000 to back Samuel Andrews, an owner of a still and an oil technician, in setting up a small refinery. Andrews was one of the first to adopt a scientific approach to the refining process. He was able to extract a high percentage of kerosene from the crude oil and could also draw useful by-products from the well. His methods and especially the excellent demand that accompanied his efforts excited Rockefeller. He sold Clark his share in the produce firm and then bought out Clark's interest in the refinery.

Thus, the pallid, narrow-boned Rockefeller, whose small eyes glistening in their tight eyepits were virtually the only energetic feature of his phlegmatic bearing, was now launched on a spectacular career. It was to make him the most important industrialist, and eventually the greatest philanthropist, in the history of America.

There is not much question that he was molded in his formative years by the peculiar and diverse pressures of his parents. An often indigent father, who sometimes had to flee from the authorities, taught him about things practical and exposed him to his own philosophy of always seeking new

opportunities. The dealer in quack medicine, freely expressing his own mercurial nature, also liked to trick his sons,
explaining, "I want to make 'em sharp."

But the mother, who more often than not was the head
of the family, was a stern disciplinarian, given to use of the
birch switch. Faced by the irresponsibility of her spouse, she
fought bitterly any tendency of the family to slide, with beat-
ings and urgent evangelistic calls for obedience.

Young Rockefeller had only minimal schooling, worked for
farmers, and saved his money. Once, he loaned a farmer $50
and was delighted to find that he could obtain a legal rate of
7 per cent interest. The family moved to Cleveland where he
studied bookkeeping, an activity which pleased him because
it suited the precise turn of his mind. After two years, he
joined a commission house as a clerk and bookkeeper. In 1858,
when he was only 19, after meticulously learning all he could
about produce, he invested his sole savings of $800 to become
a junior partner with Clark, an Englishman.

After he chose oil refining to produce, he took in as a
second partner Henry M. Flagler, a bold, entrepreneurial
type with good connections, who brought in an additional
capital of $70,000. The Rockefeller, Andrews, and Flagler con-
cern, which up till then had been only one of thirty-five refiners in the Cleveland area, now expanded, opening a
second refinery. Within two years, it became Cleveland's
leading refiner.

The way in which this was accomplished, the intricate,
daring planning down to the last fine detail of freight rates,
secret rebates from the railroads, and conspiracies against
smaller refineries, set a grand, almost malevolent pattern for
colossal growth. This culminated first in the incorporation
of the company as the Standard Oil Company of Ohio and
then into the awesome, monopolistic network that it was to
become in the 1880's. Hundreds of competitors were squeezed
out, deliberately ground under the pious heel, so that by the

mid-1880's Standard Oil was earning about $15 million a year after taxes.

Still fervently evangelistic but pragmatic and moody to an extreme degree, the young man in his thirties carefully laid out a campaign of industrial aggrandizement of proportions greater than had ever been drawn before. It involved a consolidation of several hundred oil refining firms by persuasion and then coercion. Conspiring with the railroads, which were run by dominant opportunists, Rockefeller struck favorable freight rate agreements that gave him a prime competitive edge. By controlling the flow of crude oil to a small group of refiners and by restricting market supply of oil producers to these refiners, a consortium of the most efficient monopolistic power was built. It could wield power domestically and even internationally. And, as Rockefeller effectively plotted it, the monopoly could dictate crude oil market prices, fix profit margins by regulating costs, and stabilize the oil business around itself virtually forever.

First, by calm, reasonable explanation, then by forceful action, then by constriction, competition was throttled. In a three-month period, twenty-five Cleveland competitors gave in to Rockefeller. The pattern was to follow across the country, but it was accompanied by a swelling uproar and by villification of the generalissimo of the industrial war. By 1879, the Rockefeller monopoly controlled 90 per cent to 95 per cent of the country's total refining capacity. But, in 1906, the federal government filed suit, charging violations of the Sherman Anti-Trust Act. In 1911, the U.S. Supreme Court decreed a dissolution of the combine's holding company, Standard Oil Company of New Jersey, from its subsidiary companies, which then became independent corporations.

While Rockefeller continued to head Standard Oil until he retired in 1911, he had become increasingly involved in philanthropy and from 1895 had gradually relinquished the company's rule to his colleagues.

Amidst a series of investigations and resulting notoriety which caused the great monopolist to be defamed and hated, he preserved a cold, aristocratic aplomb that dismayed and disarmed his critics. His vast, unbelievable success, which he attributed to his piety and to the will of God, he fervently maintained raised him above the clamor of the multitude. Even in his last years, his powerfully withered face and his immense charities dispensed with equal reserve to a foundation or dimes handed out to children on the street, contributed to give him a gargoylelike aspect, as with a long-forgotten but awesome relic, even through the gray years of the Depression.

And, to his last breath in Ormond Beach, Fla., in 1937, he remained omnipotently apart, perhaps America's greatest and most controversial self-made man, inscrutable and intent only on living "according to the dictates of my conscience."

10. CARNEGIE: FROM STEEL MONOPOLIST TO PHILANTHROPIST

THERE is a story, never fully substantiated, that while supervising the transportation of wounded Union soldiers after the Battle of Bull Run, Andrew Carnegie suffered a sunstroke which caused him in later life to journey to Scotland during the summer to enjoy the pristine coolness of the glen.

It is probably a true story. Yet, it is not difficult to imagine that the tiny, zealous entrepreneur would want to return to the land of his birth for other, important reasons.

At the age of thirty-three, after only twenty years in America, he already had attained an income of $50,000 a year and was seriously considering retiring to become a scholar. Returning to the Scottish hamlet of Dunfermline, where poverty then was a way of life, might have dramatized for him how far he had come since he had left it as a boy.

And, seeing his home town again, to which he later bequeathed public baths and a trust for the civic benefit, would have renewed for him the appeal of the simple way of life that he had given up years before.

It may have been all of these reasons that drew him back to Scotland, perhaps even simple nostalgia.

His quest for material attainment and personal stature in the frenetic, industrial center of nineteenth-century Pittsburgh had given him great success, but a strong feeling, too, that he was engaged in a "degrading pursuit." ". . . the amassing of wealth is one of the worst species of idolatry," he wrote in his diary in 1868. "No idol is more debasing than the worship of money. . . ."

Few of the great American tycoons had the good fortune, native ability, and purposefulness—the elements that make up the platitudes of the "rags-to-riches" saga—as did Carnegie. From a bobbin boy in a clothing factory, he became a clerk; attended night school to learn bookkeeping; became a messenger in a Pittsburgh telegraph office; and had an opportunity to be a relief telegraph operator. Then, because he had prepared himself in telegraphy, giving every job all he had in him, he became a regular operator earning $800 a year.

His enthusiasm, his quick intelligence, and his obvious admiration for the successful men with whom he came into contact brought him the sponsorship of Thomas A. Scott, division superintendent of the Pennsylvania Railroad. Scott asked him to become his telegraph operator and personal clerk. In a short time, the eighteen-year old Carnegie became valuable to the railroad man.

He gave Andrew a tip to buy the stock of the new American Express Company, which became the first of many of Carnegie's successful speculations. In all cases, Scott guided his young protégé, and when he himself was promoted to be the railroad's vice president, he recommended Andrew, then only twenty-four, to succeed him in Pittsburgh.

Six years later, when he was offered the post of assistant

general superintendent of the Pennsylvania, Carnegie resigned instead to devote himself to the iron industry. He had already managed to acquire the services of several master mechanics to work in the companies in which his investments had grown. Now, he began a career as an entrepreneur for the iron-making companies which was to have no parallel. By increasing his capital and his ownership, by adding more foundries and men, and by drumming up business for his factories by a constant round of travels and contacts, he became the operating head of the combined companies and a millionaire before he was thirty-five.

Although he was impressed by the development of the Bessemer converter, Carnegie was reluctant to make the switch in his own plants from iron to steel. But when he saw his competition capitalizing on the railroads' eagerness to shift from iron to steel tracks, he decided to build the country's largest steel mill for $1 million. By 1877, Carnegie's furnaces were dispersing the heaviest clouds of smoke about Pittsburgh, producing about one-seventh of all the Bessemer steel in the country.

He had also learned the game of finance well from Scott and the other entrepreneurs with whom he met in his spreading circle of contacts. And this, despite his continuing investments in his own and other companies, enabled him to retain enough resources to capitalize on the Panic of 1873. He bought out several of his partners, who hadn't been as lucky in their investments as he, but, at the same time, declined to go to Scott's aid, when the older man asked for help.

More powerful and affluent than ever before, Carnegie in 1882 acquired the giant coke-making operations of Henry C. Frick. This allowed Carnegie to both add that basic steel-making ingredient to his already massive complex and to bring in the talents of Frick, a less omniscient but dynamic industrialist of near-Carnegie proportions. Promoting his business endlessly, pitting one executive against another, giving incentive to the promising young men in the mills by making as many as forty of them partners, Carnegie built the largest steel-making company in America, with numerous related subsidiary concerns. In 1899, he organized the Carnegie Steel Company as a New Jersey corporation with a capitalization of $320 million. The following year, the company earned a profit of $40 million, of which Carnegie's personal share was $25 million.

In 1901, after he had promoted the potential of his "trust" to J. P. Morgan, then the great financier of the era, he offered to sell his business to Morgan for $300 million. Only a few days before, Carnegie had consented to let Frick have it for $100 million. The usually crafty Morgan quickly accepted the offer and combined it with other steel mills to form the U.S. Steel Corporation. It was America's first billion-dollar company.

From that time until his death eighteen years later, Carnegie devoted himself to philanthropy with the same zeal that he had shown in business.

And, from his bench in Central Park, he looked back with warm satisfaction on the fruits of his "idolatry worshipping." He wrote a series of books and many articles revealing his sensitivity to the pressures and boons of an industrialized society. One of his most persistent messages was that the rich should distribute their wealth while they still lived.

11. MORGAN: FINANCIAL JUPITER

In one of the more ludicrous confrontations of aggrandizement, violence, and confusion in American railroad history, John Pierpont Morgan, a heavyset, dullish-looking, hulking scion of a successful financier father, emerged to his great surprise as a popular hero.

The incident occurred in 1869, when Morgan backed J. H. Ramsey, president of the Albany & Susquehanna Railroad, against the acquisitive moves of the masters of the Erie line, Jay Gould and Jim Fisk. After a series of clashes in the courts and between paid thugs of both lines, a new battle was touched off. Morgan and Ramsey dispatched several hundred men one morning on a locomotive leaving Albany to take over the Gould–Fisk operated stations in the western part of the state. The opponents, hearing of the foray, did likewise from Binghamton. The two locomotives met head-on in a deafening, smoking collision, the dazed but surviving battlers then fighting it out on the ground. Soon, the larger, better-armed forces of Morgan and Ramsey took the day.

Although the fighting then resumed in the courts and ultimately the disputed line was temporarily taken over by the state, Gould's salty, buccaneering reputation caught up with him and in the fall of the year he capitulated to Morgan and Ramsey. A new face among the freebooters and plunderers of the day, young Morgan stood out dramatically as the victor of the infamous Gould and Fisk. The public took him to its heart, thinking him a hero of virtuous qualities. But, in time, his public image tarnished and turned black.

In the context of his life, the incident was small when viewed against such later Morgan exploits as acquisition of control of much of the nation's railroads when they were bankrupted in the crash of 1893 and his masterminding of the steel merger that resulted in the formation of U.S. Steel. But it allowed him to emerge from his shell, to prove to himself and to the world that he could indeed ignite the fire and display the wily skill of power exploitation that he had vainly wanted to for years.

His problem was the not unusual one of the frustrated, seemingly inadequate son of a self-made man. In the case of John Pierpont, whose father Junius was a grim, hardy merchant-banker who liked to control his son at all times, the son's aspect was like that of a giant dullard who stands meekly and dumbly awaiting his father's instructions. But, even if that were actually the case in those early years, J. P. Morgan's rise and impact on the national and international scene was to far eclipse those of his father.

He was guided by his parent toward a good formal education, first in Boston and then in Europe. "Pip," as the young man was called, had an independent streak but it was beaten down by his father until he was twenty. Then, after several apprentice years at George Peabody & Co., a London banking house, in which the older Morgan was a partner, Pip returned to New York in 1857 as his father's banking agent.

Slowly, young Morgan injected his firm and himself into an increasing number of financing arrangements. One of his first ones later brought him considerably bad publicity. He backed Simon Stevens, a munitions agent, who bought defective carbines from an Army quartermaster in Washington for $17,486 and then sold them to a western military outpost for $109,912. When Morgan sued for the full amount, a congressional committee declared that "he cannot be looked upon as a good citizen. . . ."

But nothing seemed to dismay him, now that he was feeling his strength, not concern over the public's reaction or even what other financiers, including his father, thought of him. By then, he had gone way beyond caring about any censure from Junius. After a series of partnerships with other bankers, including Charles H. Dabney and Anthony Drexel, Morgan in 1895 founded his own company, J. P. Morgan & Co.

Among those exploits was his role in helping to sell the $260 million federal bond issue of 1877, in which his firm, Drexel, Morgan & Co., made a clear profit of $5 million. In 1879, Morgan formed a syndicate to sell 250,000 shares of New York Central in Europe for William Vanderbilt for $25 million without causing a ripple of concern about the railroad on Wall Street. He was much admired for this effortless deal.

From the deck of his imposing yacht, *The Corsair*, the

supine six-foot, 200-pound Morgan would map plans for "trusts" in railroads and steel, harsh terms for loaning gold to the federal government in 1895 and, later, mobilization of the banking muscle of New York to avert widespread financial ruin as a result of the 1907 Wall Street panic.

The most daring, most dangerous exploit came in 1889. The day after New Year, a "private and confidential" circular was issued by three of New York's largest investment-banking houses summoning the country's great railroad magnates to meet in J. P. Morgan's house at 219 Madison Avenue.

There, six days later, the brusque financier boldly laid out a plan for an iron-clad combination or monopoly which would declare a halt to competition among its members and give them control of the country's railway system. The banking houses would guarantee that they would prevent the negotiation of any securities that would invite competition. This way, a monopolistic executive committee could effectively control the construction of parallel lines or the extension of lines. The point was that a thumb jammed against the artery of new enterprise was better than a gun pointed at its head.

The proposal was a direct violation of some of the high statutes of the land, punishable by confinement in a federal prison, but no one summarily walked out or rose to argue. The intent of Morgan and of the group came near fruition when James J. Hill, who controlled the Great Northern Railroad, and Edward H. Harriman, who controlled the Union Pacific, struck a peaceful settlement plan in their opposing desires to acquire the Chicago, Burlington & Quincy line. They would partition the disputed line's territory and thus help each other by keeping out competition.

J. P. Morgan, whose firm held a substantial block of shares in Northern Pacific, which, in turn owned a large interest in Chicago, Burlington & Quincy, was appointed arbitrator for the plan. Characteristically, instead of serving passively, he sold all the major parties the idea of organizing a vast holding company, the Northern Securities Company. This new entity would hold title to both the Great Northern and the Northern Pacific, the latter also holding a substantial interest in Chicago, Burlington & Quincy. It would be the effective owner of three lines.

There was a sharp, irate outcry from many who feared such a combination. The federal government brought a suit against Northern Securities, and the Supreme Court deemed it an illegal corporation.

Not long after, Morgan had brushed off his defeat. That same year, he negotiated the U.S. Steel formation. And, while monopolistic trusts were a violation of federal statutes, the trust-makers succeeded by 1903 in having the imprisonment clause struck from the anti-trust law.

When the "Jupiter of Finance," as he was called, succumbed in Rome, in 1913, at seventy-six, he was generally eulogized as the greatest of American magnates and financiers. Calumnied and hated on one hand, he was respected and even idolized on the other—an image of an adventurous pirate in an age that was confused and amorphous.

12. FORD: 15,000,000 MODEL T'S FROM THE WOODSHED

In 1893, Henry Ford, a thirty-year-old ex-farmer and mechanic, began building a motor car in the woodshed of his home on Bagley Avenue in Detroit.

Three years later, at 3 A.M., on a rainy June morning, he excitedly broke down the wall of the woodshed. With a flashlight and umbrella held by his wife, Ford wheeled his first car down the alley and into the street. A friend rode ahead on a bicycle to forewarn any on carriages or on horses who might be on the streets.

The auto worked but not the two companies formed to produce it in 1899 or in 1901. The first one, the Detroit Automobile Company, produced only twenty-five cars before it petered out. The second also gave out, mainly because Ford went off on a tangent of building racing cars and ignoring what he later became most famous for, production.

In 1903, the Ford Motor Company was organized and incorporated. By 1908, only eight stockholders remained of an original twelve, the others having been bought out by Ford. Those survivors in the founding year had represented an investment of $33,100. By 1920, they had gotten something like $33 million in dividends and were bought out by the founder for $105 million. This was a fantastic profit, of course, but not compared to what Ford derived. Only a scant few years later, the lanky, zealous visionary of the production line spurned an offer for $1 billion to buy his company.

In a life that began in the middle of the Civil War and endured until two years after World War II, Ford spanned the era of America's greatest economic growth, and, in his own way, was one of the mightiest contributors to it. It is one of the singular characteristics of those eight decades that a master mechanic of sparse education, with a complete distrust of the world of finance and a lack of sophistication of business practices should have become the master-mind of industrial production, influencing more than anyone else not only his own industry but numerous others.

Ford could not read blueprints, but he decided in 1909 that the Model T would be his only model, sell for a basic price of $850, and, as far as color was concerned: "Any customer can have a car painted any color that he wants so long as it is black." It was a durable, ornery, road-hugging, sky-climbing, metal jackass. He sold 15 million of them before the Model T was discontinued in 1928, 1.7 million of them alone in 1923.

Long before Ford's cars changed to more stylish, more varied, and more expensive models, he became one of the best-known Americans, an authentic native genius, as much and perhaps more than even Thomas A. Edison, for whom Ford had worked before building his first car. He was as American as apple pie, as tart as cranberries, and as immovably stubborn as a backwoodsman.

All his life, he spurned outside financing, unions, intellectuals, and stockholders' rights. Yet, in 1914, he created a storm by announcing that his workers would receive double their minimum wage or $5 a day and they would participate in a profit-sharing plan that would distribute up to $30 million a year among them.

And yet the next year, he was also the sponsor of the ignominiously unsuccessful Peace Ship, a sincere but baldly naive effort intended to stop the spreading world war, wandering aimlessly from European port to port until the U.S. entered the war; he fought unionism and combatted it with the use of goons and other unpleasant tactics until only six years before his death; he treated his executives with considerable disdain and even cruelty; and engaged in an anti-Semitic campaign in his own newspaper, the *Dearborn Independent*, for which he was later compelled to apologize.

Thus, the man, complex and paradoxical in his very marrow and temperament. But, by his adoption of the moving assembly line—the work moving to the worker, rather than vice versa—he revolutionized American industry. He injected the worker into the production mechanism like an essential cog, ironically hastening the power of unionism rather than halting it.

If this was not all his own concept, as even some of his closest associates admitted, he espoused it, instituted it in his plants across the country, and refined it. Perhaps what made him the country's most important manufacturer was his pioneering premise and action in offering millions a low-priced, efficiently operating automobile which cut down time, distance, and led to a massive change in social habits.

13. WHAT WERE THEY?

THESE were the ones with the principal roles, the ones who marched down American economic history leaving ineradicable footprints, who departed larger than life-size in the wake of astonishing accomplishments and a continuing chorus of sharply mixed applause and grave accusation.

Were they plunderers, pirates, hunters, and stealthy men of the night?

Yes, most, if not all, were, in varying degrees. Only the truly naive would entirely equate their exploits with the stresses of the time, the lack of formation of the society, and the ineffective legal force of the government. Nothing, under any circumstances, can condone the worst perpetrations of the great American tycoons. They were products of their time, yes, even as men are today in the second half of the twentieth century. But ethical and moral principles do not change, even if time, law, and society do.

That aside, the positive accomplishments of these progenitors remain etched more clearly and more deeply today than do their misdeeds, if only because the passage of time dims all, while life goes on, the living society profiting from the faltering steps that men took in the past. Nothing in a study of the entrepreneur is revealed more clearly than that—the individual's deeds successively contribute to the attainments of the present and future. Conversely, the cruelty, the violence, the chicanery, and the immorality that may have constituted the means to the end remain part of the past.

It can be put perhaps more simply, if more starkly.

Misdeeds belong to history and give it its true color. But achievements are seeds flung into the future.

Four

———— •• ————

PROTOTYPES OF TODAY

1. THE DYNAMIC INNOVATORS

LIKE history, politics, science, and art, business has its Hall
of Fame and its Chamber of Horrors. It is full of heroes and
knaves, wise men and fools, leaders and followers, nobles and
les nouveaux riches, its dragoons and its dragons.

Businessmen often ignore the public, overlook its needs,
and militate against its better interests in their zeal for
profit, according to one highly articulate school of thought.

But it can be just as forcibly argued that business is creative, that it builds employment, a better standard of living,
and inevitably results in higher levels of education and culture.

In a nation literally begun as a "business enterprise," business progress has immense ramifications. Giant steps are taken
with creative breakthroughs, a new invention, a new system
or a method, a trail-blazing corporate program that obtains
wide application. What then is more important—the invention
or the method of applying the invention to practical and
widening needs? Obviously, the invention, but the applica-

tion is certainly very significant, the lifeline that the invention needed.

Some of those who "knew a good thing when they saw one," the dynamic innovators and users, have occasionally assumed a role virtually as important as that of the inventor, the developer of the concept, and, in a few cases, more so.

Thus, Henry Ford will be remembered longer than Carl Benz or Otto Daimler, two of the inventors responsible for the development of the auto. Andrew Carnegie, who was slow to adopt the process of converting pig iron to steel and then became its greatest exponent, may have made a far wider impact on modern civilization than the inventor, Henry Bessemer.

Adaptors and entrepreneurs like Ford and Carnegie, because of their pragmatic skills, their ability to bridge the technological and marketing phases, became not only great industrialists but industrial prototypes. They established a model for others and the result was the birth of a great new industry or the explosion of a new phase into another great industry.

There have been many who became a symbol of a particular industry in America—Eli Whitney, Charles Goodyear, Cyrus McCormick, Thomas A. Edison, Gail Borden, the Wright Brothers, Lee de Forest, and others. Many have passed on but some remain—living legends.

Several of the greatest of these contemporary prototypes, who deal in basic human needs—communications, shelter, and clothing—were interviewed on a normal business day, so that they replied to questions with minds still vitally attuned to immediate concerns.

Having made their astonishing impact on industry, it appears, did not mean that they had removed themselves from coping with the situations and responsibilities faced on a normal day by the average businessman. One might say that men such as these live in a crucible in which time pressures constantly grate against one another. These include the burdens of grappling with the turmoil of the present, living with the decisions of the past—wise or foolish as they may have been—and preparing for the largely unknown challenges of the future.

2. DAVID SARNOFF

I got most of my help from older men
and my envy from younger men.
—DAVID SARNOFF, *on looking back on his
sixty-year career.*

PERHAPS the most impressive observation to be made about David Sarnoff, the chairman of the board of the Radio Corporation of America, and now in his late seventies, after a conversation of several hours with him, is his acuteness. A disciplined mind comes through and it leaves one somewhat with the sensation of having just emerged from a swim in a cold-water pool.

Asked, "Would you recommend to young men just out of college that they join a big company, or try to start their own businesses, or does it all depend upon the individual?" he quickly replied:

"First, they should get some experience for themselves at the employer's expense. After that, they can make a decision about the future."

As to "What is success in business?" he answered:

"A man can be a great outward success but be inwardly a failure. Every man must ask himself, 'What am I here for?' The answer must be that he is here to express the forces that are within him, whether he be an executive or a bricklayer. Success in business or in any endeavor depends on expressing what forces a man is endowed with and is able to develop."

On "As the head of a giant business in a giant industry, do

you think there are opportunities for new, self-made men in the electronics and other major industries?" he said:

"More than ever. There are people now in the electronics business who are new to it. After all, the electronics industry did not reach its present sales of $20 billion in just a few years. It is made up today of many companies of many sizes. That means that there are numerous small entrepreneurs in it now, in addition to the giants.

"But the main thing is that we are in a big world that is getting bigger and communities that are constantly growing."

A disciplined mind is the mark of many highly success-ful businessmen. It often seems to come "with the territory," *i.e.*, the staggering responsibility and the constant pressures on a variety of levels which are the daily burdens of such men. Certainly not all, perhaps not most, have a finely mesh-ing coordination of thoughts, its transfer into words and then into action, as does Sarnoff. His life shows it.

At seventy-five, he decided to catch up with a longtime de-sire by learning how to swim, under the tutelage of Florence Chadwick, the English Channel swimmer.

At sixty-nine, he declined to back away an inch in his faith in compatible, all-electronic color television. That year, 1960, RCA, had already spent the staggering sum of more than $130 million to pioneer and develop that concept without having yet realized the potential that Sarnoff had been pre-dicting for years.

When he was twenty-eight, the United States government asked the General Electric Company and several other con-cerns to form RCA to protect American patents in wireless and radio by taking over the Marconi Company. Sarnoff fought off prejudices against his youth, his training, and his religion to hold on as Marconi's commercial manager and then as RCA's general manager.

In his early teens, he became head of a family of six when his father died. Too poor to continue in school, the young immigrant (he had come to America from Russia in 1900 at the age of nine) became a newsboy, a delivery boy, and then a messenger for the Commercial Cable Company. There, he decided to learn to operate a telegraph instrument, saved his money to buy one and learned the Morse code.

When he was fifteen, he became an office boy at Marconi. At seventeen, he took advantage of the opportunity to become a wireless operator, even though it meant leaving home to work at Marconi's lonely wireless station on Nantucket Island, in Massachusetts, for two years.

It all, of course, seems too good to be true. A boy who strove so hard to learn, to be worthy of recognition, to achieve stature by leaving nothing undone, to miss no opportunity, probably irritated those whose temperament was more passive and who accepted life as it was. One can easily picture him in those days—the scrubbed face and the hand-me-down clothes straight out of Horatio Alger, too eager, too bright-eyed, too ingratiating, too inquisitive, and too, too quick to do everything.

And yet, even for the jaded and the cynical, there are strains in the Sarnoff life and in those of self-made men like him that defy the frequent charge that success comes from being there at the right time and in the right place.

"When I came back from Nantucket and spent some time in Marconi's New York office," Sarnoff said, "I realized that the company's two engineers knew nothing about business and that the general manager, the traffic manager, and the bookkeeper knew nothing about the technical side of the business.

"Neither side, in other words, knew about the other's activities. So I decided that my future lay in combining the knowledge of both and in serving as a bridge."

A *bridge*. The word epitomizes Sarnoff's role over the decades. He bridged the efforts of the scientists ("Sometimes, I have more confidence and faith in the work of the research man than he does in himself") and of the administrator and marketer ("I could easily envision the growing development of mass and individual communications and I had no doubt whatever about their ultimate usefuless and the services that the new devices would make possible.")

Sarnoff had a way of converting laughter and ridicule for his ideas and concepts into sweeping victories. In 1915, when the young man pointed to a primitive wireless set and proposed a "radio music box" that could eventually become as popular in the home as the piano or phonograph, he was the butt of a lot of jokes. He won that battle, of course, and resoundingly. In 1929, the same guffaws arose in the electronics industry when he decided to subsidize research on Zworykin's iconoscope tube. That tube, of course, became *the* television camera tube.

In 1950, when he persisted in pushing compatible electronic color television, the laughter rose to its highest decibels but it had its frantic aspect as competitors anxiously tried to safeguard their investment in black-and-white television.

That year, however, the laughter almost submerged Sarnoff when the Federal Communications Commission licensed the CBS mechanical color TV process nationally and rejected RCA's. Sarnoff went doggedly back to his research men. Less than a year later, they developed a new system that ultimately pushed the CBS method out of the way. This victory, delayed as it was, was all the sweeter.

If Guglielmo Marconi, Lee de Forest, E. H. Armstrong, and Vladimir Zworykin were the inventor-fathers of America's vast electronics and communications industries, Sarnoff served those industries as a most imaginative guide.

These industries acknowledged his role as "our most distinguished citizen" at a dinner on September 30, 1966, at the Waldorf-Astoria, honoring Sarnoff's sixty years of service. It was an unprecedented testimonial event, sponsored by the three largest organizations in the electronics and broadcasting industries.

As the head of a company with annual sales in excess of $3 billion and employees numbering about 124,000, Sarnoff has tremendous resources behind him—and that includes speech-writers. Yet, the alertness of his mind in his late years is obvious in an interview, in which spontaneous responses to spontaneous questions can receive little benefit from material prepared by others.

However, the granting of this interview was based on his request that he be given a look at the resulting article. When he did so, he removed several comments that he had made, apparently for reasons of personal taste, concern at their critical content, and some sensitivity about possible reaction to them.

Q. What was the biggest obstacle you had to overcome in your long career?

A. There were different obstacles at different periods. In the beginning, the biggest was poverty. My father was sick and there were younger children. I had to support my mother and the family at an early age, when my father died, and I couldn't go to high school or college. Getting an education was something that I couldn't afford. Early, very early in my career, I was determined to overcome poverty. At a time when most boys just think of fun, my objective was survival.

A few years later, when I was working at something better, my obstacle was youth, a lack of background, and no social standing whatsoever. It all seemed to me to be so overwhelming. I tried to appraise all the factors. How do you overcome obstacles like these? I decided to acquire knowledge, to learn what I didn't know. I decided, too, that I would have a great willingness to work and not to be the type of worker who watches the clock.

When I worked for Marconi, there was little that I wouldn't do. I carried Marconi's briefcase, when he would allow me to, and I used to deliver the boxes of candy that he would send to his friends.

While I worked for Marconi as a wireless operator, I studied at night in different schools. When I was in Nantucket, I took a correspondence course in technical subjects. I never minded doing anything, if it meant learning something new and adding to my knowledge. I knew that, sometimes, when you were very willing, people didn't mind letting you do the dirty work, but if it had benefits for you, it should be done. For example, while I was still a messenger boy for Marconi, I would go down to the ships that Marconi had to clean the operators' equipment. They didn't mind letting me do it and I learned how to take the equipment apart and put it together again. I also used to get a good meal aboard the ship.

Q. What was your greatest obstacle?

A. That came during the formation of RCA. When it was formed by the U.S. and took over Marconi, I was in a key position because I had handled the Marconi Company's commercial affairs and I remained in that post when Marconi became RCA. I ran into a tremendous barrage of criticism from certain GE men and the other companies that controlled RCA. Everyone wanted to know, "Who is this kid who is running everything?"

They took special umbrage at my proposed "radio music box." Each company thought in a different area—GE thought in terms of power, AT & T in terms of the telephone, and so on. In either case, the "music box" was useful to them only insofar as it would further their own particular interests. "Who would want to listen to a radio-telephone?" they asked.

I said, "The greatest advantage of the radio-telephone [radio] was that through it a single voice could be heard by millions." This was something different, a voice to be heard by the mass rather than by the individual. So, in effect, what the oldsters regarded as its limitations, I saw as its greatest asset.

But, as the "radio music box" began to sell in growing numbers, the same critics were jealous of its potential and their hostility toward me became even greater.

The pressures were enormous, fed by political and commercial considerations on the part of my enemies. I found myself engulfed in a whirlpool of intrigue, not because of anything I had done but because of what I was.

Owen D. Young, who held the dual jobs of chairman of the board of both GE and RCA, received all kinds of complaints. But, by then, he had developed a confidence in me. So, the complaints didn't register with him. But that didn't stop my enemies. They demanded that I should be put back into communications, that I didn't know anything about business, manufacturing, or marketing. And then GE hired an efficiency expert to look into the matter.

The report which he turned in to Owen Young recommended that I should be fired for neglecting the transatlantic communications phase of the business and for spending time and money on broadcasting over radio, which would never pay off.

I had occasion to see the report and now I knew that I was at the crossroads of my life. Should I remain or quit under fire? That night, I walked around and around the blocks near my home trying to come to a decision. I had no one to advise me, only a young wife preoccupied with her home and family.

Then, I knew that I could never quit. Outside of ill health or being in jail, which are beyond the ability of man to control, I decided that anyone has the choice of fighting adversity. I would fight back hard and I would fight clean. I asked Mr. Young to come down from Schenectady and I told him in the most honest way I could about how I felt, the story of my life, and why the report was wrong because the efficiency expert just didn't know or understand the potentials of our business.

During the four-hour conversation, I began by explaining to Young what it means to be a penniless immigrant boy and wound up by telling him that the electric companies were cutting off their noses to spite their faces by trying to prevent RCA, the only expert in its field at that time, from broadcasting.

When Young returned to his office, he threw the expert's recommendations into the wastebasket.

Q. Did you falter at any time when in the fifties and sixties RCA was spending so many millions on color television and consumer acceptance was coming so slowly?

A. I never had any doubts. It was the same problem in black-and-white television. We spent $50 million on it before it caught on. No, I never had any personal butterflies on the expenditures for color TV. I simply never had any doubt of its efficacy or practicability.

Q. How does one achieve such great self-confidence?

A. First, you have to believe in yourself as a person. You build self-respect by pondering on all the alternatives of your position, on all the ramifications. Thinking these through will either reinforce your convictions or remove them. Thus, when I faced all the criticisms against our color television concept, they seemed insignificant when measured against the potential dimensions of the system and its benefits to humanity.

Q. What field other than electronics would you have selected as your preferred one?

A. I would have been a lawyer, or a teacher, or perhaps an editor. I don't think I would have been excited by making money as a merchant. I really got into wireless purely by accident. After I had been a newsboy for a while, I decided that I wanted to be a newspaperman. I went downtown one Saturday morning, when I was fifteen, to the New York *Herald* building. I approached a man behind a window in the lobby and said that I wanted a job, any job. This man, it seemed, did not work for the *Herald* but was in the outer office of the Commercial Cable Company. "I don't know if there are any jobs open on the *Herald*," the man told me, "but we can use another messenger boy in our shop." I took it and so got into the field of telegraphy. Later, after I had learned how to operate a telegraph key from the operators, I got a job with the Marconi Company, in wireless. And so I remained in electronics, not newspapers.

Q. Has the entrepreneurial climate changed in the electronics and communications fields in recent years?

A. Opportunities have to be viewed as though they were a barrel of apples. You pick out one you like, rub it briskly, and sink your teeth into it. In other words, you have to pick out the opportunity and make the most of it.

Today, there are more opportunities than ever in electronics and communications. These are service industries that will grow and grow—businesses that are good for individuals. Today, you don't have to sell the public on any new product or service. You don't have to go through the tortures and delays of the past anymore.

Q. In retrospect, how do those past years look to you now? Any observations at this stage?

A. I was always fortunate in being associated with older men. Most were at least ten to fifteen years older than I— men at the head of Marconi, GE, Westinghouse, AT & T— and I learned more from them than from books. In turn, they liked having a young man come in and consult them.

But I was very fortunate. I got most of my help from older men and my envy from younger men.

Q. What are the most important ingredients for success?

A. There are a number of factors in any man's life over which he has no control—his birth, his parents, the traits of heredity, his health, and where he was born.

Assuming that these elements are favorable to him, he must then have certain qualities or factors over which he does have control. He must have a willingness to work hard. He must be conscientious and apply himself. He must fix on a goal early in life and not be a drifter. And he must have character, integrity, and patience.

Frequently, new college graduates come in recommended by friends and I ask them, "What would you like to do here?" And they reply, "Anything." I tell them, "I'm sorry, but we don't have a Department of Anything, so we probably can't use you here. But we do have research, advertising, sales, and numerous other departments. Didn't you develop any intellectual curiosity during your four years in college?"

A man also has to be complete by being a family man, with a happy home and children, and later grandchildren. Otherwise he has to do things to compensate for that lack of family and that can get complicated.

A man also has to have an identification with his time, his government, his society, his community.

He does not have to strive for perfection, but for excellence and for improvement.

To the extent that he does these things, he will be happy, regardless of the extent of his income or of his degree of recognition.

3. WILLIAM J. LEVITT

I Read, I Study,
I examine, I listen, I reflect,
And out of all this,
I try to form an idea
into which I put as much
Common Sense as I can.
—MARQUIS DE LAFAYETTE, DECEMBER 16,
1777. (*William J. Levitt's favorite maxim,
reprinted and distributed to his staff.*)

No less than a man, any business, or any segment of business, must search out its own identity. Is it in a trade, a craft, an industry? The quest is even more important for an entrepreneur. The right answer will provide a successful direction.

In the midst of opulent surroundings, William J. Levitt speaks plainly. The man who revolutionized the American home building industry sits in a large, vivid office, with golden rugs and lush canvases of modern Italian and French masters, and volunteers, "We had to put our business on a business basis."

Frowning but with a fond gesture, he strokes the flank of a dog who dozes on a sumptuous sofa nearby, adding, "To try to convince the public of what we were, we had to first know what we are. What were we in this particular industry? Were we crap-shooters? Speculators? No. We decided that we were manufacturers of shelter."

A nonconformist among builders, Levitt put up a community in 1946 for thousands of war-weary GI's and their young families. Seventeen thousand homes, arranged in clean, geometric lines, were raised on six thousand acres of potato farmland on Long Island. Families camped overnight in tents to be first in line for the new $7,990 homes. From the first pioneering Levittown, L.I., Levitt has since built many other housing developments, diversified styling and decor, expanded internationally, and become America's best-known home builder.

A lean, demanding, intellectual type, Levitt in his sixties is irked by an industry still as archaic as the craft guilds of the Middle Ages, the inability of the federal government to help meet the housing needs of an expected population boom by 1980, and the circuitous thinking on the part of many that avoids grappling with urgent problems.

Of his own firm, he says, "We decided we were simply manufacturers of real property as distinguished from personal property. We were certainly not just builders. This identification of ourselves was our initial step in getting our image across to the public."

He adds, "What this amounted to was that we took a business that wasn't a business, that wasn't an industry, and simply gave it a frame of reference.

"That's really all we have today and it has worked well for us."

Pausing to gaze meditatively through the broad windows of his office in Levitt's ultra-modern Grecian headquarters structure in Lake Success, L.I., he continues with what seems an expression of painful realism, "Here is an industry on which possibly twenty-five per cent of America's population depends for a living, directly or indirectly. It represents a huge dollar and unit volume, and yet ninety-five per cent of the production is done by people who make what business today would call not profit at all.

"Oh, they make a living—ninety-five per cent of the building put up today is by builders who produce five units or less. This is unique in American business. I mean the production of an item that should, from standpoint of sheer logic and economics, be made by a mass producer. It would be like asking the corner appliance store to make up a color television set for you. He could do it, of course, but it would take him at least six months and cost you three thousand dollars. Or to ask the neighborhood service station to produce a car for you. It would probably take three years and cost you thirty-five thousand dollars."

As with many other successful, self-made men, Levitt has a consciousness of his own importance and of his role in the sphere of business in which he operates and even outside it. Nonetheless, his criticism of his contemporaries is based on a foundation of singular accomplishment over two decades. In that time, the Levitt firm has built more than eighty thousand homes.

What is particularly noteworthy about Levitt, and which could have unusual meaning to other businessmen, is that the most spectacular phase of his career came after he had suffered a bad business setback in 1960.

That year, after thirty years in business, Levitt and Sons had a deficit of $763,000 and its sales were $16 million, which represented a decline of 66 per cent over a decade. The public had just lost interest in Levitt's huge developments. Over a fifteen-year period, the postwar seller's market had turned to a buyer's market.

Levitt had tried to avoid such a reverse. He had revamped the architecture of his homes and changed the street planning to relieve the monotony of his first two seventeen thousand-house Levittowns, on Long Island and near Philadelphia. The third, located in New Jersey, had done poorly by comparison with the others. Of a planned twelve thousand units, only about seven thousand had been sold within the first seven years.

And a dash of salt was dropped into the wound. In 1963, or about five years after the new development was begun in New Jersey, the residents voted to change the name of the town from Levittown back to Willingboro, the original name.

Even before the year of the big loss, Levitt had been considering decentralizing his operations. It made sense, too. Since the big building boom had limited the availability of land close to the center of metropolitan areas, builders had begun to find it difficult to locate sites to put up four thousand to five thousand units in a group.

The alternative was to build a number of developments simultaneously and in different locations. Now faced with the deficit, Levitt knew for certain that he could no longer build massive numbers of houses in a single location and show a profit.

The new policy was put into effect and its benefits have been cumulative, rather than immediate. From erecting mammoth Levittowns, on which his fame was based, Levitt turned to building smaller ones on sites along the east coast from Stony Brook, L.I., to Cape Kennedy, Fla. What is more, the stamped-out look of the older developments has given way to a rolling landscape and curving streets. Houses are much more varied in design and no identical models stand side by side.

Bigger and more expensive houses are now grouped around a club, a golf course, a lake, or a recreation area, in an effort to provide appealing community amenities and environment.

Satellites are being built on satellites, such as two near Willingboro, and none in the continental United States any longer is being called Levittown. Levitt, too, has gone abroad, with new developments not only in Puerto Rico but also in Paris. Five other French cities are due for Levitt projects, as are Spain and Italy.

The directional change pushed Levitt's sales to about $74 million in 1966 and his net income to $3,254,000. In 1967, everything Levitt did seemed to catch fire. Sales rose to $120 million and earnings were commensurate in rate of growth.

With all that bounce, Levitt demonstrated that he was one of those self-made businessmen who are simply too strong and too creative to be downed by a reversal, shocking as it may have been to his ego.

Honors and accolades have come to him in profusion. The American Institute of Architects has given two awards to Levitt homes. Media have commented ecstatically on him. "William J. Levitt is the only home builder to win membership, along with Henry Ford and Henry Kaiser, in the small circle of businessmen whose names are known to the man in the street," the *Wall Street Journal* said.

Commented *Fortune* magazine: "A good case can be made for the proposition that the best thing that has happened to the housing industry in this century is Levitt and Sons, Inc."

But perhaps the greatest recognition came in July, 1957, when International Telephone and Telegraph exchanged $92 million of its stock to purchase control of Levitt and Sons.

Levitt, who in the merger became the largest, individual holder of ITT stock, said that the marriage would enable the company to broaden its operations, particularly in the planning and building of entire communities, and in increasing its international scope.

That is Levitt today. Covered by such a halo, how did he get there, anyway?

There are three chapters in the story of the Levitts' rise. One involves the entry of the family into the home building industry. The second centers around their construction of a 750-house development in Norfolk, Va., for the U.S. Navy during World War II. And the third tells of their adaptation of mass-building techniques learned during their defense contract work to the housing needs of civilians.

In 1929, Abraham Levitt, an attorney, held a 25 per cent interest in a Rockville Center, L.I., property owned by some of his clients. For some unexplained reason, the village chose as a site for a new sewage disposal plant not a remote location but an unsuitable, twenty-acre tract immediately adjacent to the land owned by Levitt and his clients. The clients promptly sold the site to Levitt since its appeal to home builders seemed to be at an end.

Not quite knowing what to do with the property, Abe Levitt and his son, Bill, built a house on it and quickly sold it. During the next year, they built eighteen houses there. Two decades later, the Levitt assembly-line crews would be building eighteen houses every morning, and, after lunch, eighteen houses every afternoon.

After Pearl Harbor, a government ban precluded all building except that having to do with the war effort. The Levitts had the choice of either going out of business for the war's duration or of building low-cost housing in critical areas. They chose the latter and were given priority to build 750 houses to rent to naval officers. Told that speed was essential, the Levitts experimented. They learned to frame an entire wall on the ground and then to raise it into place. An obstacle was the building of septic tanks for sewage disposal in concrete blocks, a process that took half a work day. The Levitts decided to use pre-cast, concrete, burial vaults instead, which lopped off most of the normal installation time.

Back in the civilian home building field, they applied their wartime knowledge and picked up a few ideas from the assembly-line techniques of the automobile industry. They broke a building of a house down into twenty-six basic steps, starting with digging house footings and ending with painting the exterior trim. Each step was handled by a specially trained crew. Time studies developed differentiations based on the degree of labor skill each step required.

For example, one crew installed wall framing, while another more skilled crew framed the roof and put in the special rafter cuts to determine the façade variations. A basic ingredient in the system was avoiding use of the handsaw and substituting shop pre-cutting of all house parts and shop pre-assembly of plumbing and heating units. This assembly-line technique became more and more refined over the years.

By the time Levittown, L.I., was finished, the Levitts had learned something else—that, as Bill Levitt put it, "A house is not enough; it's only thirty per cent, at the most fifty per cent of a home." Besides the house, the residents need utilities, streets, shopping centers, schools, playgrounds, parks, churches, and more. All these were included in the Long Island community. Before they moved on to the next Levittown, the Levitts built a $250,000 community-center building and gave it to Levittown, L.I., for Christmas.

Bill Levitt had attended New York University but left shortly before graduation to join the family business because he was impatient to begin his career. In 1954, he bought the interest of Alfred, his younger brother, who later died. As Abe phased into retirement, Bill gradually took over the company's reins.

One of the open secrets of Levitt's success is his use of research to root out prospective sites for new developments. Using a computer, he put 207 of the country's metropolitan areas under an intensive demographic study and analyzed 165 aspects of each. Utilization of such research techniques is an important innovation in an industry wherein the vast majority of entrepreneurs are graduate bricklayers or carpenters, who are still steeped in "craft" thinking.

Use of research is now also being put to a new stress on marketing. When Levitt decided to mass produce low-cost housing at a time when returning soldiers and sailors had to raise families in small apartments or in their parents' or in-laws' homes, the overwhelming response to his effort showed that he had "sense pitch" for the public's needs. But today, says Levitt, "We are becoming persuaders. We solved the problem of mass production and now we are solving the problems of mass selling."

Levitt's answers to questions in an interview are thoughtful and candid.

Q. What business principle would you say is enunciated by your company's success?

A. Building is as old as prostitution, but a few of us, such as we at Levitt and Sons, have tried to do something different and that is probably my answer to your question. I believe also that our stress on people has helped us greatly. Each man has his own responsibility. He's got to be able to think for himself. And we have a sophisticated recruiting program—we compete in the colleges but we also seek out those with experience and talent.

Q. Can a small entrepreneur or small builder get into the field today?

A. Not very likely, unless he takes a different approach. Today to succeed you need organization, talent, know-how, and experience.

Q. Does that mean that the little builder is on the way out?

A. That's a hard question to answer. I believe that there will always be a place for the small builder but that the problems of the next five, ten, and fifteen years will cause many changes in the structure of the building industry, including the rise of many larger companies representing consolidations of smaller ones. By the end of this century, we're going to need about 52 million new homes in this country. The Department of Housing and Urban Development has published a figure of 22.5 million new homes needed in the next ten years. Who will put these up? We've never come near it in this industry—the most the industry ever constructed is less than 10 per cent of that figure per year. The answer to that must lie in the birth of new, bigger, building companies, not smaller ones.

Q. Your new concept, the Primary Employment Town, known as P.E.T., has excited a great deal of interest. The principle has stirred everyone's imagination—the concept of the town with the economy, the culture, and the social needs all wrapped up in a community of fifty thousand people, with the factories, the offices, the homes, schools, churches, and so on included in it. When will this become a reality? Will it require government financing? Where will the first one go up?

A. I think the problem to be solved first is that it must be dramatized. I don't want to debunk other planned communities, but they will not prove to be self-sufficient and the error will be compounded as time progresses. The P.E.T. will come into its own after some of these lessons are learned by others. In the meantime, we are working right now on several suitable locations. The first one will not require government financing. We will be able to finance it ourselves.

But the frustrating thing is that the government doesn't seem to look at the problem of increasing population realistically. I have testified before Congress on housing legislation but I see no recognition of the fact that we cannot go on dumping people into big cities. It's already becoming increasingly impossible to enjoy day-to-day living there anymore. We must begin to build throughout the country in the great, open spaces that are available. And to do that, we need a concept such as the Primary Employment Town, self-sustaining in individual livelihood and social needs.

Q. As a self-made man, do you have any concern about the future of the company that you helped to found when you will retire?

A. None at all. While it is true that one of the main reasons for General Motors' success was the fact that Alfred P. Sloan was a management genius, it has been perpetuated after him because he passed on his knowledge to a team. You can't run a business without a team. We have carefully built up such a team. We have put into writing procedures of company continuation if the top executives are away. If, through some bad fortune, an accident should overtake the entire Levitt top echelon, the written memo on that subject provides for a committee to run things until a new top level is chosen.

In my old age, I've become a very conservative guy. I have no question in my mind that the company will continue and I have so delegated authority. In recent years, I have not even gone to see every new development we have started. The properties were bought without my seeing them. Reports were made by various of our departments and conclusions were reached by our team. I would be a supercilious, overbearing fool if I didn't rely on the talents and skills of my associates.

Q. What key qualities do you look for in them?

A. We have made and lost a lot of money, but we learned. Our slogan is "Get the job done—and don't make the same mistake twice." We have to be able to spin on a dime. I insist that our executives make decisions without sleeping on them too long. I don't want any vacillating. Eighty-five per cent right is better than delaying decisions for fear of making mistakes.

Q. Why hasn't a success such as yours tended to create more competition for you?

A. I don't know the answer to that one . . . and yet I suppose I do know. I suppose it requires not just experience but the motivation to continue to invest and build for the future. Many companies started before we did but somehow many of them petered out. Poppa builds up a company but the sons or the grandsons just don't have the interest or the stamina to continue on.

Q. If you could have chosen another field and applied your talents to it, which one?

A. None. I have lived, breathed, and dreamt this business. There was nothing I wouldn't do yesterday—or today. You've got to love the business you are in in order to get ahead in it, and I mean not be afraid to clean ashtrays, sweep floors, or answer the telephone if you have to. I've always maintained that I've never met a chief executive of a major company who wasn't basically a salesman, and of major proportions. He had to sell his product, his beliefs, and his people. I consider myself basically a salesman.

4. DAVID SCHWARTZ

> There's no philosophy of business.
> You're in the style business. You have
> to think straight and be on the job.
> The successful people are always on
> the job.
> —DAVID SCHWARTZ, *chairman of Jonathan
> Logan, Inc.*

SOME kibitzer (jester) who spent a lifetime working on New York's Seventh Avenue, that teeming center of America's fashion industry, once said (well, not once, but many times), "You don't have to be good to make a million in the garment industry. You just have to have a lot of brass and everybody thinks you know something and then you got it made."

However, like many other indigenous comments about a business, the kibitzer's observation assumes that the listener understands the trade's foibles and mores. Thus, a few definitions are needed to properly understand it or discount it.

"Brass," of course, means nerve, and even something more that is tantamount to leadership, for the garment industry is largely composed of apt followers of a few, creative, self-starters.

"Everybody thinks you know something" signifies a search for self-confidence. This is the lifeline of an undercapitalized industry in which everyone banks on the season at hand, or for those who have more resources, on the current season and the next one. Confidence, too, breeds a like reaction among the retail buyers, so that it is self-sustaining.

"Then you got it made" is, at the least, an expression of sheer bravado. At the most, it is an uneasy yearning for security which must be bolstered by constant attention to what you are doing. No one ever really has it made on Seventh Avenue—only those who run scared. They fervently hope that what they have staked so much on in styling, fabrics, trimmings, production, advertising, and promotion will not be scorned by an ultimate consumer who never really knows what she wants until she sees it and tries it on in the stores.

If it all seems a great, big gamble, it is. Yet the fashion industry is still one of the most remunerative for an entrepreneur and one of the easiest ones for entry, that is, if you have about $100,000 on which to stake all for one good season. Even with that kind of kitty, at least one out of every four or five new garment producers still fail.

Today, in an industry which has grown one hundred years in the last twenty, with the advent of electronic data processing, market research, time and motion study, cost accounting, automation, and even the corporate developer (merger specialist), there are plenty of entrepreneurs. But of these, only a few important self-made men are left. Most of the others running the haute, midi, and "low" couture companies are sons of successful fathers, who have been staked by others, either a fond relative (father, mother, uncle, aunt), or function under a corporate "umbrella," which provides the financing, and accordingly pulls the strings.

Of the industry's self-made men, the biggest of the big is David Schwartz, a thin, intense, raspy-voiced man in his late sixties, whose restless drive and willingness to take risks have created the largest, most envied, and most copied company.

Schwartz, the chairman of Jonathan Logan, Inc., went into business with a capital of $7,500, which he shared with an erstwhile partner, more than forty years ago.

Jonathan Logan, some say, is actually a kingdom with twenty-three principalities, seemingly self-governed and self-sustaining, but actually tightly ruled, if in a paternal manner, by Schwartz and his son, Richard. This is undoubtedly a one-dimensional appraisal, since their management of the giant apparel maker has helped to bring about a new aura of stability to the frenetic garment industry, as well as a new respect for it from outsiders. The ten divisions added through direct acquisition by the Schwartzes have all grown in sales, profits, and scope under their supervision, which at least indicates a beneficent rule.

Besides the two dozen divisions and subsidiaries, Logan maintains affiliates in three other countries, sells its millions of garments to twenty thousand American retailers, operates a dozen showrooms in this country and abroad, owns twelve plants and leases fourteen others from Canada to Arkansas, and includes the industry's largest, integrated (from yarn manufacturing to finished garments ready to be worn) knit goods complex in Spartanburg, S.C. Its salesmen write more than $200 million in annual orders, a small sum by steel and railroad industry standards but a vast one for the highly fragmented (4,700 companies) women's apparel industry.

The man who put it all together never completed high school and hasn't worked for anyone else since he was nineteen. During the Depression of the thirties, when everyone else was apparently selling apples, he made money and kept the company alive. In the late fifties, he had practically sold his business but couldn't sleep at night worrying what his children would do without it and so never signed the final papers. In 1965, five years after Logan went public, he turned the reins of the business over to his then twenty-five-year-old son. It was one of the most daring moves in a business life full of daring moves. But it was calculated to succeed and it did.

Since then, the older Schwartz has voluntarily taken a back seat role as board chairman. But, outwardly, he hasn't changed much. Schwartz eating the fineries of the 21 Club and fretfully coexisting with its waiters is the same Schwartz sitting broodingly on the edge of his desk or darkly pacing his showroom in New York, as pink-cheeked, sharply dressed salesmen warily look on.

His mind racing as much in his quasi-retirement as it ever did, he seems equally restless in both environments, mentally stalking over what he may have missed that moment or that hour but deeply happy over two things. These are his singular accomplishments in a tough industry and his pride in the way his son has grasped hold of his responsibilities.

Schwartz, the older, has made some important discoveries for himself, and, because of his stature, for the industry. One is that, despite all the rapture expressed by fashion writers over styling innovations, especially the offbeat or the more daring ones (Carnaby Street, Mod, Op, Pop, the Nude or see-through look, the mini-micro-midi-skirts, or the meditation look, to mention those that arose in the past few years), the instrument or organization which can produce fashions for the millions is more important than any particular "hot" style which it can put on the market.

After decades in the fashion business, David Schwartz is sure that he has the right formula:

"The heart of our business is to be able to take large orders from retailers who used to have two stores and now have eight or nine and to ship goods fast to them. This isn't the kind of business that depends on whether you're hot or not hot. Our business just isn't dependent on any one fashion trend. Each division caters to different customers who go for different trends."

His pattern of operations has led to the growth of other large companies which closely follow his example. But some do not. Either they base their success on the broad styling of one division and every so often find to their dismay that they have badly misjudged a market, or else they go in for the "kooky," pace-setting fashions which generally fail to establish a sound sales foundation, although these attempts do influence the styling mode of the day.

Schwartz also has learned that a man who builds a company himself inevitably needs help and advice from others and a harmonious relationship with labor. Without these, he has learned, he is likely to stay small, perhaps to witness a creeping decline in his business or to be outpaced by his competition.

Shortly after he decided not to sell his business but to keep it for his family, he engaged McKinsey & Co. to determine what he needed to capitalize on his potential. The management consulting company studied his mail, his reorders, his history, and his production capacity. To reach toward the indicated, larger role, he was told that he needed a new, bigger distribution center out of the heart of Manhattan. Schwartz built it, in Jersey City.

In 1949, twenty-three years after he started on his own, he

decided that his operations were growing too large for him to remain a nonunion producer. He needed the union's help and he needed the stability of knowing he could obtain experienced workers. He met David Dubinsky, then the powerful president of the International Ladies' Garment Workers Union, one afternoon at the Harvard Club in New York and, even before their respective lawyers had arrived, the two had shaken hands and verbally agreed on a contract.

This direct approach toward the union is not very typical of the garment producer. Even when they become convinced that they must become unionized, most will skirt the issue and then find themselves reluctantly backing into an agreement.

Schwartz displays a warmth and a welcome toward younger people, sales executives, salesmen, designers, and others. His brusqueness, which can be forbidding and is famous in an industry where brusqueness is both offensive and defensive in nature, is lacking toward any newcomer of serious intent.

"New people come into our business and they bring fresh, new ideas that help us," Schwartz explains. "Frankly, I think that every generation comes smarter to the job than the one before it. My kids are smarter than I am and theirs will be smarter than they are. I see it, too, in the stores, our customers. How many times does an assistant buyer do a better job than the buyer that she replaces?"

In the classical pattern, Schwartz came from a poor family and left school early in his teens to work. At fifteen, he was earning $5 a week; at seventeen, he was earning $10 a week as head shipper in a garment loft; and, at eighteen, he was an executive earning $18 a week at the J. C. Stratton Company, a prominent dress firm operated by a dour, elderly Scotchman.

A year later, David invested his savings to start his own business, joining with a production man. The tiny firm had initial success but Schwartz soon saw that he needed greater resources to compete effectively. One evening, he arrived unannounced at the big house on Riverside Drive where the eighty-six-year-old Stratton lived.

"Yes, David?" the old man asked, with surprise. He had not seen the thin, nervously energetic young man since he had left his employ two years before. "How is your business?"

"Fine, Mr. Stratton, but I'll never get anywhere unless I get more machines," Schwartz replied, quickly. "How about lending me twenty-five hundred dollars so I can buy another fifty sewing machines?"

Schwartz left with a check. Two years later, he repaid the old man. The young entrepreneur was always grateful to Stratton for his faith in him and his generosity. Scotchmen, Schwartz is convinced, aren't stingy—just careful.

The early years were full of long hours and back-breaking efforts for the factory owner and his employees. "I used to sell all day and help to ship the goods all night," he recalls. Propelled by sheer momentum, an instinct for opportunity, and never allowing any disappointments to overwhelm him, he became the first manufacturer to produce dresses of rayon, making thousands in this new synthetic fabric to retail for $4 and $5.

In the midst of the Depression, he invested in a cotton dress company, then in others, and, by 1932, he had a chain of manufacturing businesses and even ventured into the textile field. Thus, during the Depression, Schwartz was already operating a miniature of the big, diversified complex he was to build in the fifties and sixties.

The lessons he learned from that experience came in handy later. "The companies we owned that we watched did well," he said, "but the others went to pieces."

By 1936, the small complex had begun to right itself, and, as he says, "I was the driver again." Three years later, as the country's economy began to reflect the war in Europe, the

Depression ended, and business generally, including garment manufacturing, picked up sharply.

Just prior to the sixties, when his company's annual sales were about $26 million, Schwartz agreed to a merger of convenience with Butte Copper & Zinc., a metals holding company, which wanted to divest itself of its stock. He wound up with a listing on the New York Stock Exchange, an equity for his interests, and cash for expansion. Butte sold its physical assets to Anaconda Copper.

Since then, Jonathan Logan (a name chosen for its consumer appeal) has become big business, operated with a surface latitude by David Schwartz. But the truth is that the volatile Schwartz is a tough, hardheaded trader and a stern master, who watches the business carefully, although his son is the operating chief and has authority at least as great as his father's.

In the midsixties, the older Schwartz had a severe, traumatic experience when he was quoted in a *Fortune* magazine piece on Jonathan Logan as saying, "If I drop dead, so does the business." Although he claimed that he was misquoted, the company's image suffered sharply as a result on Wall Street. The financial community itself was having a difficult time trying desperately to decide if investment in fashion businesses would be wise, in view of Seventh Avenue's feast-famine history.

If a company could go down the drain when its founder passed on, Wall Streeters reasoned, why invest in it? The fear passed on, however, but the Schwartzes felt the incident's lash, that Jonathan Logan, the giant of them all, might really be a one-man company, for a long time. Much of the Schwartzes' financial and public relations efforts have since been geared to establish the opposite contention.

Richard Schwartz's promotion from executive vice president to president at twenty-five, making him one of the country's youngest chiefs of an important company, was partly intended to remove the "one-man" stigma. His father, however, had always shown confidence in Richard's opinion, frequently writing him at Cornell for his analysis of a decision the older Schwartz had made.

Relaxed, confident, and untroubled, David Schwartz preferred being interviewed in the 21 Club but the routine of questions-and-answers in the midst of the hubbub didn't seem to bother him.

Q. In your early years in business, did you have hopes of becoming the biggest garment producer?

A. No. I just had a day-to-day ambition. But I was consistent. I never gave up. I was always in there pitching. Sure, I had plenty of disappointments, but if you always try, the averages are with you.

Q. Where did you get your ambition, anyway?

A. Those were the days when a fellow had to fight. I'm talking about 1926 and that time. I always wanted to grow. But I still go into the office at 8 A.M. You always have to be on the job to be a success. That's been true for forty years. I'm a very happy man today and I'm enjoying it all.

Q. Why do you think you became so successful in an industry as competitive as the garment industry?

A. Here are a few reasons: I never did anything that I couldn't afford and I was never afraid to take a risk or gamble on something new.

We always tried to be the first with the right things and that's the way you have to be. It hasn't changed—it's the same today.

We kill ourselves to have something the next guy doesn't have, to give a good value and still make a good profit.

You're never alone with everything for any time in the garment business. But if they don't copy you, it's no good, either.

We're in a very interesting business that most people in it hate because they're not successful.

We influenced the garment business. Because of us, people reached out and tried to do things, too. They saw our example and they've been following us ever since.

The main difference between me and others in the industry is that they don't think as big as I do.

Today, we've got the great good-will of the world. We're honest and people love us. If they couldn't make money on us, they would drop us.

Q. Can a young man or even an ambitious older man still do what you did?

A. I had $4,000 of my own to go into business, but that was a long time ago. If you want to go into the fashion business today, you need to pay $25,000 just for the showroom and for the designer and for the salesman. . . . You can drop $100,000 for one season just like that. When I was just getting started, it used to cost me sixty cents to get a dress sewn. Nowadays, it takes between four and five dollars, plus fringes. I think smart young men would be smarter to go with us than to go on their own. They can get good salaries, stock options, and other incentives. We've made more people rich. . . .

Q. Many people were surprised when Richard became president of such a large company at twenty-five. How did it happen and how did it work out?

A. The fact that Richard was my son didn't matter. He was executive vice president for two years before he became president. We—the board of directors—felt that he was the best man for the job.

I was the most criticized man in America after that. But look how well he has done. He's grabbed hold of his responsibilities and he's doing real well. There's not an important merchant who doesn't know Richard. He knows how to get the most out of business and that's the most important quality. We've got other young fellows that are like that, too.

Most rich men lose their sons because they don't give them the opportunity to show what they can do. In their growth, they forgot about their kids. I know men with much greater wealth than mine who just aren't as lucky in their children and it's a lot their own fault. They never gave them the chance.

And then there are some who don't have sons or sons-in-law in the business. I know one man who just took a bad shellacking and he would not have made the mistakes that he did if he had a son in the business or someone he could talk to in the business.

Q. After four decades of running your own company and of enjoying your success, are you now diversifying your interests, especially with your son having taken over?

A. Well, I think so. One of my great joys are the contributions we have made to charities, schools, hospitals, and to other philanthropic causes. In the last ten years, I gave millions away.

I keep in close touch with the business, too, but Richard calls the shots. Then I have other investments—a shopping center upstate and different stocks that I own and follow.

I socialize, too, more than I used to, but mostly outside the industry. If I didn't, I'd clash too much with people in the dress business. They'd ask me too many questions about business and I'd have to lie. This way, I enjoy myself and I don't have to lie.

Five

---•---

ON A PSYCHOANALYST'S
COUCH—I

1. X-RAYING THE PSYCHE

BEHIND drawn blinds in the hushed atmosphere of a psychoanalyst's office, successful, affluent, powerful businessmen, or
members of their families, unburden themselves of their emotional problems. Most are there to plead for help. Others just
want someone to talk to.

Who are they?

A hard-driving, millionaire contractor who hewed stubbornly to a twenty-year goal, achieved it, and then for the
past two years has concentrated on destroying everything
that he attained by drinking himself into oblivion. The reason: the tremendous obligation he felt not to make his dead
father seem to be the pitiable failure that he was.

The sensitive, family-minded head of an importing firm
who was chaste and moralistic all his life. Suddenly, he
turned to extra-marital relations, and, in doing so, showed

severe sadistic tendencies. The psychoanalyst described the man's problem as "beating his mother."

A publishing company chief who felt an increasing anxiety because his friends, and especially his employees, hated him. Under psychoanalysis, he admitted that he was consciously "breast-feeding" his staffers, being overgenerous and over-solicitious to them, so that they would feel unusually obligated. Because they were receiving a "life-sustaining flow" from him, the businessman was told, he expected them to work harder. But what he was really showing his employees, he was informed, was not magnanimity but contempt. "The breast-fed practice not only dehumanizes, but also infantilizes the workers," the doctor said. "No wonder they don't like you."

The aging, self-made tycoon who stubbornly refused to retire. He told the psychoanalyst that his thirty-eight-year-old son was simply incapable of running the business. But what he really had, the businessman learned, was a Samson psychology. He wanted to bring "the temple crashing down on," refusing to believe that the company could exist without him, nor did he, in fact, want it to. He would rather it died with him.

The wife of an inventor-entrepreneur who was suffering a severe form of depression because her husband was having business problems and didn't seem to want or need her anymore. "Stand up—and show some aggression," the psychoanalyst advised her. "You are important to him, and let him know it. You stood by him all the years he was struggling—and also bore him three children in the bargain. Now you want to share in the better life you both worked for, even if it does entail some problems."

Why do a disproportionate number of sons of self-made men exhibit homosexual traits? Several were told by psychoanalysts whose help they sought that it was because their dynamic fathers had no time or opportunity to show interest or love in them. In some cases, it developed, the mother took over the father's disciplinary role, with disastrous effects on the son. Since they were cast adrift by this disturbing relationship, it was suggested that the sons make lives for themselves independent of their parents—marry and seek careers of their own—proving themselves in all possible ways.

In a country in which the individual's initiative and business acumen built the world's mightiest industrial force, it is often assumed that many businessmen are psychoneurotic, not infrequently psychotic, and sometimes even worse. To achieve great entrepreneurial success is to sacrifice normal social life, family relations, and rapport with others less dedicated and less successful. So the theory goes, and many subscribe to it.

But, those who should know best, those psychiatrists who have attended most to the businessman's emotional ills, do not agree. And, while they refute the venerable "sacrifice" theory, they point out that without some of the driving, hard-nosed, anti-social traits that form the superficial portrait, most of the highly successful businessmen of today would be working for someone else, probably in a low-ranking job.

Do businessmen, especially those who built a company from the ground up, visit psychiatrists or psychoanalysts more frequently than do other types of people? No, the doctors say, they don't.

But what they do have are emotional problems perhaps more indigenous to them than to others who pursue a less dedicated, less frenetic way of life. Their problems, however, do not emerge as much from this particular type of existence as they do from the individual's own traits.

If there is one area of virtually unanimous agreement among those who attend to the problems of the psyche, it is that, despite the emotional travail that brings self-made men (and their families) to the psychoanalyst's couch, such people are no more prone to psychoneurotic ills than, say, a truck driver, a clerk, or a postman.

In fact, some psychoanalysts believe that the highly aggressive businessman would be less likely to have the type of neurotic problems that would cause him to seek psychiatric help than would writers, doctors, attorneys, actors, or musicians. The businessman is usually "outer-directed," dealing more or less effectively with environmental realities. The others tend to be more "inner-directed," grappling often with a reconciliation between reality and their "creative" interpretation of the facts.

Nonetheless, if one visits a psychonalyst or a psychiatrist, it is because something hurts, just as is the case when one visits the family doctor or the dentist.

If the hurt or the emotional problem stems from the individual's own nature, what is the self-made man like inside, in his mind, his nervous system, and his personality, where even he cannot know himself?

Discussions with a number of America's leading psychoanalysts and psychiatrists elicits this composite X-ray:

> The really successful self-made man has an underlying grandiosity. He has a dream in which he is a crown prince and so he feels entitled to riches. This creates in him enormously high hopes. . . . He has an exquisite sensitivity to his employees, especially as to whom he can trust and whom he can't. It amounts almost to paranoia. But he must be like this. Almost all of the men of this type have had great teams. You don't become rich or powerful without having a team. No one builds a great empire by himself—so it is a matter of self-protection and an essential to success to find out who will screw you or who won't. . . .
>
> The man who builds a great fortune is often a man without talent. If he were, for example, interested in a specific process or phase of business, manufacturing, advertising, design, he might easily lose sight of his primary object of making money. This distraction by being committed to a skilled specialty could

be more disastrous to the entrepreneur than to the corporate executive. So the self-made man does have one talent—he knows how to make money. . . .

He sets certain goals—sometimes, it is a temporary one, such as becoming a millionaire at the age of thirty. Beyond that, the future is vague. Sometimes, it is a long-range goal, such as making his company the biggest one in the industry and himself the biggest man in that industry. But, mostly, it is a short-term goal, or several of them, laid end to end. . . .

Nonetheless, short- or long-range, the goal builds up a head of steam—a kind of inner pressure that drives a man endlessly forward so that often he never seems to accomplish his purpose, because new goals arise. In some cases, astonishing success comes so quickly that the self-made man raises his aims to heights he never thought he could attain. But now he is sure of it. . . .

Men such as these have a prodigious, natural endowment. This is a phenomenon, in the sense that it has survived tens of millions of years of evolutionary sequence. Man is a genetic entity, a fortuitous conglomeration of genes and constitutional endowment. . . . Now, having said this, it must be added that perhaps the greatest attainment of the business dynamo is that he has not fallen into the pitfalls which have been the fate of others who may have been as well endowed as he but did not achieve the eminence or the success that he did.

What are those pitfalls? Mostly, they are physical events or happenings—illnesses, accidents, which would have reduced, crippled, or destroyed his effectiveness. Also, speaking from the psychiatrist's view, as important as anything else is the fact that successful businessmen have escaped the problems of the ill mind. For the mind is prone to the vicissitudes of distraction, disorganization (of thinking), and of fragmentation (a psychotic breaking down of the mind). . . .

This hardly means that the self-made man is of a pattern. He is, as much as any other man, subject to this truism: That in the human species, the evolutionary trend like the concept of the expanding universe is toward an increasing diversity, or individuation of people. Not two company founders are alike. A study of their individual profiles brings out certain common traits, such as drive energy, dedication, vivacity of thinking, resourcefulness, an amazing ability to channel attention, effort, and aggressiveness. But no two of them have the same "style."

Each man, like fingerprints, is one of a kind and he has no exact counterpart anywhere. . . .

2. THE BUSINESSMAN AS PATIENT

THE self-made man is a problem to his psychiatrist.

The very assertiveness that the employer of hundreds and even of thousands, the mover of men, finance, and events, brings to the psychoanalyst's office represents an obstacle that sometimes raises the doctor's hackles. These patients are difficult. They often can't and won't lie down on the couch. They sit there and talk, quite imperiously. They have built up a set of defenses over many years that won't allow them to humble themselves by confiding their innermost secrets. Some do, sooner or later; but others don't.

Because they are loners in the midst of a crowd, a good many have a problem of communication. Even with loyal confidants, the seemingly hardboiled entrepreneur has a gnawing feeling that he is being listened to for an ulterior motive, a motive that he doesn't care to examine. But it is disillusioning and disturbing to him. Isn't there such a thing as sincerity anymore? he wonders. He wishes that he had someone to talk to, who has no axe to grind, no selfish motive in listening to him. Sometimes, the self-made man has to pay for this pure ear.

For several years, a businessman of great attainment has made regular weekly visits to a leading psychoanalyst. He has no apparent emotional problem and he is not even really lonely, according to the psychoanalyst. But he wants to sound off to someone. And the psychoanalyst is a good listener. This particular executive will continue to make his visits indefinitely, his psychoanalyst believes, adding that the sessions have some sort of therapeutic value for the businessman. Yet, his problem, which can best be described as a minor anxiety feeling, appears hardly serious.

Businessmen go to psychiatrists because they have a pain, which their own MD, or perhaps they themselves, attribute to a psychoneurotic or a more serious problem of the emotions or the personality. And what can the psychiatrist or psychoanalyst do for them?

"What we seek to uncover in a patient, businessman, or otherwise, are those things that vitiate, paralyze, or distract them from their normal course of behavior," observes one veteran New York psychiatrist. "In the case of the businessman, it is to determine why he is being diverted, to a lesser or greater degree, from his dedicated, devoted course of action and behavior.

"In a superficial sense," he adds, "if a man is running backward, we do our best to make him run forward."

But the psychiatrist or analyst doesn't have a simple time of it. He can't see the totality of the self-made or any other man who comes into his office. The doctor's field of vision is limited to the management of the patient's emotional difficulties. Beyond that, he knows little of the man. The patient, especially the business tycoon whose success characteristically stems from a guarded calculation of the world around him, is able to hide much.

Otherwise, the psychiatrist comes well equipped to the challenge. He has attained an MD degree, and, after internship, he has taken at least three years of psychiatric residency and special training.

In addition to this educational and professional training, the psychoanalyst has also attended and graduated from a psychoanalytic institution. An essential part of the regimen at this specialized school is that the training analyst must himself undergo a thorough analysis. Its purpose is to evoke in the training psychoanalyst those emotional difficulties that he may have submerged in his personality.

Unless he has the subjective experience of this self-searching cathartic process, he cannot fully understand what he is seeking to arouse in his own patients. And, unless he becomes aware of what his own emotional problems are, as a microcosm of what he will unearth in others, he cannot hope to adequately treat the illness range that he may find.

A specialist in the major branch of medicine known as psychiatry, as cardiology is a specialized branch of internal medicine, the psychoanalyst like the psychiatrist is concerned with the study and treatment of disorders of the mind such as neuroses or psychoses. But psychoanalysis is the method area of psychiatry which treats such disorders on the basis that they are the result of the rejection by the conscious mind of factors that then persist in the unconscious as dynamic repressions.

The resulting conflicts on the individual's personality may be resolved when the analyst discovers or analyzes the repressions through the use of techniques such as free association or dream analysis.

Not infrequently, the businessman opens the psychiatrist's door uncertainly, not quite sure why he is there, troubled by some physical ills rather than by any apparent emotional problems. Sometimes, he is sent there by his own MD; other times, he comes on his own.

"We see a lot of wealthy men because of psychosomatic problems," reports a busy analyst. "It comes from their syndrome of overmobilization and their excessive feeling of self-sufficiency. They complain of a 'little ulcer,' or a 'small heart-attack.' In the overwhelming majority of cases, a physical examination reveals no existence of such problems, and usually, once these anxious men have broken down and shared their experiences and their problems, they are all right.

"The burdens of being on top exert a great deal of pressure. Few of these very wealthy and powerful men can deceive themselves that they cannot be easily toppled and they therefore must be eternally alert. And, as a result, they frequently react to the pressures by becoming convinced that they have a 'little ulcer,' or have had a 'small heart-attack.'"

Not all analysts agree that the businessman as a patient is generally more difficult to handle than others. Declares the chief of the psychiatry department of one of New York's largest medical centers:

"Before coming to the hospital, I had more than three decades of private practice. Between sixty per cent and seventy per cent of my patients were men, and many were businessmen. It is simply not true that they are difficult to help. They make excellent patients. They knew something was wrong with them and they knew that they needed help."

The same degrees of resourcefulness, energy, and the "ability to make courageous decisions" that helped them to achieve success were brought to bear on helping themselves to solve their emotional problems. In other words, says the psychiatric chief, they were as well motivated in this respect as in their business life.

Other professional opinion differed. In the case of one psychoanalyst with considerable experience in treating the country-club set, his contacts with businessmen patients show a great variance in behavior in his office between the very wealthy and those who were merely wealthy.

"Those patients who are really affluent demonstrated a certain cynicism, even a skepticism about the psychoanalytic process," he says, "but they were there to cooperate, to listen and, hopefully, to be helped. The others, let's say, the new millionaire, the new, little, rich guy, was aggressive, even resentful. Chances are his wife, or his family, compelled him to come to my office and he was really not prepared or not willing to unburden himself to me."

Some businessmen visit the analyst's office not to cure an illness or to ease a disturbance, as much as to seek advice on a personal matter. Frequently, such an instance involves problems with children. A son or daughter who is rebellious;

or who has departed from the family home to live in free squalor as a hippie; or a worrisome situation with a child whose future for various reasons seems uncertain.

And, in such cases, the parent's behavior can be typical or it can be peculiar. A strange, if not irate reaction came from a quite wealthy businessman after he brought his son to be treated by a psychoanalyst. As the doctor relates it:

"The boy, seventeen, was born a schizoid. His father refused to believe that it was the boy's nature to merely sit all day before the television set, or, if forced away from it, to wander aimlessly through the city or countryside, with no interest in a career, education, or his future. When I finally told the father that I could contribute nothing to help his son, that he was simply a harmless, foolishly happy person whose life could be relatively calm if his father would continue to support him for the rest of his days, the parent lost his temper and berated me. In my twenty-five years of practice, he was the only one who refused to pay my bill."

3. MOTIVATION

THE magnified picture etched on the public eye:

The squat, overdressed tycoon sits tensely in his overstuffed chair in an immense, gaudy office. Frantically, he punches buttons, muttering, even yelling. Lieutenants, secretaries run in, their hearts pounding with fear. He stabs the air with expletives, gesturing contemptuously at them. Later, that day, he is traveling in a jet (preferably his own), simultaneously talking into a phone and dictating into a tape recorder. As the plane nears the field, instead of fastening his seat belt, he throws it aside and goes forward to the pilot to personally direct the plane's approach to the landing strip. Soon, the tycoon is directing a large meeting around a polished oval table in the city's largest hotel, laying plans for a national or international multi-million dollar deal. Late that night, he is back on his jet, relaxing or trying to, a bottle of tranquilizers and a bottle of Scotch at one hand, a striking, sloe-eyed young woman in a negligee waiting his pleasure at the other hand. Discreetly in the rear, an earnest young doctor stands by, adrenalin-filled hypodermic held at the ready.

Exaggeration—in depth? Of course. A caricature? Of course.

But no more exaggerated in principle than the fact that since the days of Horatio Alger, the average person has had a completely false idea of the well-springs, the stimuli, the motivation of the American entrepreneur.

The facts are, according to analysts who have probed the businessman's psyche, that he is not driven by his neurotic suffering; that poverty is not the major stimulus for the self-made man's success; that he is not carried forward relentlessly by a constant goal; and that he does what he does not because he has to but because he likes doing it.

Here is what psychiatrists say on these points:

"The general public has been brain-washed to believe that the struggling, suffering, and adverse circumstances, and, in a great sense the connotation of the clap-trap of Horatio Algerism is the secret of success," one analyst said.

"Such men as make a big, personal business success have a prodigious endowment of a natural manner. This includes a creativity, imaginativeness, resourcefulness, vivacity of the thinking process, single-mindedness, dedication, and a great ability to channelize their effort and energy. He is, in short, just about a phenomenon."

In no way, however, the analyst said, does this mean that the self-made man is not as prone or as vulnerable to becoming neurotically ill as anyone else. But if he is unfortunate enough to show signs of stress, or neurosis, at the time he became successful, people are inclined to say, "What happened to the poor guy? Did his success cost him his health? Or was the success the end result of his previous, neurotic problems?"

The analyst continued, "If his neurotic disruption had taken place in childhood or youth, or at any other time in the sequence of his success, people would not be much inclined to comment on him. But for some reason, because he has become successful, it is as though he were suddenly and unceremoniously disrobed. The face is that the vulnerability and frailties of the successful are no different from those of the underprivileged or, for that matter, the mentally defective."

On poverty as the spur, another analyst observed, "I don't agree that it is the big stimulus for the success of the self-made man. The venality, the drive, their very success involve individual traits that are an intrinsic part of their own makeup, have little, if anything to do with the environment of their upbringing. If it was only poverty, why didn't the other ninety-nine per cent of the poor kids in the same neighborhood also make it?"

And, on the matter of goals, said a third analyst, "It is a misconception that the self-made man has a constant goal that pushes him on.

"He always enjoys what he does. He gets a great emotional thrill out of its challenges and he scarcely ever thinks of reaching a lofty, long-range goal. He wants to do a good job, to win out in an immediate or short-term quest. The long-range objective is not with him, not part of his consciousness."

If that is the case, if the self-made man achieves his huge success not because he is driven to it by neurosis or poverty but by natural traits that lend themselves to his succession of short-term goals, where do these traits spring from? In most cases, they are not inherited, nor do they represent a new strain that can be passed on to the next generation. They are instead natural and evolutionary, but not necessarily genetic, or hereditary.

What of cases in which the son exhibits a business drive and creativity of enterprise greater than even his successful father? Aside from their rarity, such cases usually show that the son acquired traits not so much from his father as from his mother, a grandfather, or an uncle, or not from anyone at all. Such a suspected connection with a relative is, at best, conjectural. The psychiatric community, for one group, believes that a natural evolutionary endowment is the primary if not the sole basis for the entrepreneurial skill.

"The self-made man's creative imagination, that most important part of his makeup, springs from an isolated nuclear endowed center, which depends upon all other aspects of the individual for its expression, support, and fruition," declares one psychiatrist. "This dependency is much similar to the body's blood vessels and muscles which depend upon the skeleton for support."

The "nuclear center" lies at the heart and core of the human being and represents a combination of physical, physiological, and psychological factors. Its dependency on the physical and mental conditions could, of course, cause problems if those factors are affected by illness. But not more so than in the case of any other person.

"A disruption of the supporting matrix of the creative stream of the individual may or may not affect that stream," the psychiatrist adds. "So, for example, if an individual has become emotionally traumatized or assaulted, it may or may not encroach upon his creativity."

But, lest the layman become entirely convinced that the self-made man's undeniable attainments spring purely from normal instincts, the experience of a number of psychoanalysts is that often the man of great enterprise is a paranoiac. In the simplest of terms, this is a person who has consistent delusions either of grandeur or of persecution, or of both.

"Some I have treated have an overt paranoia, particularly because of their belief that people are out to harm them," reports an analyst.

"While this disorder—and it is a serious disorder—was one

of the reasons that brought the businessmen to my office," he says, "it also played a role in their success. There is in the paranoid person a certain amount of fear and distrust toward everyone and this characteristic in the successful person is put to good use.

"He studies the situation carefully at all times. The fear in him compels him to look more closely at every aspect of his working and personal life. He becomes a student par excellence. He doesn't take anything for granted. Because of this fear provoked, he makes superior decisions. He develops a megalomania. It's the old story of the man who 'isn't afraid of anybody, because he's really afraid of everybody.'"

He adds: "Men like these fight not just their competitors but the government, their families, everyone. They'll try to learn the things that other people can't do and then they will find a way to do it."

The analyst described the unusual behavior of a wealthy oil man, the founder and head of his own company, who was both a friend and a patient. On several social occasions to which he had invited the doctor, the businessman pointed to several men of varying ages and said, "Watch them. This is how I do it in my business. I study what they do with their hands, their feet, how often they light a cigarette. I study what their behavior is like. That way, I put together little bits of information and I know what type of man each one is. The impatient guy, the nervous guy, the real insecure guy, and the guy who smokes all the time because he can't concentrate—they give themselves away every time and I get the edge on them. You can't miss."

The oil man, of course, was paranoiac and has a history of severe paranoiac attacks involving his wife and family.

The drive of the most successful corporate founders is so intense and their preoccupation and dedication so complete that an analyst who has had long experience in treating them is convinced that their megalomania is so successfully structured that they could rise to the top in any political structure.

"Many of them would either end up as Stalins, or at least as commissars, if communism, rather than capitalism had succeeded in the Western world," he asserts. "As it is, they became powerful industrial tycoons in a democratic but capitalistic society."

And, in that society, it is apparently possible to wield tremendous power in such a role without arousing the ire of labor unions or the workers, he observes. Witness the birth of the new breed of millionaires who have achieved vast success, power, and wealth through the manipulation of money. The issuance of convertible debentures, warrants, notes, and other paper may be a controversial move, but it is certainly legal, unless fraud can be proven. Nonetheless, this new form of acquiring power, which has been variously described by critics as "printing counterfeit" or "playing Scrabble," has been fostered without the labor–management difficulties, more than token government interference, or personal bitterness that would seem to be a natural result of such activities.

Putting it all together, what is the enterprisers' profile of motivations? Its major features, not very coincidentally, represent the very elements of their success:

An underlying grandiosity, in which a dream must be lived of enormous aspiration and entitlement to power.

An expression of an unusual, natural endowment, involving creativity, resourcefulness, and dedication.

A paranoialike, "exquisite" sensitivity to others, particularly employees and competitors, which provides the skill to develop a "great team" and to analyze competition.

A desire to pursue and a talent only for the money-making practice, and an ability to concentrate on this goal without diverting interest to subsidiary phases of the business.

A yearning for power on a dominant scale to achieve either a tycoon or a commissar status.

A driving urge to throw oneself into the business, hence an enormous devotion and love for the task.

4. HAPPINESS

THE bulky, middle-aged man sat nursing a drink on the country club veranda, his rather prominent cheekbones and somewhat high, hooked nose creating an odd combination with the benign blue of his eyes. He felt a smile easing onto his face and inwardly he was conscious of a warmth that did not emanate entirely from the liquor. The waiter hovered overanxiously nearby. Acquaintances sauntered past with a wave or a hello. He sighed. It was 6:15 P.M. and he was more than content. He was happy.

But he really shouldn't have been.

Early that day, he had had an unpleasant scene with his wife. He was away too much; she was by herself too often. Without saying so, both knew that a yawning gulf had developed between them, almost imperceptibly over the past few years. Each new contact, each deal, each new project provided him with new layers of attainment, sophistication, almost a deepening of his feeling of growing omnipotence. Her world was static—membership in a women's organization, alternate days of shopping, a matinee, a museum, visiting the children, supervising the housework. She had surprised him with her bitterness. He had thought she was settled on her own level of fulfillment, such as it was.

The later hours at the office had been disconcerting, too. Two competitors were pulling some tricks. His secretary of the past two decades had committed several errors, one of particular embarrassment to him. His long-time general manager, who was a few years older than he was, had seemed more inadequate than ever lately and the boss's thoughts turned again to the question of retiring the man early. He wondered if the big salary and the generous stock options he gave the executive were not more of a sinecure than an incentive.

And, as he had walked through the sales department in the early afternoon, he had been dismayed at the number of men who sat, apparently listlessly, at their desks. In his day, he had made it a practice never to be in the office in the afternoon, unless he had to. Even on slack days, he would be either making contact calls, or, if he had run out of names, he would take in a show or a movie and call in late before going home.

The day ended with a disagreement in principle over the telephone with his attorney; a vaguely disturbing indefinite answer from an official in a federal agency in Washington to a request; and an accusing phone call from his daughter who had accepted her mother's version of the morning scene without question.

He had been in a bad mood as he left the office for a quiet meal at the club before going to a night meeting. His chauffeur was waiting for him and as the Continental pulled away and he looked over his shoulder at the building that bore his name and he saw the stream of home-bound employees emerging from the twelve floors that housed all he had worked for, his troubles seemed to lift. Then, as he entered into the friendly circle of respect and social acceptance at the club, the inner warmth began to suffuse through him and his day of unusual troubles receded onto a back burner of his mind.

Are entrepreneurs happy? Yes, say their psychiatrists, they are, as long as they satisfy their drives and reach their goals and then go on to new ones. The disorganization of the day and the discomfiture of family problems slide off them with ease as long as they do not unduly disturb the mainstream of their life's effort, their work and their business.

"It is possible for the businessman to be serene," a psychiatrist says, "even amid external chaos.

"The exception to this, the unhappy businessman, is the one who has the kind of inner pressure that drives him endlessly forward but never seems to enable him to accomplish his purpose."

Such a man, he adds, is not only unhappy but ultimately unsuccessful. Happiness (even amid chaos) and success (especially personal) go hand-in-hand, he is convinced.

"What is happiness?" poses another psychiatrist, rhetorically. "Happy people are sometimes the sickest sort of people around—for despite the smile on their faces and their general contentedness, they experience unresolvable problems in life.

"Quite a few people tell me that they are happy because they feel an absence of sadness or pain," he says. "But sometimes this is devastating to the personality because one has to have a contrast. If you know or have pain, it is then possible to enjoy pleasure.

"Otherwise, the personality is like a piece of music all in one note."

A self-made man who became a self-lost man is included in the case file of a prominent midwestern analyst.

The businessman involved had built a chain of stores in Indiana to a successful point and then eventually lost most of them because he was an "unhappy" man. A Jew who elected to fight bigotry by trying to "pass" to the other side, he showed anti-Semitic tendencies. The spur to this behavior was that not only did he crave acceptance from the gentile community but he also had a flair for politics. To achieve a political career, not to mention recognition from his non-Jewish neighbors and acquaintances, he raised his family as non-Jews. All his three sons had to go to Exeter and all three ultimately married gentile girls.

But, as such stories often seem to go, all his pretensions and the sham that was his life were not successful. Gradually, he became aware that he was not respected, that he would never amount to anything in politics, and that rather than acceptance he was drawing ridicule.

His normally violent temper raged out of control. He railed at everyone and the confidence and trust that he had carefully built up over the years waned. Ultimately, his credit lines withered and he was forced to drastically curtail his business.

A misconception over the personality of many of the most successful businessmen is probably the reason why many people consider them to be frustrated, discontented, and strange. Why, for example, do so many wealthy and powerful business leaders seem to put on a different face during different occasions, swinging widely from seeking publicity and notoriety at times to eschewing it at other times as though it were leprous?

Paul Getty, the oil billionaire; Howard Hughes, the mysterious empire-builder; and Frank Sinatra, the movie actor, producer, and entrepreneur come easily to mind in this regard.

The question has puzzled not only Americans, who tend to look on some of their most successful businessmen as either national heroes or as pariahs, depending upon the man's individual image, but many people abroad. Foreigners see American culture as basically still business-oriented, money-minded, and noncreative, and, at the same time, status conscious and ostentatious. It all denotes immaturity, they believe, and aren't surprised when Americans act willfully and even capriciously.

When the question was put to one of New York's most prominent psychiatrists, he replied, "To assume that a successful industrialist or businessman consciously or deliberately behaves differently in his personal and business lives, that he must be all of one type, all of a rigid profile, is erroneous.

"One can't expect a businessman to operate the same at a board of directors' meeting as he would swimming, driving, having dinner with his family, or playing golf. This would presuppose that the armamentarium, the totality of his resources, is in use at all times. If there is a breadth and a depth to an individual, the fact that he appears as a different person in different situations doesn't mean that he is striving to be different.

"In other words, the fact that certain features of his profile may be more prominent at one time than at another doesn't mean that he necessarily changes from one time to another."

To stress his point, the psychiatrist selected the peacock as an example. "The most prominent feature of the peacock are his feathers, but there is much more to him than just that. All peacocks look alike, until a closer scrutiny of them shows that there is a leader among his kind. Certainly, the pecking order in a barnyard is evident—there is a first-degree pecker, then a second-degree pecker, and so on.

"So with the self-made businessman. The most characteristic of the species is his individuality. There is simply not a second edition of him. But there is more to him than his individuality, and, in each, the collection of traits is different than in the next self-made man, and the behavior of each is different and varies as the occasion demands of him."

So much for one psychiatrist's reaction to a widespread misconception.

In its simplest terms, according to another analyst, the businessman's happiness depends on the sense of well-being that he derives from his work. "When work becomes the greatest form of play that there is," he added, "you have a worker or a businessman who is happy."

But, it is not that simple. The businessman may be personally happy, but, if he has the classic self-made man's trait of near-total absorption in his endeavors, chances are he is punishing his family, robbing his wife of companionship and his children of their father's time, solicitude, and counsel. Result: an unhappy family situation. It is the self-made man's lot to create this problem, as well as to suffer from it, more than from any other personal situation in which he finds himself. But there is one more problem, rare by comparison. It was

alluded to earlier: the pitfalls of any human being, the vicissitudes of the mind, which "vitiate, paralyze, cripple, or distract these men from their dedicated and devoted course of
action and behavior."

A psychoanalyst who had put a depressed businessman
through psychotherapy to solve the man's repressive obligation
to a dead, unsuccessful father had several other cases in
which businessmen in their late thirties sought to destroy all
that they had built.

One, already mentioned, tried it through alcoholism; another through depression; and a third through sheer apathy.

In all cases, the fathers of these businessmen came from
lower socio-economic circumstances. Their education was
minimal, because opportunities were lacking, and their financial attainment was very modest. But each had been ambitious, although success had eluded him.

As a result, the successful sons were "endlessly apprehen-
sive" that they would upset and bring embarrassing ridicule to
their parents, even though they were dead.

If this tries belief, the analyst took another tack.

"Every child at some time threatens that when his father
spanks him, 'One day, I'll be as big as you and I'll beat you
up!' The son's drive, with this underlying threat, becomes a
great source of energy which propels him onward to a business
success.

"But when he reaches his goal or a pinnacle for him of the
greatest attainment, the child (the businessman) finds that
he doesn't want and doesn't dare to be bigger than his father.
And, so, in fact, he begins to break down what he has built.
He has lost his joy in life."

In other words, the analyst concluded, the child-man, after
reaching maturity and earning great success, finally winds up
his punch at his father but he never quite uncorks it.

Six

ON A PSYCHOANALYST'S
COUCH—II

1. TURN A BUSINESSMAN INSIDE OUT AND . . .

AMERICA's entrepreneurs often come through with surprisingly little human dimension. The worn decal sticks: the corporate swashbuckler leaning beady-eyed and sweating over a deskside Dow Jones ticker, money on his mind and avarice in his soul.

With all his frailties and strengths, the human being inside the businessman appears to elude equally the ordinary layman and the many observers either in the academic world or in the management associations who study him as carefully as they would a pinned butterfly. But, always from the outside.

To the psychiatrists, however, businessmen do, of necessity, reveal themselves as they are, and the aspect is often pathetic and sometimes tragic.

Some stories that analysts tell are cases in which they were the therapists. Others are related, as it were, from a distance.

Th did not treat the people involved and so were compelled to stand by helplessly even though they suspected the turns of the drama that would soon unfold.

Sad and yet revealing is one such story. Burly, flamboyant Ralph Markenstein, a rich, power-loving, self-made man, decided after forty years to relinquish his post as president to another. He hired a management expert, a Joseph X. Steiner, to take the job on a five-year contract at $150,000 a year. The names of both men are necessarily fictitious.

The first year, everything Steiner did was more than right in Markenstein's eyes. There were comments among the staff that "even when Joe goes to the men's room, Ralph stands up and cheers." Steiner was a forthright, courageous type who had a record of accomplishment and of standing by his principles.

One reason that Markenstein had tapped him for the job was that he wanted people to know that not only would he step aside for someone else but that the someone had to be a man of unquestioned integrity and conviction. For too long, Markenstein felt, he had been judged a dictator, the head of a one-man company, and too egotistical to admit another strong man at the top.

But, almost at the anniversary date, the two had their first cheek-by-jowl confrontation. Steiner won out, but Markenstein was shaken down to his toes. Suddenly, he began to fear Steiner, as he suspected all along he might fear a rival.

From then on, Markenstein fought the younger man, often countermanding his orders. When Steiner accused him of it, he denied it. But soon the founder knew he had to rid himself of the tough-skinned president by trying for his jugular. In successive steps, he removed Steiner's principal responsibilities, gave his decision-making rights to others, and then secretly forbade anyone in the main office to communicate or even to converse with Steiner, except the president's secretary.

Steiner found his office becoming a cell. He knew, of course, what was going on but he was powerless to change it. His entire career had been successful; however it wasn't long before he began to believe that he was at fault. "What I can't get through my head," he told a friend, "is why Ralph turned on me so suddenly. What did I do?"

He could, of course, have broken his contract, but he hated to walk away from a job as a failure. Every so often, he would meet Ralph in the hall and the big man would give him an affable, even a gracious greeting. Two years went by in this tortured, eerily isolated way for Steiner. One afternoon, he jumped through his office penthouse window to the street forty stories below.

Markenstein was aboard on a vacation at the time but he just managed to make the funeral. It took him almost a decade to hire another president.

If Markenstein literally destroyed a potential rival by humiliation, an act that is not less than psychological homicide and which brought him much opprobrium, a drive to suspect rivalry in others and thus to render them powerless is a trait of many self-made men.

Observes Dr. George J. Breitbart, a New York psychiatrist who has treated numerous businessmen, "The aggressive trait of the successful businessman who drives people out of his employ is frequently a statement to the effect that 'there is no room here for the two of us.' That phrase is the realistic assessment of the employee's qualities and potentialities, leading to the employer's conclusion that they are more or less identical with his own."

When the supply of rivals runs out and the competition wanes and there are no sons to take over, the company founder may find himself faced with his greatest dilemma.

One alternative can be simple, if abrupt. After thirty years of building one of the largest firms in the materials construction industry, the aging owner decided to retire. His sons were successful in their own right. He and his wife had more money than they would ever need. Much of his business had become automated and the number of employees had been substantially reduced. He was not anxious to sell the company or to see it run by other owners. One morning, he simply closed its doors forever.

Self-made men like to build dynasties.

As in the great Roman and Egyptian royal families, the patriarchs hope that they will personally remain the most noted members, sometimes even exhibiting a lively jealousy of their talented offspring. But, say the physicians to whom they bring their emotional ills, they suffer their greatest pain when their sons do not emerge as successes in the manner of the fathers.

Even a weaker, more pallid facsimile would be acceptable, perhaps even preferable. But when the sons are clearly failures, the fathers are bitterly disappointed. Somewhat less are they troubled by their difficulties with wives and daughters.

"Problems with children seem to be the main thing that brings the self-made businessman or corporate executive to me," notes Dr. Milton R. Sapirstein, a leading psychiatrist who is in charge of the organizational psychiatry department at Mount Sinai Hospital, in New York.

"You can't raise children on an estate surrounded by a high, electronically guarded fence as easily as you can in Levittown with a back fence facing the next one and the mother in the kitchen," he adds.

"The children of the affluent business families are aware of the fact that their parents are special and this sometimes leads to difficulties. They tend to turn problems with their parents around to mean problems with money and so they become anti-money and anti-business. That's why more and more children of the wealthy are becoming 'hippies' and leave home to live in a 'free' or bohemian environment," he says.

Stick a pin into a self-made man and he will yell just as loudly as any other man, bleed as much or as little, and rub himself just as hard.

But the traits that he brings to his work, that lead him to his success—the dedication, the restless mind, the creativeness, the grandiosity, and the paranoiac sensitivity—make him perhaps even more human, perhaps more prone to generate problems than other men.

One businessman in his late forties bragged to his analyst that he had had thirty women in one week. The doctor scoffed mildly at this almost unbelievable medical phenomenon. "Loverboy" then readily admitted that he had been exaggerating. He had really had liaisons with only two women, he said, but had craved at least twenty-eight more. He listened sheepishly as the analyst explained that the patient's tendency to brag about his sexual exploits was related to his great urgency for success in all he did.

If the urgency produces problems in businessmen who have such a dominant trait, it often brings unhappiness and difficulties to their families.

The principal reason is neglect. Psychiatrists who treat the businessman often find members of his family in their waiting rooms. "It's not infrequently an unintentional neglect," says one physician. "They're so wrapped up in their work that their families may rarely see them for long stretches. The family ties break down and the result are neurotic difficulties of various types."

So, in all too many cases, the successful businessman and the entrepreneur are caught in a trap of their own human frailties. Turned toward their businesses, those frailties are attributes which make them rousing successes and indomitable competitors.

A most spectacular success today is a youngish egotist whose instinct for corporate gambling and whose brash courage has turned enemies and fair-weather friends into reluctant admirers. But, to his attractive, young wife, his excesses such as high-living, inordinate restlessness, and frequent absences, have turned him into a "problem" child, a child she loves because she knew him and was warmed to him when he was penniless and humble. She has threatened many times to divorce him. But she hasn't and she probably never will. She is caught in her own trap of human frailty.

The businessman's stereotyped aspect to the public is paradoxical from the standpoint that Americans often tend to make national heroes of their countrymen who have made astonishing business successes but the hero-image is cold, brutal, austere. Politicians, athletes, military men, and entertainers represent warm, human personalities. However, only businessmen and scientists appear to have the problem of joining the human race, American style.

As Dr. Lebert H. Harris, a prominent Manhattan psychoanalyst, puts it, "The self-made man's image is pseudotypical, rather than prototypical. There are certain stereotypes which many people formulate in their minds. An actor, for example, is pseudotypically polygamous, virtually by definition. It is not a fact statistically. But a prototypical aspect is that of a primary model. In that case, the image is based upon the knowledge of the behavior of a specific person or persons."

Most businessmen, especially those of the entrepreneurial element, are reluctant to expose their human side to the public except when they can entirely control the result. This, of course, is simply not possible, and it accounts for the rapid turnover in the public relations men whom the entrepreneur employs.

But the businessman keeps trying. He hopes his philanthropic contributions, often made to assist worthy causes while at the same time being tax-deductible, will help to show his humanity. The public, however, is not generally willing to cooperate in this plan. Philanthropy, for whatever good causes, is still part of the process of the exchange of money, in the average person's view, if he ever thinks about it at all.

2. THE FAMILY RELATIONSHIP

What type of women do self-made men marry? Pretty much the same variety that other men marry. But there are a few differences in the inclinations that the go-getter businessman on the rise has toward the woman he wants to share his home.

First, the young entrepreneur knows instinctively that he will have to neglect his family at least the first few years and possibly for many years. So, he tries to find a spouse who will not be so possessive that his absences will cause her much alarm and result in family scenes that will divert him from his main objective. He doesn't always succeed in this objective, of course, because it is not easy to predict how another person will behave.

Second, the young man who has a habit of looking at himself in the mirror and agreeing that what he sees is a handsome, virile tycoon of the "new breed" is also inclined to seek out a woman whose beauty and grace will add another jewel to the crown he is convinced he will wear. This choice is probably an easier one to obtain than the other, but, of course, it can give rise to many other problems, if the attributes and characteristics of the bride are in any way incompatible with his own.

Third, instincts that the suitor hardly suspects come into play. And they are probably no different from the ones that many men of totally different callings exhibit. But the fact is that women whom self-made men marry generally fall into two classes—the weak-willed and the strong.

If, for example, the young businessman with his head totally immersed in his business has had dominating characteristics and has an unusually outward personality, he will probably gravitate toward a girl who is happy in her home and does not want to be part of his business life. She will admire and respect him for his attainments but she will not seek to become part of them. In her own way, she will try to match in her home something of the triumphs he has reached in his business. And, if the young man's instinct has been sound, they will both be happy.

But, if the budding self-made man has had a possessive mother in his background and hasn't overtly fought her but has instead accepted her dominating role, he is likely to settle for a bride from the same iron-backed school. If, other things being equal, she provides a pleasant home and doesn't interfere too much in his business, they, too, will be happy.

However, the obstacle in all these inclinations is the simple one of the unpredictability of behavior, humans being what they are, and, as a result, many family problems arise in the homes of the successful businessmen.

"Businessmen have a different relationship with their wives and children than other men do," observes Dr. Oscar Sachs, a New York psychoanalyst. "Their unintentional neglect of their families produces conflicts, mainly because of the demands of their acquisitive drives and their dedication to their business. And, so far as the types of women they marry, there is a wide range and many opposites of types."

A midwestern businessman in his thirties married a woman who had been a minor executive in the same company in which he had started his career. She encouraged him to go out on his own. As his successful efforts led to the development of a big and important company, she counseled him and often personally involved herself in his work.

Their growing family evolved into what is one of the classic patterns of the self-mader's problem:

As the father neglected the home, the strong-willed mother replaced him and became the disciplinarian. The son, dominated by his mother and yearning for his father to provide an example, became a homosexual. The only daughter grew up to be a mature and full person, but, for reasons that no one could seem to understand, the man she married developed several paranoidal tendencies and she ultimately divorced him. When the father died, the mother truly became the matriarch and also took over the running of the business.

As Dr. Sachs implied, different businessmen will marry opposite types of women.

A southern banker married a pretty but flighty woman who had never matured from a childhood narcissism. Despite the fact that the couple had four children, the mother spent considerable time enjoying herself and exposing her beauty. The husband was away a good deal, cementing relations for the bank which he had founded and partly for whose benefit he had decided to wed an attractive, outgoing woman.

All four children developed neurotic and emotional problems of various kinds. But, even with that, they were more fortunate than other children in similar circumstances. Their maternal grandmother, who sadly knew her daughter too well, devoted herself to the children and helped to ease their troubles as they grew up.

How many of the self-maders' families are troubled? The answer is hard to come by, even among some of the country's most outstanding analysts. The main reason is that they have no way of telling, since they are only brought into the situation if there is a problem.

But the answer probably is that such families have no more problems than those of less affluent families. Many laymen, in fact, appear to think that the wealthy families have even fewer difficulties than those in poor circumstances. Emotional disturbances and broken homes among the poor have received considerable emphasis in recent years as a result of the publicity over social aid and anti-poverty programs.

Comments Dr. Breitbart, "The one thing that is not apparent to the observer of the affluent businessman is his home situation, the demands of the wife and children and the pressures that these create on the man himself. Nor is his own internal state obvious, for that matter.

"The notion that is being pushed today is that broken and impoverished homes are the cause of most of today's human emotional difficulties. But I have seen no less an escalation of pressures in the homes of the wealthy. They may appear to have less because they have cadres of servants to shelter them in the comfort and peace of their homes. And they have social and private secretaries and doormen to shelter them; and doctors, psychiatrists, lawyers, and accountants and every form of consultation to help them. But all this does not help when the emotional pressures are more than the normal health of the wealthy can sustain."

Adds Dr. Harris: "The closer the businessman's main activity in life is to the main forces of his childhood, the family drama in which he participated and the primitive forces that brought about its tension, the more difficulty he will have in his later personal life."

Dr. Harris maintains that the problems that a man has with his sons are derivative of the problems that he had with his own father. How does the businessman deal with his own son, other than with the knowledge, experiences, and instincts that he retained since he was a child? And how much, poses Dr. Harris, does the son contribute to his father's degradation of him?

In an eastern city, the seventeen-year-old son of a wealthy manufacturer drunkenly lurched over to the gaudy, illuminated waterfall in a local night club and calmly urinated into it. When the police arrived, he rather incoherently explained that he couldn't find "the john." But the police learned later that the boy had been having a running battle with his father and had been committing a series of minor social infractions as a protest against his father's demands to live up to his responsibilities.

Childhood prejudices well up under pressure.

An industry leader proudly watched his thirty-two-year-old son take over his own post as president and two years later joined in the applause that greeted the young man's successful performance. Suddenly, to his dismay, the father found that his son was not only opposing every idea that the older man proffered but was taking every opportunity to ridicule him.

The climax came one evening, when at a dinner party, the son flatly and publicly told his father, "You don't know what you're talking about, I've accomplished more in two years than you did in the past thirty. Why don't you just keep your mouth shut from now on?" The company founder walked out in tears.

Later, from a mutual friend, he found out what was bothering the young man. It seemed, the son told the friend, that he just couldn't take his father's foul mouth and coarse ways anymore. For years, he said, he had been embarrassed by them and now, having come into his own, he felt he didn't have to take them anymore. Although the son apologized in due course, neither was again quite happy in each other's presence and the father began seeking a buyer for his substantial interest in the company.

But the reverse happens, too. A semiprofessional prize fighter when he was a young man in Baltimore, a big, burly food processor deliberately held his son down on the executive ladder in the company he had organized. Although the young man had achieved an excellent scholastic record, had received a master's degree in business administration, and was showing exceptional supervisory talent, his father seemed to be deprecating all he did.

When the time came to choose a new president, the father ignored his son, a slim, wispy and somewhat academic-looking type, and selected a six-foot, three-inch, 220-pound manufacturing executive. Somewhat later, the latter analyzed the situation:

"Joe never forgave the boy for not being the big, strapping guy he is. The fact that the kid has more on the ball than either of us didn't seem to matter. But I'm going to try to convince that hard-headed, old bastard that he's all wrong."

And, eventually, he did.

Perhaps the most common reason for the personal problems that the dynamic businessman has is that they emanate from the sacrifices which he voluntarily makes in order to succeed.

Dr. Harris observes, "There is no doubt that the one who builds a business from the ground up has to make sizable sacrifices in his marriage, in his family life. This is observable at all levels. This even penetrates to avocations, at times, and even when an avocation represents an important personal expression. One man I knew, for example, had a considerable talent as a painter but this interest could not compete with his primary drive to express himself in his business and he gave up painting."

One of America's most prominent psychiatrists, who declined to be quoted by name because he didn't want his present and former patients to be embarrassed by association, emphasized that virtually every examination of the troubled tycoon revealed "an impossible family situation."

He added, "Their depressions and anxieties emanate from repressions caused primarily from troubles with wife, sons, and/or daughters, even though a good many of the businessmen I have treated show a fear of various degrees over the possible loss of their good situations. This comes from their concern over government intervention in their businesses, over a possible spread of communism, and, lastly perhaps, over their own inability to keep up with competitors.

"But none of these concerns provide the basic causes of the businessman's problems to the extent that his difficulties with his family does. Often, such difficulties arise because the man has-moved ahead but his wife has stayed behind, or the fact that his children do not give him the respect he feels he deserves. Yet, the biggest disturbance may come from the loss of his inner craving for immortality when his children fail him.

"Great success tends to build a feeling of omnipotence— the tycoon is inevitably convinced that he knows all the answers. This omnipotence (megalomania) compels the man to buy immortality, and he tries to do this through many contributions, providing fellowships, endowing hospitals, museums, colleges. He would like to top it all off by also buying immortality through his son's imitating him when he passes on. But, when the son is inadequate, the pleasure and the power of the father's attainments frequently turn sour."

If, as some psychiatrists have pointed out here, the father's treatment of the son is a throwback to how he was treated by his own father, when are the formative years of the relationship between the second and the third generations? Analysts differ here. Some, as Dr. Sapirstein has already said, believe that the sons run into neurotic difficulties because "they know the parents are special." But, others such as Dr. Breitbart, feel that "the father is to the child what he is whether he is a self-made man or a civil servant."

Dr. Breitbart adds, "The formative years of a son are mostly complete by age eleven or twelve, long before he can conceive that his father is a real success or not. Up until the boy is fourteen, or so, the father represents a security symbol, and the mother is just the most beautiful woman in the world. After that period, the son's convictions can only be augmented along the lines he reached in his formative years."

Regardless of which school of thought is correct, the undeniable fact is that the influences of the formative years last a long time. They affect not merely the son's life, but that of his parents, even those of other relatives and certainly those of the woman he marries and their children.

An evolution of such problems, traced back by one analyst, involves a wealthy family in the publishing industry in an eastern city. Fictitious names must be used.

Two brothers, Richard and Henry Topping, founded a tiny trade publishing business in the Midwest in the late thirties and moved to the East just before World War II. After the war, the great demand to capture a share of the ripe consumer market brought the brothers considerable advertising from businessmen shifting their factories from defense to civilian work. Thus, advertising and circulation boomed and the business grew tremendously, particularly when the Toppings decided to add related magazines, news letters, and annuals to capitalize on the opportunity.

Through the forties and fifties, all went brilliantly. Richard, the older, was the company's top man, the chairman of the board, and he functioned as the inside man, carefully watching all business and administrative phases of the company. Henry, seven years younger, was the president, functioning as the outside man. He feted the advertisers and concentrated on sales and marketing by keeping a close touch with the industry.

George Topping, Richard's son, was the heir apparent. This was so because he was always considered to be a very bright young man and it was obvious to all that his father was getting up in years and his uncle was not equipped to run the business. Henry may not have liked that arrangement but he could hardly deny that without his older brother, the company's operation was beyond him.

In the early sixties, the Toppings began to run into difficulties, mainly from the rise of new competition. They decided to institute changes in policy and none was more active in this regard than the young man, George.

He soon dismayed his elders. Although a "figure" man, George nevertheless seemed to find difficulty in interpreting them. But, seeking to wield his growing influence, he began to establish his own communications network within the company, a hegemony of his own. When the brothers went to check something, they found that George had already been there, had discovered the problem, attempted to solve it, and not particularly well.

Richard defended his son against Henry's complaints. But it was obvious to both that George, in his impulsive zealousness, was attempting to build a company within a company.

In the midsixties, the company's problems grew serious and the Toppings borrowed on their insurance to keep their business alive. Shortly afterward, Richard realized that he was getting too old to cope with it all and that the business was running away from him. Frankly, he told Henry, "What we're doing is running a horse-and-buggy business in a computer age." Never a strong-willed type, Henry agreed. He soon agreed again, when Richard prevailed upon him to sell their company to a large, multi-division publisher. The Toppings, including George, got more than $12 million for their ownership.

Within six months, the new owners fired George (the systems and controls that he claimed to have instituted just weren't there) and soon afterward they retired Richard and then Henry was let out. Rather bitterly, the new proprietors said, "The new management we thought we were buying, and it was one reason we bought the Topping outfit, turned out not to be management at all."

George, then thirty-five, was a sorry sight. His inability to find a new job was compounded by his decision to divorce his second wife. He had asked his first wife to give him up because he no longer wanted to be tied down. Five years later, he had married again over an infatuation. He was now the father of three children.

His father was anguished over the son's predicament and he often discussed with the young man's mother, who was prominent in charitable affairs, what could be done. Between the two of them, they managed to arrange for a new opportunity for George without telling him of their efforts. George took the new job, after almost a year of fruitless efforts to land something and gave it a considerable effort. He is still trying.

But, says his analyst, the "pathology" of the young man is implicit in his parents. This kind, easy-going, and indulgent father presented no offsetting catalytic force to the smiling but forceful discipline of the social-minded mother. As an officer in a national women's charitable organization, she kept both her home and her social-philanthropic activities hopping all the time.

"All his life, George had been told he was wise, he was smart, he was brilliant," the analyst says. "And for years, he spent his time in a frenzy trying to live up to the expectations of him, especially under the maternal lash that his vivacious, youngish but overenergetic mother used on him and on everyone else.

"He could never take the time to study a situation, to analyze it. He had to hurry and succeed. As a result, all that he did was impulsive, not planned or well considered. People felt sorry for him and took pains to help. But that can succeed only so far. He seemed the epitome of the earnest, bright, young man who just needs a bit of help to straighten him out. He may always be that way, but now, at least knowing what his problem is, he may be able to help himself."

3. THE MARITAL RELATIONSHIP

THE self-made man has a tendency to carry his omnipotence into his home and even into his bed. And this frequently is the direct cause for the problems that will send him to see his psychiatrist.

But, because these particular difficulties are the most sensitive in the analyst–patient relationship, few doctors are eager to be directly quoted on such experiences with their patients.

They do not mind, however, discussing it in the anonymity of their offices:

"The self-made man enjoys his sense of power and he believes that his wife should recognize his omnipotence," one analyst said. "But that doesn't always follow. The couple may be getting up in years, but the husband insists on being active in bed. The wife is perplexed—she doesn't understand him."

"A lot of the tycoons have sexual problems," another analyst declared flatly.

"They have trouble functioning. It's not necessarily either fatigue or age. I think that these men always expect the best of things for themselves. Being the best, they also have to be sexually great and so they make great demands on themselves," he said.

"But, in sexual intercourse, as in, say, taking a written examination, you are completely on your own. No one can help. No one can do it for you. The problems that often bring the businessmen to the psychiatrist arise when they think that they should be able to function sexually as they do in their offices where they can press buttons that make hundreds and perhaps thousands of people jump. . . ."

A third psychiatrist observed, "Sometimes, the successful businessman of forty, fifty, or even sixty loses his desire for his wife and becomes impotent. He may become seriously concerned by it. It depresses and curbs the conviction of megalomania that is often his most prominent characteristic.

"Then, one day, either accidentally or because he is on the prowl, he meets a different, perhaps young woman and his desire returns. Suddenly, he is potent again and he begins to have extra-marital relations."

Neurotic problems among the successful businessmen which are caused by family difficulties often involve a serious incompatibility with one's wife. But hardly all businessmen, or, more particularly self-made men, experience this problem.

Many remain happy, faithful, and untroubled in their family lives, and are not neurotic.

Psychiatrists seem to have varying definitions of a neurosis: "a disrupted state of psychological functioning"; "a kind of personality compromise formation, consisting of a drive and a counterdrive"; "emotional maladaptations due to unresolved unconscious conflict. . . ."

But what it boils down to is that a neurosis is a nervous disorder, the seriousness of which depends on the degree of the sufferer's physical and emotional ills. When the marital relationship is responsible for a man's anxiety, depression, compulsion, obsession, or phobia, he may or may not seek psychiatric help. It is usually his last resort.

"Most disturbed businessmen turn to alcohol, sedatives, women, sports, pretty much in that order. A very tiny number of them will then turn to the psychiatrist for help. Most of them think that they are psychologists because they know people so well. And many of them do, because they have paranoidal tendencies and it makes them keenly sensitive to people," declares one prominent analyst.

So, it may be safely assumed that most self-made men lead relatively happy existences with their wives and families. But the troubled ones who do not have such peaceful lives may be more fortunate than the less affluent, less powerful men in similarly unhappy situations. "At least, the man who founded a successful company or who is a well-to-do businessman can break up his home, if he has to, and be able to afford the price much more than most people," observes another analyst.

And, as to a compulsion to seek out extra-marital relations, says a third analyst, "the businessman can be more selective, more discreet, and usually more successful in this goal than others because of his means."

What happens when a businessman finds that he has seriously outdistanced his wife in knowledge, taste, sophistication, finesse, even manner, so that two strangers are living in the same home? Usually, compromises are made allowing some semblance of compatibility to remain. But, when this is not possible, there is a strong likelihood of either husband or wife, usually the former, breaking away in pursuit of a happier home.

"Sometimes, when a rupture occurs in an otherwise normal, long-time relationship," declares an experienced psychiatrist, "the businessman reaches a stage in which his conscience is like that of a woman; it can unexpectedly change its 'mind.'

"For most of his life, the man operates in most areas of his existence in a way which would be considered entirely virtuous and socially acceptable, except for some totally unexpected activity in which the conscience suddenly gives way.

"In one such case," he reports, "a businessman became involved in romantic liaisons in a way which showed that he also had some unfortunate sadistic traits. Why did that happen? I would suspect that it was due to a neurotic or traumatic experience relating to his past. There is an old Victorian tradition that wives and mothers and chaste sisters are good and that all other women are not. Lots of men and women still sustain that idea. It has a lot to do with the disillusionment that everyone acquires in regard to their mothers.

"Nevertheless, it is normal to regard one's mother as being either good or bad. This particular man saw his mother in two images, one good and one bad, and it is not normal to regard a mother as two separate women."

Problems a businessman may have in his married life affect not only the couple but their children as well. And not infrequently, psychiatrists say, the children bear the brunt of the problem. An example was cited by an analyst:

In a Pacific Northwest state, a man developed a large business, becoming a millionaire before he was thirty and a multi-millionaire by the time he was fifty. But he had an unhappy marriage. Partly to compensate for his lack of education, he had married a woman who was intellectually and in worldliness much superior to him. She was pretentious but she was also a very effective community leader. And, in that respect, he had achieved his goal. He had at least in part married her to have a showpiece, a possession.

Rather quickly, the couple had three children, two boys and a girl. But, within a few years after their marriage, the couple ceased having sexual relations. He then proceeded to indulge himself with various mistresses over the years, a fact that he didn't care to hide in his bitterness over his wife's indifference to him. The void between them grew like a chasm.

As they matured, what happened to the children? The daughter adjusted sufficiently, and, in time, in fact, began to resemble her mother in many ways, which did not endear her particularly to her father or her brothers.

The older son showed an intense drive and a love of money, not unlike his father. After a few false starts, he entered the real estate field, did well, went out on his own and by the time he was thirty he was almost the millionaire his father had been at that age.

But the big problems descended on the younger brother, who developed a passive, masochistic attitude toward people. He also experienced sexual adjustment difficulties. Moreover, he never felt comfortable with his father who by now was a virtual stranger. According to the analyst who treated him, the boy had "a strong, homosexual desire to be loved by his father, while at the same time he regarded his mother as just a bitch."

If the father had been around instead of disappearing for two or three days at a time, either on business or in pleasure trips with his mistress of the time, the younger boy's depression and generally psychoneurotic condition would not have been so bad, the analyst said.

The situation was also complicated by the role played by the older brother who for years had happily persecuted and beat up the smaller boy. As a result, the youngest in the family had to cope with two overbearing men and possibly his greater passivity was toward his aggressive and cruel brother.

The analyst's remedy: "Get married and go into a diametrically opposite field of endeavor from your father and your brother. And move away from home."

The young man listened carefully and ultimately took the advice. Today, he is happily married, and is an assistant professor in a small college hundreds of miles from his former home.

If the self-made man was a villain in that particular family situation, he is only a quasi-villain in another.

A good many entrepreneurs achieve a great measure of satisfaction and even happiness by accumulating big bank accounts and substantial portfolios of securities. But one, whose marriage had badly deteriorated, achieved happiness when he fell in love again at sixty-three. He was reluctant to divorce his wife because he didn't want her to lose face among her friends. So he continued to have a clandestine but continuing liaison with his girl friend until he was sixty-nine, whereupon he died.

Happy, according to his analyst, to the very end.

4. THE EMPLOYEE RELATIONSHIP

PEOPLE are expendable in the tight, frenetic world of the self-made man.

But not necessarily because he is deliberately cruel or inhuman.

He has those traits, too, depending upon his own individual characteristics, much as men in any other field of endeavor.

Mainly, however, he demands much of his employees in

the same manner that he demands much of himself and frequently more than he is willing to reward. Because he is overdedicated to his task and finds his great love-play-hobby in it, he will almost childishly assume that those who work for him should devote themselves and enjoy the effort virtually as much as he does.

What he doesn't realize in all too many cases is that those he employs are not at all like him. They do not have the endowment or the drive. And so his employee turnover, particularly of executives, is sizable.

Say the analysts:

> The businessman's reaction toward his employees is to always think of them in terms of his own problems, not of theirs. . . .
> One businessman who came to see me admitted [that] on two occasions that he had brutalized his employees. In one case, he began by bragging about it. In another, he concluded that he had been wrong. But, his over-all reaction was that he felt guilty about both incidents. Remorse? Not at all. His guilt came from his dissatisfaction over the results. "If I hadn't blown up at my employees as I did, I could have gotten more out of them." . . .
> Sometimes, the self-made man feels a contempt for those who work for him. This may stem from our habit of nonhumanization in business (a company or corporation or a staff is *it*, not *he* or *she*), or the reverse, humanizing nonhuman events or articles (a boat is *she*, for example). Perhaps, this seems far-fetched, but from the businessman's standpoint, the staff is there to help him achieve his goal, as is his computer, his factories, and his marketing research department. . . .
> It is difficult to find a pattern in the tycoon's treatment of his employees. He doesn't resent them but he demands a great deal of them. . . . A perfectionist, and many of them are, does make great demands. . . .
> The most successful businessmen live on a sequence of people who can tolerate the pressures put on them and be reasonably happy in the process. I do not think that the average self-made man is more difficult to work for than executives in a large, public corporation. But, if he has to change thirty people in thirty days, he is not dismayed by it. People are highly

expendable to him. The vitality of the business which he is able to operate is such that he can tolerate that kind of employee turnover. If he appears to resent those who work for him, it's basically more the reaction of an individual who sees someone in his employ behaving like an idiot and he wants to shake him by the collar and say, "Be a man!"

It's not so easy for the employees to decide whether the boss happens to be preoccupied to the exclusion of others or whether he is just basically an S.O.B. Sometimes the method to his madness does not unfold until he is in his coffin. . . .

One analyst observed, "The self-made man's attitude is that he has to be tough and cut out the deadwood. To build a business empire, he obviously feels that he can't worry about his worker's mortgage or the college education of the worker's son."

This particular analyst, who had a spell of government service in Washington, pointed out that the private business sector was not imbued with any more efficiency than the government service, nor does it have less deadwood, despite all the clichés about bureaucratic malaise and nepotism.

These are the psychiatrists' views of the self-made man as an employer. But what the self-mader's employees and colleagues think is something else again.

In brief, they think he is lovable, hateful; petty, but sometime very big; stingy, but occasionally generous; not often very understanding about people; demanding of loyalty but not inclined to give it to others; and definitely overzealous.

5. ETHICS AND MORALS

If you are an extrovert, beware. You are likely to have ethical paradoxes.

"The person whose main energy discharges are outer ones (*i.e.*, the self-made man) is more likely to have ethical paradoxes, to be more opportunistic, to be more expedient, and to have moralistic contradictions, than those persons with a more balanced energy investment," observes Dr. Lebert Harris.

Morality is a very broad area of concern to the entrepreneurial group, adds this New York analyst. Some base their morality on the proposition that as long as any questionable action is not generally visible, it is proper. A derivative of that system of morality is "what's right is what you can get away with," he said.

But, from a psychological point of view, Dr. Harris says, this type of morality represents an arrested development or immature growth. Its opposite is a "fully internalized system of conscience."

Self-made men are about as honest as anyone else, notes Dr. Milton Sapirstein, but when they get into trouble anything can happen. In the grip of the megalomania that many have, they can't conceive that it is not possible for them to get away with whatever they want to.

This is tantamount to a dictatorial trait. One of the characteristics of the business tycoon is that he must have absolute power, to be above the law, in the manner of an oriental potentate, Dr. Sapirstein says.

And, in Dr. Harris's view, the ethics of businessmen are somewhat lower than those of professionals. Much of this derives from the self-made man's headlong drive to amass wealth.

In his book, *Money and Emotional Conflicts*, Dr. Edmund Bergler, a psychoanalyst who served as assistant director of the Psychoanalytic Freud-Clinic in Vienna before emigrating here, writes that "every neurotic harbors what I call an 'elastic fraud corner.'" He adds,

Basically, it represents remnants of the old megalomaniacal idea of 'being an exception,' as Freud named it in another connection. Having suffered so much, such an "exception" can allow himself (or so he believes) to cut corners with respect to the usual moral requirements. The fraud corner is elastic and frequently given to rather fantastic stretching, which, in turn, produces masochistic results.

Hence, the tendency on the part of every neurotic is to cheat in money matters. This does not imply, of course, that every neurotic acts incorrectly in his handling of money; it does mean, however, that every neurotic has, to a quantitatively differing degree, that tendency. . . .

6. THE PHILANTHROPY, CULTURE, AND HUMANITY KICK

WHY do so many self-made men, as they get up in years, become philanthropic, magnanimously charitable, and addicted to culture and the arts?

There are three answers to this question, according to a consensus of analysts, but not all are compatible.

One is that the donor or *nouveau* culturalist is buying status.

A second is that the new philanthropist is buying immortality.

A third is that he is not buying anything. In other words, he is not more charitable or inclined to the arts than those who were born into money.

The seeking of name perpetuation through grants and endowments has already been discussed. Numerous quite wealthy businessmen will form charitable foundations bearing their names and the names of their wives, hoping that they will be able thereby to aid worthy causes, to perpetuate their names, and also to amass assets under a tax-free structure.

"Philanthropy today is being paid for by Uncle Sam in the form of deductible contributions," admits one entrepreneur. Thus, he said, his contribution of $100,000 for a listing as a donor at the Lincoln Center of the Performing Arts cost him only $20,000 a year over five years and was fully deductible on his income tax return.

According to some analysts, such philanthropy by the newly

affluent represents a current status symbol. "They have to be seen on the opening night of the opera," one says, "and they have to be on a special list of donors, virtually competing with one another. As far as culture is concerned, the trend is toward competition and competition is based on the finding of new, intriguing art sources. The latest is twentieth-century oils."

First-generation tycoons want to enjoy their wealth and success in a blaze of public display, observes another analyst.

"Many of them are interested in the show aspect, in big, gaudy things," he says. He cited the white yacht of Onassis, the Greek financier, while with others it is a shiny maroon or gold-colored Rolls Royce, or a vast Hollywood-type home overlooking the highest rise in Affluence Park.

But, he goes on, the ostentation scales downward with the sons of the founders, the second-generation tycoons, who prefer that their evident success is enjoyed in more confined but discriminating circles.

Nowhere is this more true, he says, than in such a conservative city as Boston, where second-generation wealth is hidden by a cool but confident reserve.

7. SOME CONCLUSIONS FROM THE CHAIR BESIDE THE COUCH

THERE can be little doubt that most psychiatrists have a sneaking admiration for the self-made man. He may be a difficult patient to handle, but he is forthright, he has many clear traits, even his problems are traceable to obvious personal characteristics, and, once his natural suspicion has been broken down, he brings his considerable resourcefulness to bear in helping the analyst to solve his problems.

But some—and these are in the minority—do not admire him. They compare his frequent exhibitions of paranoia and megalomania to those of some of history's most infamous dictators, Hitler, Stalin, Genghis Khan, Napoleon. Thus, they see those traits as dangerous and disturbing. There is nothing personal in this appraisal. As a patient with problems, the self-made man who has such traits must be helped and analysts will exert every bit of professional skill to help him.

Even when they freely discuss his emotional problems, an evident touch of sympathy over the patient's frequent disappointments with children and his incompatibility in the home creeps into their talk. Perhaps the only time when the analysts display scorn or register concern over the implications for the country's future is when they cite cases of tycoons whom they do not personally know but whose exploits are widely reported.

"Once in a while, one comes along with a Hitler type of mentality—if he could put his hands on an atom bomb, he would have used it, in other words," one analyst says. "Such is his degree of paranoia that nothing that he has built can possibly exist without him. Such men would prefer that the vast businesses they built go down the drain when they die, all who worked there would lose their jobs, and they could just leave their money to their children. The great memory of their past deeds would be their monument."

The waste and the cruelty implicit in such actions are what disturb psychiatrists. They are much more sympathetic to the founder who wants his company to remain after him, and run, if possible, by his sons, more or less as he did, if that is possible. That form of immortality, at least, they feel, leaves behind on earth some measure of good-will.

One of America's best-known psychiatrists is among those most disillusioned with the tycoon. He had not only treated him but he has socialized with him and he has been left with "little to respect." But it was not all aimless. By his many contacts over the years with such men and by "listening to them spout off," this famous analyst has been through a veritable training course in finance. Some years ago, he embarked on an investment program with other members of his family that has since made him a rich man.

What do the psychiatrists who treat the self-made man think of the future of the species?

Most believe that the traits which have made him successful in the past will continue to make others who also possess them become similarly affluent and important in the years ahead. But there are others who say they have thought about it deeply and are hardly sanguine.

The self-made man of the thirties, forties, and the fifties, who intuitively applied himself and "flew by the seat of his pants," was quick to sense people, times, events, opportunities. His personal style was a "telling aspect and component" in the organization of the business. Because of this, note these analysts, there was a quality of communication and an employer–employee relationship which permeated all aspects of the business. His idiosyncraçies were an asset—the boss's toughness or even his badness (or, if he had other, more endearing qualities, too) was a welding, a cohering element.

They liken such individual idiosyncracies to Churchill's cigar-smoking and his shaping his fingers in the V for victory sign, or DeGaulle's fierce Gallomania, or Franklin Roosevelt's greeting to the nation, "My Friends," or Harry Truman's swearing.

However, in the seventies and eighties, the expected massive trends toward more formal educational enlightenment and to more acculturation, both already well under way, will have profound influences on business and on the conduct of business management, they believe.

"Today's self-made man would find his idiosyncracies a disruptive handicap," one psychiatrist says. "Because the intricacies of management will be too great for him to handle alone, there will have to be a dispersion of his responsibilities. If he is to be part of the active managment, he will have to be more humble and democratic, and fit into a scheme of management in which the whole is greater than the parts."

Underlying this concept, of course, is the presupposition that the trend toward business giantism will continue and flourish to the detriment of opportunities for small business, admit these analysts.

"In the socio-economic sense," one notes, "there is an evolutionary change taking place whereby the old, self-made, successful man is an antiquity, a memento, and a phenomenon of the past. This is so because there are few heads of very large companies who have the security today no matter what their stock holdings are. They are constantly being appraised by the other directors and shareholders, in terms not only of their performance but of those of the competition and the national and international economies."

Up till now, the company was the matrix and the self-made man its core. "Now, the complexities of management and the socio-economic trends are such that it is becoming clear that no one man in any business can know all and be all," the analyst continues. "That means that the head of the business can only be window dressing in the future. The business, therefore, will continue to be the matrix but it will select its own core."

One sign of this organizational complexity is the fact that the "new breed" of executive trainee hired by business today rarely meets or knows those in other departments. This, some analysts think, is creating a cohesive fragmentation of the company, with the only communication channel being the computer.

Another sign, says an analyst, is that the young men being educated and prepared for business are being trained to master the techniques and the knowledge of the giant companies. This empirical trend of business education, now generally accepted in an age of sophisticated electronic data processing, cost accounting, and time-study engineering, would be useless to the same upcoming executives if they were to become heads of smaller businesses because they could not afford to use such techniques unless the company organization was large and diverse.

If the self-made man of the seventies and eighties will be unrecognizable from the recent and current models, he will also hardly fit into the "technostructure" of the emerging corporate giant as it is posed by John Kenneth Galbraith, in *The New Industrial State.*

Some in the psychiatric community point to a new, interesting development in the framework of modern society which may have an important bearing on the future business elite. It is a "selective inbreeding" which is occurring among the families of affluence and importance. Increasingly, their children are marrying others of like circumstances and environment. The implication of this, in the view of psychiatrists, is that the issue of such marriages will represent a new generation of endowed children inclined by a socio-economic environment toward a business and professional career.

And, in pointing to it, not all analysts see it as a desirable development because of its limitations on the infusion of other cultures and social levels.

Outside the analyst's examination room, other efforts are being carried on to help the businessman who finds himself increasingly beset by troubles. These include businessmen's retreats such as one in Silver Hill, Conn.; seminars for corporate executives held by the Menninger Clinic, in Topeka; and the "sensitivity training" program sponsored by the American Management Association under the guidance of psychologist-businessman, Alfred J. Marrow. The AMA project involves a group-organized self-examination by businessmen from which comes an increased knowledge of oneself and an awareness of one's role in the world at large.

As they seek to ease the emotional problems of the

troubled tycoon, psychiatrists are candid in admitting that their efforts are circumvented by the limitations of the patient himself.

But only a few mention in this context the greatest dilemma faced by the psychiatric community today—knowing the difference between the man who can weather emotional turmoil and the man who can't.

"We see the man and the woman who needs help," observes a much respected analyst, "but we don't see the person who has gone through similar problems and has been able to effectively cope with them. It would be most helpful to see the differences in ego organization, personality structure, and character. Why does one man break under stresses and strains and another one not? We simply don't know."

This problem has been stirring much thinking in recent years among analysts. "What is normal?" was basically the theme of a 1966 meeting of the Institute of Psychosomatic and Psychiatric Research and Training of Michael Reese Hospital and Medical Center, Chicago. In the texts of ten of the speakers which appeared in the September, 1967, *Archives of General Psychiatry*, a broad-scaled examination was made into the need for research into normal behavior.

One of the most intriguing approaches was made not by a psychiatrist but by Dr. Abraham Kaplan, a member of the philosophy department of the University of Michigan, at Ann Arbor. "How does it come about," asked Dr. Kaplan, "that the category of the normal has been so neglected in psychiatry, that we are here at a conference on new directions on research on normal behavior, as though we stand at the frontier of a new territory which one might expect to have been explored long ago?"

After criticizing by implication that normality is viewed as an average or as "health," he said, "The actual content of the prevailing view seems to me to amount to this: A normal person is someone who doesn't make trouble—trouble, that is,

for whoever is doing the classifying. This outlook is familiar
to all of us. I am told that there are hospitals where a 'good
patient' is one who doesn't make trouble and there are uni-
versities where a 'good student' is thought of in the same
way."

But his own view is that a wider perspective is needed.
Emphasizing the importance of "philosophical sophistication" for psychiatric research, Dr. Kaplan added, "We must
investigate the style of individual human beings in art, politics, religion, interpersonal relations, and everything that is
characteristically human. I believe that psychiatry has focused
too much on a narrow band of the whole spectrum of behavior. . . . We must study man, not only as he reveals himself in his abnormalities, but also as he is seen to be in his
literature, in his art, in his science, and, of course, in his
philosophy."

He concluded, "At bottom, a normal man must be defined
as one who is fulfilling the human potentiality of being a
philosopher. Perhaps this frank egocentricity is the most significant thing I can put before you; it may hold a mirror to
your own egos. For whatever we seek, if the search goes on
long enough, what we ultimately find is—ourselves."

Seven

---◆---

THE RULERS
OF NEW YORK

1. ASTRIDE AMERICA'S DISTRIBUTION
CHANNELS

ON a warm summer night recently, at a party on an estate in White Plains, N.Y., eight well dressed, smiling men were gathered in a close huddle.

A good meal sat comfortably in their stomachs, reinforced by a pleasing variety of liquors. But they had other, perhaps more substantial reasons for the good nature that oozed out of their eyes and rounded their features.

They were only one of many such light-hearted groups, buoyed that evening by the occasion, the annual birthday party and outing of Leon Lowenstein, a textile manufacturer well into his eighties.

Across the vast acres of the Lowenstein grounds, other groups traded talk and banter, drinks in hand. White-coated waiters wandered through the hundreds of guests, offering hors d'ouevres and liquids, not forgetting to stop at the large pool frequented by the younger element. An orchestra played lightly, discreetly, seemingly unheard. Behind the mansion, a large tent capable of holding all the guests awaited the time of toasts and gifts for Mr. and Mrs. Lowenstein, to be followed by a buffet supper and dancing.

If the point of Lowenstein's annual parties seemed to be losing its pertinence each year, particularly after he had reached his eighties, the mood on the balmy June evening was one of amiability, even of happiness. Continuing good health and longevity are, after all, worth noting, even if formalized in a lavish, outdoor-indoor party. And being invited to it was at least a mark of some recognition. Even the wives and children present felt appreciative.

As new arrivals, conversation, greetings, and visits of waiters eddied around the group of eight, few others joined them. It may have been the close, if casual way in which they stood together, although it was not overly forbidding since they were occasionally overheard to be exchanging jokes and kibitzing about the rise and fall of their favorite stocks. But even those who knew them well on an individual basis or who wanted to know them better approached but could summon up only a faint "Hello, there," and continue walking by. A newspaperman who had been invited had the temerity to come over and greet the group but quickly left after receiving only a superficial welcome.

It was probably the knowledge of who they were, their role in the ruling rank of entrepreneurs in New York's tremendous, monied, merchandising world, that kept them sacrosanct that evening. One man did approach and was admitted, the warmth of their welcome showing that they all felt he belonged, too.

But, shortly afterward, the group disbanded, the men walking away in ones or twos to join others across the flowing lawns and lavish gardens. Immediately, each one's entry into a new group brought not only a change in its composition but a new emotional level to it. For individually, all eight were merchant princes in their own right, tycoons of a substantial province of New York's business colossus. They were some of its biggest employers and its prime movers of commerce, money, and influence

That is what they are individually.

But, together, they rule New York.

Within a short period prior to or after their casual meeting that summer evening, most of them were involved in some interesting doings.

One cleared a profit of $2 million in twenty-four hours by arranging to buy stock in another company he knew was about to announce merger talks. It did; the stock he had just bought rose in value as he expected; he sold it and made a killing.

Another took over a company twice as large and at least ten times as famous and respected as his own, mainly because he wanted to run a tremendous company and he projected a "father image" to its largest stockholder.

Two of them, millionaires many times over, sold the companies which they had founded. One did it because he wanted to retire and devote himself to his family and to the management of his substantial charities. The other sold his and his family's shares for $32 million because he wanted to realize the equity in his firm now. Yet today, both are active in business, but not as owners. Instead, one works for a boss whom he could personally buy and sell many times over; the other puts in mild, happy days, enjoying his millions.

A fifth, already the founder and major stockholder in the biggest firm in his industry, acquired another big concern, merged it into his own and now heads a "super-giant."

The sixth sold his manufacturing interests at what was held a "low" price, retained his real estate holdings, and spent months in Las Vegas and the Caribbean "recuperating."

Today, as the purchaser of his company grapples with an
armload of inherited problems, the seller and many others
are now convinced that the selling price was hardly "low."

Individually, all continued during that time to add to their
power, their assets, and their growth through frontal moves.
In a boom time, business control can only increase, even
without expansionary efforts through acquisition or merger.
But businessmen such as these are never content to sit by and
let an opportunity go to anyone else or be reluctant to create
one with "leverage" possibilities.

These eight men rule New York—New York in the sense
of its largest industries, the multi-billion-dollar mercantile,
apparel, and textile sector, with vast individual and collective
influence extending throughout the United States and abroad.

All of Jewish background and fiercely proud of it, they
are always willing, if not anxious, to help one another. And,
they are, in fact, successful in extending their sphere of influence and power by doing so. Yet, they are also avidly
competitive with one another, seeking ways to capture opportunities first. Rarely, however, does bad blood boil up
among them because of it.

And, in this push-pull way, by helping and competing with
one another, they have in the past two decades become some
of the most influential businessmen in the country and have
cut a swath in its largest city that is certainly due to broaden
and deepen.

The "Jewish Mafia." This is a name put to them by the
unkind and probably the envious, or by the simply critical, or
by the racists who always see dangerous religio-national overtones to any successful endeavor by several of the same
religion or ethnic background. Notwithstanding this or any
other appellation, the eight are among the most viable self-
made men of their time—a loosely functioning version of the
merchant's trade guild, the entrepreneurial European combination of the Middle Ages that defied tradition and titled

rulers to give expression to the expansionary instincts of its members.

Aside from any other considerations, one thing is certain about them in today's America. No comparable group of individuals is in such strong control of the nation's important distribution system. That system, through its multitudinous ramifications in all phases of business, is nothing less than America's lifeline.

2. THE SURPRISE PARTY

ON September 2, 1966, in Byram, Connecticut, in the palatial home of Mr. and Mrs. Albert List, some eighty people in unusual costumes waited impatiently. Attired in typically collegiate, graduation caps and gowns, they sipped martinis and sherry behind drawn blinds at a surprise party as they waited for the guest of honor to arrive.

They hardly looked the part of university students. Most were too old and too worldly looking. Their undergraduate years were decades behind them. This was natural, considering that they were almost all highly successful businessmen and their wives.

They represented an elite from New York's main three thoroughfares strewn with money: Wall Street, Fifth Avenue, and Seventh Avenue. They were mostly New Yorkers but they came from as far west as Minneapolis and from as far east as Tel Aviv.

A hush spread over the group as a lookout motioned that the honored guest was approaching. A servant admitted him. He was escorted into a darkened room and the shadows and stillness exploded a moment later into lights, people, and the classic shout, "Surprise!"

The cherubic face was dismayed, the soft, manicured hands groped at the back-swept hair for reason, and then he took in the dress of the entire assemblage and he understood. Meshulam Riklis told himself, as he accepted the proferred hands, the throaty congratulations, the women's kisses on the cheek, "Rik, you came a long, long way." Nineteen years before, he had arrived in Minneapolis from his native Palestine with his wife and he hadn't known a soul.

But he wasn't being honored that night for his singular accomplishments in his new country, although that was implicit in the attitude of those at the party. He was being feted for something perhaps more unusual, if not rare.

At forty-two, after building a $1-billion business empire in an astonishingly short time, Riklis had just completed his master's thesis and had been granted a master-of-arts degree in finance at Ohio State University.

If that was unusual, the contents of his successful thesis were even more so. Entitled "Expansion Through Financial Management, Case Studies," the eighty-page study spelled out in detail the precise manner of how he had raised a vast company literally from a point of zero.

It may well be one of the few instances of a successful businessman starting with a theory, putting it into practice to erect a gigantic organization employing more than forty thousand persons, and then retranslating the reality back into a proven theory.

The pitch of the thesis was unusual, too. It stressed "the effective nonuse of cash."

This intriguing method of empire-building involves the using of the cash or "cashable" assets of one company either as the collateral to obtain credit to buy another company or as the funds to acquire another firm. The former is preferable, in Riklis's view. But if the latter became necessary, Riklis said in his thesis, he would agree to pay cash only if he could project an immediate generation of equivalent cash from the acquired company.

It was an approach that was to bring him distrust from the traditional-minded business world, opprobrium from Wall

Street, and much, much success, after learning several hard lessons.

In 1951, when he was a twenty-nine-year-old security analyst earning $110 a week in a Minneapolis stock brokerage, Piper, Jaffray & Hopwood, he set himself a goal of creating a $1-billion business in ten years. He would do this, he reasoned, by obtaining control of undervalued companies (whose asset book value was greater than the price of their shares on the stock market) and by building them into companies of "strength and promise."

It didn't take him ten years to accomplish this objective. It took him fifteen. The reason for the delay was that he made a few, serious mistakes along the way. One, in fact, almost tumbled him all the way down from the pinnacle.

3. ALBERT A. LIST

"I AM blessed with the power of making money."

The tall, burly man with the gray hair-brush mustache admitted this without any apparent conceit. Albert A. List gazed with satisfaction and some longing out over the veranda of his twenty-two-room home in Byram, overlooking Long Island Sound.

"I'm contented all right, but I don't mind telling you frankly," he said to two friends sitting alongside, "that I would feel more so if I could do something for society. I can be content and happy because I suppose I derive a great satisfaction from my work and I enjoy giving money to institutions so that I feel I help. But I would like to do more—much more."

He sighed, arose heavily, and motioned to his guests to accompany him inside where he showed them his latest, non-corporate acquisitions—new additions to an imposing collection of paintings and sculpture.

Between 1945 and 1965, List once estimated that he contributed at least $20 million in philanthropies. A few years ago, when he donated $6.5 million to the Jewish Theological Seminary of America and to Mount Sinai Hospital and Medical School, he announced that thenceforth he would give $5 million away each year. It would go to his favorite causes, medical research, social services, education, and religious institutions.

The continuing concentration on philanthropy and his feeling that he simply could not do enough in this connection are not typical to the same degree of most self-made men. In List's case, in fact, these convictions amount to a compulsion.

He came from Fall River, Mass., where his family ran a grocery store. An opportunist, List was briefly a retailer and a wholesaler, always using the money he made in one enterprise to buy his way into another. His forte became buying ailing companies cheaply and then building them up. For a long while, he was so successful in this *modus operandi*, the end result of which was to sell the acquired company at substantially over what he paid for it, that he was known as "the liquidator."

However, he suffered a major setback when his company, Glen Alden Corporation, failed to obtain control of Endicott Johnson Corporation, the big shoe manufacturer. That company's employees, rallied by an incumbent family management, bought enough company stock to deter List from his plan. He gracefully bowed out eighteen days after making a tender offer for the stock and sold it back to the employees' pension fund.

List, whose real name is Hyamowitch, retired twice, once in 1937, when he was thirty-six and had made his first million. Why? "I told myself once I had $1 million, I'd retire. I had it in 1937. That's the only time I knew what I was worth. From then on, it was all plus," he said, some years afterward.

Bored, he returned to business four years later, but he retired again in 1965. That year, he sold a 49.6 per cent interest in Glen Alden to the McCrory Corporation, headed by Meshulam Riklis.

Long a major figure behind the scenes in many takeover deals (anthracite, textiles, tanneries, theaters), and a heavy contributor and mover in philanthropic activities, List had warmed to the brash, younger, eager-faced Riklis. The Israeli entrepreneur and advocate of the "nonuse of cash" was just the man to guide Glen Alden and safeguard its financial future. For List, the sale could only represent the additional means to give money away to good causes without his having to burden himself anymore with the making of money.

And that was why he saved Riklis from the wolves.

4. CHARLES C. BASSINE

CHARLES C. Bassine gave up eating lunch or dinner in public places during at least two periods in his life. Both occurred during times of severe personal aggravation. One was when he was ashamed of his company's low profits. The other was when his securities hit a bottom on the stock market.

He didn't want to be seen and he didn't want to see anyone himself. A man who seemed to have the touch of success in his very fingertips, he didn't care to face the hidden hypocracy that others would show him as they tried to make it seem that nothing had gone wrong. It was enough to make him want to hide.

Those intervals quickly ended and the rest of the time in a brilliant, money-making, power-building career, spanning more than forty years, he was seen, heard, and applauded everywhere. There was a coiled strength, even a threat of unleashed raw power in his dark, lined face, the heavy, black eyebrows leveled outward in a stern challenge that made strangers and opponents wary and friends proud.

By 1966, when he was fifty-seven, he had amassed more than $30 million (some were convinced it was more like $100 million) from a garment manufacturing and retailing complex he had founded in 1936. Born in Brooklyn, he became a clerk in a shirt plant, studied law at night, and in ten years emerged as one of the company's top executives. But he was anxious to strike out on his own.

He knew the South offered opportunities for ambitious, knowledgeable businessmen with some capital. A southern railroad and a small town, Sparta, Tenn., were only too eager to help. The rail-line was anxious to carry more freight on its track. And Sparta was anxious to develop more jobs. Bassine leased a building there at a very nominal figure. The carrier hastened to grease its rails for him. He began producing shirts, naming his firm after the community, Spartans Industries.

Success came slowly but it was the kind that lasted. Bassine now began to diversify. From a growing number of plants, an endless flow of not only shirts but almost all other types of garments spewed forth to be sold by Sears, Montgomery Ward, J. C. Penney, and other national merchandisers.

In 1958, when his sales hit $30 million, Bassine shipped thirty-two million garments. That year, too, he set up manufacturing operations in Hong Kong to help him meet foreign competition.

A raging success as he was in that period, he was, nevertheless, filled with an unsatisfied drive. So he decided in 1960 to enter the budding discount store field. A powerhouse when in high gear, Bassine had twenty-six discount stores in operation within four years. But while the sales of the Spartan stores jumped, store-opening expenses and high organizational costs brought first a dip in corporate profits and then a deficit that lasted several years. For a man of Bassine's success urge, this was a disaster. It almost ruined him.

But he rallied, absorbed the high expenses, and put the

firm back on a solid footing. In 1965, he acquired a forty-store discount chain, adding it to his own, and in 1966, he also took over a large apparel company.

By mid-1966, Bassine's annual sales were running at a rate of $375 million. He was now at the top of the heap of low-price garment makers and an important figure in the discount-retailing industry. As a philanthropist, he contributed several million dollars a year. His advice was sought by many on business and on personal matters, too. He was one of the most vibrant personalities on the New York business scene, part of or a soul-mate of many business deals. "If Charley likes it or wants in on it," the word went out, "it's got to be good."

As effectively as he could thunder at his executives or competitors, he could charm shareholders at an annual meeting or other wealthy people at a fund-raising dinner. Few businessmen had as much right to feel as self-fulfilled as he. He seemed to be one of those rare and fortunate people who had reshaped the world to meet his fancy. But one thing was lacking in the fulsome spectrum of his attainment. He had always wanted to run a $1-billion company.

That was why he heeded a plea of another, younger businessman for whom Bassine had a "father image" to take over his company. Bassine could merge the much larger company into his own, thus achieving his $1-billion empire, and run it all as he saw fit.

And that's what Bassine did.

5. CHESTER H. ROTH

IN one hour on a recent March morning, two annual shareholders' meetings were being held. At the earlier one, a short, irate shareholder jumped up to revile management in the form of pale, tense Louis Epstein, president of the Colonial Corporation of America.

"This merger stinks to high heaven!" the little man shouted, referring to Colonial's pending merger into the Kayser-Roth Corporation. "Colonial is in great financial shape. We bought our stock when it was $19 to $22. Now, we're supposed to sell it for a lot less!"

Because terms of the deal called for an exchange of Colonial shares for under $10 each, similar resentment was echoed by other small shareholders. One complained to Epstein that the Colonial chief was "smirking" at his remark that the merger was unnecessary. "I'm not smirking," Epstein replied. "I'm really smiling. It's just how you interpret it."

The volume of complaints rose to unmanageable proportions and Epstein peremptorily adjourned the meeting. He and three colleagues stalked out, redfaced and resentful, to a volley of charges hurled after them: "Shame on you" . . . "You sold us down the river" . . . "It's a sellout . . ."

Only a half hour after the second meeting started, a heavy, confident man in his early sixties rose to tell the Kayser–Roth shareholders that the merger with Colonial had received the approval of 91.3 per cent of the company's 4.5 million shares. A spattering of applause went through the audience, not one person of whom had raised a single question during the meeting.

And, even at the earlier, stormy meeting, the unhappy shareholders had only managed to muster 45,293 shares against the merger, compared with 2,891,803 shares for it.

As he quickly closed the second meeting, Chester H. Roth, chairman of the board of Kayser–Roth, sat down with the barest of smiles. It was against his nature to show gratification that he had just completed the largest merger in the history of the American apparel industry. But, even in the easily gracious way that he accepted the congratulations of many who came up to him afterward, his pleasure was obvious.

The sharp contrast between the post-meeting reactions that both Roth and Epstein received is typical of the manner in which Chester Roth does things. It is smooth, apparently effortless, and topped off with dignity. One might think that putting together a $350 million merger, as he did that morning, was something that the stout, gray-haired New Yorker did between appointments.

The fact that Louis Epstein severed his connection with the merged company only months later, to become president of a stock brokerage, is somewhat beside the point. Epstein bore the brunt of the small shoreholders' ire, but the thin, worried clothing executive was not even a principal in the deal.

It was worked out some months before between Roth and Sol Berger, a brilliant if mercurial entrepreneur. For reasons of his own, Berger was quite willing to part with control of Colonial Corporation, a company he had founded, for one-third under the current market value for his 33 per cent interest.

Roth is considered a man who knows a bargain, but he is scarcely one to jump into anything without considerable research. From the age of twenty-six, when he used a hard-earned $1,500 to start his own hosiery mill sales agency, Roth exhibited a deliberation and a quality of concentration that moved him ahead to unexpected heights. In a few years, he became a hosiery manufacturer and then the owner of a group of companies. After World War II, he became the head and the major shareholder of a complex of companies offering many of the most famous apparel brands in America.

He joined his own hosiery group with Julius Kayser & Co., adding without much delay such other famous firms as Catalina swimwear, Interwoven, Esquire, Mojud and Holeproof hosiery, Excello and Jayson shirts, Cole of California and Martin sportswear, and others.

Sitting much as a potentate (and looking much like one) over many "states" in his sumptuous office on upper Fifth Avenue, Roth exerts an enlightened monarchism over all his divisions, helped by only a small central staff. On each day's developments, important or trivial as they may be, his habit of deliberation is evident but it is also clearly tempered by an instinct for opportunity. At Roth's core, however, is a vast pool of self-assurance.

"Frankly," he told this writer not long ago, "I have not met a man yet whom I considered as good as I am. If I did, I would make it my business to learn from him."

This combination of highly charged egotism and willingness to carefully amass facts by observation and study was in great part responsible for the creation of the great Kayser-Roth complex. Its values and potential were realized by the American Tobacco Company and the Penn-Central Railroad when they decided to diversify and both sought to acquire Roth's company.

6. EUGENE FERKAUF

"ALL I want is for this company is that it should do all the merchandising business in the United States."

This comment, probably made in a facetious moment by Eugene Ferkauf, founder of E. J. Korvette, the big discount store chain, some years ago, later brought him many moments of embarrassment and regret.

Five years later, when he took the initiative to merge Korvette into Spartans Industries and make it a division of the smaller company, the brooding, intense retailer admitted, "I'm not a front-office man. I'm a merchant and that's how I get my kicks. Korvette got so big, it was hard for me to realize that there's so much to it now, so many phases. That's where a lot of the trouble started. . . ."

Between the times Ferkauf made those two statements, he became recognized as one of the great merchants of the fifties and sixties, was voted into the Retailing Hall of Fame, and was the subject of a *Time* magazine cover article. The sixteen-year-old boy who had run one of his father's Manhattan luggage shops had hewed to the "bargain" concept when he entered his twenties and began to develop a chain of discount stores that more than any other company furthered the "discount revolution."

By May, 1966, when Ferkauf virtually came to the end of his rope, he was ringing up $750 million in sales in forty-three giant stores ranging from Hartford to St. Louis. However, profits had slid almost to a paltry 1 per cent of sales, about at the bottom of the discounting industry's performance, and the decline was laid directly to Ferkauf.

A merchant in the great tradition of John Wanamaker, A. T. Stewart, Nathan Straus, and Nathan Ohrbach, Ferkauf was frankly overwhelmed by the responsibilities of the vast administration needed to back up a giant retail business. Twice, he had relied on others to hold Korvette's operating reins only to find matters worsening.

Ferkauf (oddly enough, his name is a German derivative of "to sell") loved most to prowl the aisles of his stores, to watch his salespeople sell and his customers buy. With satisfaction, he would listen to the cash registers ring, not so much for the money flowing into the till as to its expression of public confidence in his choice of merchandise. It satisfied his almost childish, disbelieving delight in the simple process of the sale. "I still marvel that people are willing to pay money for goods that I want to sell," he once said.

Conceivably, if it were entirely up to him, he would have struggled indefinitely with the flagging return on furniture and food and even the profit problems he was having on apparel. But, while he was Korvette's largest stockholder, owning about 20 per cent of its shares, the other directors and large shareholders insisted that he take drastic steps to correct the situation. They suggested a merger with a well-run company.

He went after Montgomery Ward & Co., which had once expressed interest in taking over Korvette. But, upon checking, he turned elsewhere because he found that such a merger inevitably would have meant that "his boys," some of his long-time executives and old associates from Brooklyn, would have lost their jobs in the process. Painfully, nervously, he went down the list of merger candidates as the board's pressure persisted.

Charles Bassine, the hardheaded, hardfisted chief at Spartans, was an old friend. He had helped Gene Ferkauf with counsel in the past, had even tried to work out a three-way merger with Korvette, Spartans, and Alexander's Department Stores. And, since his own father's death, the sensitive Ferkauf had come to look upon Bassine, who was fifteen years older, as "one of the finest men I've ever known."

The lengths Ferkauf would go to in order to cement a merger with Bassine amazed everyone except those who knew the two men best. Others would have to struggle to understand Bassine's fiery ambition and rocklike determination and Ferkauf's confusion, guilt complex, and overwhelming need for relief to begin to sense why Ferkauf was willing to give up all to bring in a new boss over him and over "his boys."

7. THE TWO SOLS

IN the world that most people know, there is only one Sol. It shines brightly down on them when the sky is clear. But at the pulsating core of the New York mercantile world, there are, or have been until recently, two Sols.

Sol Kittay and Sol Berger started out with very little and became multi-millionaires for approximately the same reasons. They combined a salesman's instinct and skill with an entrepreneur's daring.

"You can't dance at every wedding," Kittay said once, to emphasize his point that a businessman has to be very selective when buying other companies. But Kittay often went to the altar, as shown by the fact that his concern, the BVD

Company, acquired fourteen other firms between 1951 and 1964. A hard driver, a shrewd bargainer, with a Machiavellian skill at keeping his executives on their toes, Kittay belongs to that large group of entrepreneurs who likes to find a downtrodden company, buy it cheaply and build it up.

If Berger had started in Detroit instead of in New York and gone into automobile manufacturing, the company he founded might well today be one of the Big Three or Four in the auto industry, instead of the big apparel-textile complex that it is.

"Giants will emerge in the garment industry," he said, on one occasion, "and their growth will result from acquisitions and efficiency of operation similar to that of Detroit's automakers."

He lived that philosophy, before his 1966 retirement at age fifty-one. His former company, the Colonial Corporation of America, operates plants which are models of streamlined, mass production instruments. Twenty-seven of them spew out more than 1¼ million garments a week. To them, he added other companies, acquiring four in an eighteen-month period through 1964.

A New Yorker, Berger began operations in 1947 with a small capital and a used Chevrolet. The first year, striving to develop new mass production techniques, Berger had sales of $300,000. By 1960, his business totalled more than $20 million and five years later it had hit over $100 million.

Berger, Kittay's junior by about five years, is less dynamic on the surface. But behind the smooth, almost gentle disposition is a fine judgment for self-survival, if not a calculation, which always seemed to bring Berger bobbing to the surface of any situation that had a churning undertow. Longtime associates are confident of his probity, his sincerity, but in retrospect they remain surprised by the evidence of his personal resiliency, which often placed him in much more favorable circumstances than their own.

Kittay, a blend of suaveness and desk-pounding determination, is an anachronism in his world. Born in London in 1911, he came to the United States at sixteen and even today has not only the clipped accent of the British but the peremptory manner of the typical English businessman.

Yet, since 1945 when he invested his $20,000 savings and a loan of $100,000 to buy a bankrupt knitting mill in Ohio, he has adopted well the habits of the American wheeling-dealing entrepreneur. In 1951, he bought the seventy-five-year-old BVD company, named after its founders, Bradley, Voorhees, and Day, an underwear manufacturer that had seen better days. Kittay then adopted the BVD name as his corporate signature. And, by a continuous practice of acquisition of many old-line but drifting companies, he built a $200-million-a-year complex of apparel and retailing companies.

In August, 1966, he sold his and his family's one-third interest in his company to Glen Alden Corporation, which had come under the Riklis control. In explaining why he had elected to sell his interests at a time when BVD was at its greatest strength, he said that the company's becoming a subsidiary of another, cash-risk company would enable it to be more aggressive in its acquisitions and to achieve much greater growth.

Then he paused, raised a glass of water and examined it against the light. He observed, "After all, if I want to sell a glass, it would be wise to make it shine, to make it glow and look most attractive. We have done this—and can operate from a position of strength." Confidently, he gently lowered the glass.

This incident, as reported in *The New York Times*, showed that he thought it proper to enhance a corporate image ostensibly for the main purpose of obtaining the best possible terms in a merger or acquisition. A controversial approach, it drew gasps of surprise along Wall Street, especially from those who still retained some idealistic notions about businessmen.

Kittay continued as BVD's operating chief, despite a chorus of predictions that two such forceful personalities as his and Riklis's would not permit a harmonious relationship for long.

If Kittay became a king of national brands by dint of acquisitions and sales promotion, Berger soon became the exponent of the unbranded or private label apparel. These are goods that are not advertised by the maker but by the seller, in Colonial's case some thirty thousand stores across the United States.

However, two years after Berger boasted of Colonial's ability to "produce a quality garment for the mass market more efficiently than any other apparel maker in the nation today— we can sell it at a lower price than any other firm and make a 5 per cent net profit after taxes on each item—" he began seeking a buyer for his 1.2 million shares. Since he offered a "bargain" price, $8.50 a share when the current market value was $12½, he readily found a customer in Chester Roth.

But why Berger should want to liquidate his holdings in Colonial at about one-third less than they were worth puzzled many people, not to mention the small shareholders. Colonial's founder, however, explained the move as an effort to protect his shareholders' investment by arranging a merger with a "fine company, such as Kayser–Roth." There were, however, many skeptics who scoffed at this, suggesting that Berger just wanted out and worse.

Berger, who retains considerable real estate interests in New Jersey, watches over them but mainly spends his time enjoying his leisure in various places to enjoy leisure, such as Las Vegas. Kittay continues to run BVD, much in the manner that he did before, except that now he has a friendly but sharp eye peering over his shoulder.

But, because they elected to "sell out," both Sols have passed through an eclipse of sorts. Yet, the swath they cut remains an important part of the world that they helped to build.

8. GEORGE FARKAS

AND, in that world, George Farkas is a loner. He is also a loner who enjoys that role.

Few in New York's giant distribution industry are as self-made or as self-sufficient as the founder of the powerful, promotional chain of Alexander's Department Stores. The more successful he became, the more Farkas hardened his resolve not to accept the merger blandishments of some of his most important competitors, such as Bassine, Ferkauf, Nathan Ohrbach, founder of Ohrbach's, and the late Joe Weinstein, the founder of J. W. Mays. Both Ohrbach's and Mays are leading New York-based chains.

Fast-talking, mercurial, sensitive, and yet demanding, the rail-thin Farkas is probably the greatest realist of New York's merchant hierarchy. He was always convinced that real success comes only to those who keep their own counsel and that control of one's enterprises can easily slip out of grasp under the satisfaction that comes with wealth, recognition, and friendship from competitors. As a result, his company remained longest in private hands of any of like size, well over $200 million a year in sales, in the city's mercantile industry.

He enjoyed his role and often demonstrated his independence with an unusual candidness. Since his substantial real estate investments bring him more of a return than his retail business, he conceded not long ago that his real estate interests were very profitable.

"But that," he added, "only represents money and money can be a very empty thing. Money does not give you an identification with something alive and moving."

For fifty years, from the age of sixteen, Farkas thrived in the art-science of selling fashions and related goods at "under-selling prices." This is a stratum of retailing roughly between the higher markup and services of department stores and the lower margins and minimum services of discount stores.

Like Ohrbach, he pioneered the importation of "high-fashion" couture and *pret a porter,* as well as the featuring of American couture clothes, at low prices. On weekends, stores such as Alexander's, Ohrbach's, Loehmann's, Klein's, and Mays attract an outpouring of housewives who frequently will do battle with each other to strip bare the tightly packed racks of dresses, coats, suits, and sportswear.

His success is a great source of satisfaction but perhaps Farkas enjoys even more the progress of his independently run business in the face of the growth of such traditional New York department stores as Macy's, Gimbels, Abraham & Straus. All are local outposts of national chains.

"I have a serious problem," he confessed. "I am so excited by every phase of the business—the merchandising, the competitive battle, the entrepreneurial challenge--that every day I have to decide what to give up."

Born in Paterson, N.J., he worked as a stock boy for his father who owned two women's shops in Harlem. George became head of the family at sixteen when his father died and also ran the family business. He managed somehow to finish high school, despite all the pressures on his time, and also briefly attended New York University's School of Retailing.

In 1928, he opened the first Alexander's store, named after his father, in the Bronx. That store was subsequently expanded thirty times. During that period, Farkas opened increasingly larger stores in the Bronx, Queens, White Plains, Connecticut, and other locations in the metropolitan New York area. In 1965, the ambitious Farkas spent $21 million to open the most expensive store to be built in New York and Manhattan's first major new one in four decades. Brashly and courageously, he chose a site just opposite Bloomingdale's on 59th Street and Lexington Avenue. And more than one hundred thousand customers mobbed the new store on the opening day.

Since 1959, when he turned over the presidency of the company to his then twenty-nine-year-old-son, Alexander, Farkas gradually relinquished his operating authority; in late 1969, ill health forced him to retire, but he remained an important figure in the company behind the scenes.

His indomitability was never better demonstrated than in 1962, when Eugene Ferkauf of Korvette bought a 42 per cent interest in Alexander's. The sellers were Louis Schwadron, George Farkas's brother-in-law, and a longtime associate, and two Schwadron sons, Jack and Arthur. Farkas spurned Ferkauf's offer to merge and a year later voluntarily forfeited $200,000 which he had agreed to put up with Korvette as a down payment to buy back the shares.

Farkas explained that he preferred to use Alexander's capital funds for expansion than to acquire its own stock. And to back up his point, he began a new, accelerated phase of store-building.

A collector of abstract paintings, which he loves to display in his stores, including using some of them on exterior walls confronting customers as well as competitors, Farkas would seem to be an extremely happy man if it were not for his natural restiveness.

In the late twenties, he married Ruth Lewis, who has a doctor's degree in education from New York University and taught sociology there for a number of years. They have four sons and so an indefinite continuation of the family line in the firm appears certain.

"You don't dedicate yourself to the glory of having been at the top," George Farkas observed in his sixty-fifth year, "but for the joy of living it every day." But there is little doubt that he has shown a boundless zest for both.

9. WHAT THEY DO

THIS, then, is the cast of characters, the managers of New York's largest business complex, give or take one or two.

They are rarely written about as a group. Why? All are so successful that they are generally regarded as examples of what the individual man can achieve if he tries. They are the shiny, modern paragons of the self-made strain that has so earmarked the history of American business.

But, perhaps because they are on the surface so fiercely competitive—and they are in fact—and because nothing collusive has ever been discovered in their activities, relatively few outside their circle are aware of the importance of their relationship.

They themselves would deny that they constitute any sort of a working, interlocking, cartel-like, or even an ideologically homogeneous group.

But, the fact is, that they are none of these in actuality but most or all of these in effect, even though they probably could not be accused of any violations of anti-trust or of restraint-of-trade laws. But their power makes it unnecessary for them to break any laws.

What, after all, is illegal about lending one another money; advising one another on what the best business move would be; bailing one another out of a hole by bolstering his stock with a substantial personal purchase; calling a bank, insurance company, factor, or other lender to put in a good word so that one of the group can obtain a loan at going or better interest rates; giving one or another the first opportunity to take a position either as an officer or an investor where permissible in one's own company; or introducing one man to another to break the barrier of strangeness and to smooth the way for a business deal? None of it, of course.

But when this activity is typical of most of them, when it

involves companies so large and so well known by the investing public that their stocks often hit the "most actives" lists of either of the major stock exchanges, when it fosters a power of bigness as contrasted with the continuing struggles of small business, when it induces a favored treatment by the financial community purely because of influence, then their relationship takes on a somewhat different aspect.

What is that aspect? Is the relationship of these who dominate New York's largest business sector good, bad, constructive, dangerous, beneficial to the nation's economic well being, or does it mask a game with sinister overtones that they play with the billions of dollars they control in assets or securities?

There is no pat answer to these questions. There is only a wholesome aspect to their relationship if their attainments are viewed as an accomplishment by eight men who built corporate properties with immense employability, capital assets, and economic leverage purely by talent and drive.

But there is also reason for a questioning pause, in which to ponder on the rights of power. This comes when their rapport is examined in the light of the extension of convenience and favors among a select group; of a protectionistic inclination and sometimes of unilateral decisions among them involving each other's companies which are rubber-stamped by management-appointed boards but not submitted to shareholders at large until virtually a *fait accompli.*

But perhaps their truest aspect is that they are what the time has made of them.

Pent-up consumer demand and a vast manufacturing capacity to meet it emerged hungrily from the conclusion of the Second World War. America's distribution system was archaic and incapable of serving as the pipeline for the consumer goods that would soon flow in a mighty torrent.

Together, these elements offered great opportunities not only for the development of new systems of manufacturing and distribution but for the rise of new entrepreneurs.

Two other groups were also impatiently waiting for the cornucopia to fill.

The nation's bankers, insurance companies, and factoring firms knew their services would soon be called into play and they chaffed at the bit. The capital funds would be needed to provide the far-flung factories. Then short-term money would be essential to buy the raw materials and to pay the factory workers. And, of course, there would have to be underwriting funds that would turn tiny private and family-owned companies into corporate giants owned in part by the small investors but still controlled by the founders. Now, these, by making the American public a partner in ownership, would be able to expand and keep expanding.

And, of course, there was the public. It craved so many things. Homes, automobiles, refrigerators, freezers, radio, and television sets, clothes that would shrug off the wartime look, nylons, pure white shirts, and all manner of leisure goods.

Everything, everyone, the entire socio-economic structure, stood ready for the appearance of the new entrepreneurs.

They were already at work.

In Fall River, Abe List had already made his first million and was involved in a variety of buying and selling activities, including a financial partnership with Cyrus Eaton. Working with the Cleveland industrialist who later stirred controversy by espousing building an economic bridge with the Iron Curtain countries, List included among his entrepreneurial activities retail groceries, iron ore development, and real estate.

Eager, intense Bassine was manufacturing men's shirts in Tennessee to the great pleasure of the local authorities. But he was beginning to sense that his ambition would require him to move his main base to where the money and the action were, New York, and he did.

At war's end, Roth was already one of the country's largest hosiery knitters, a major supplier of apparel to the armed forces. Clear-eyed and carefully premeditative, he now turned to the vast potential of civilian needs. He acquired an additional string of hosiery mills, set about attracting bright, new, young men into management, and generally laid the groundwork for his eventual "General Motors of national brands."

Riklis, discharged from the British army, returned briefly to Palestine and in 1947 emigrated to the United States. His sense of "Mabat rahok," the ability to see and plan for the future, spurred him and by 1953 he was already trying to buy his first company in Minneapolis, developing his empire-building technique. In the midfifties, when he was just over thirty, he established himself in New York, already a chairman of the board, to operate his first company, the Rapid-American Corporation.

Those first years after the war's end . . . Kittay had already bought his first knitting company and within a year he repaid a $100,000 loan out of profits. Ferkauf took off his army khakis and went back to his family's business. In 1948, he opened his own luggage shop in Manhattan, with $4,000 in savings, and also began selling appliances at discounts from a catalog. By that time, Farkas was successfully operating two stores in the Bronx, constantly expanding them as he geared himself to blanket the metropolitan area with new ones. And, in 1947, Sol Berger invested $27,000 in cash and his wife's engagement ring to follow Bassine's trail to Tennessee, where he was also eagerly received.

Since then, all of these and the others who are fitfully members of this group have traveled a great distance to achieve skills in management and entrepreneurship, affluence and power. In virtually each case, their motivations shifted from an initial escape from poverty or modest means to an indomitable ambition for position and influence and then to an unquenchable zest for industry domination or inter-industry conglomerism.

Their thrust was greased not only by a highly favorable

economic environment but by others cheering in the wings. The enterprisers' growth was abetted by a financial community eager to cash in for itself, by a government mechanism often confused by the opposing desires of wanting to foster commercial and industrial growth but of not wanting to invite monopoly, by suppliers of all types of goods and services whose liberal extension of terms and of credit paid off handsomely, and by unions who liked giant companies because these meant security and the ability to pay higher wages.

But the entrepreneurs' greatest boon was, of course, the ever-growing consumer market of millions and millions of Americans easily influenced by advertising, the power and glamor of big business, names, national brands, and aggressive public relations.

And, in the process of their climb, the entrepreneurs helped, counseled, protected, and, at times, fought bitterly with each other. But, even in those instances of strife, the rancor was neither deep or long-lasting. Peace soon returned in the manner of most families.

10. THE TRIALS AND TRIUMPHS OF MESHULAM RIKLIS

THE moment Meshulam Riklis appeared on the scene, few knew it but a new, dynamic phase of the New York mercantile world was being ushered in.

The fulcrum of that vast market would soon become money, or rather a particular use of money, its leverage by the pledging of assets to buy other companies and the use of their assets for the same purpose. Such a practice was not new. Louis Wolfson, of the Merritt-Chapman Company, had come out of Florida some years before and used the device to great advantage before a series of negative happenings set him back. From Switzerland, financier Hanns Ditisheim had come here and excelled in its practice, run into some serious problems and then committed suicide in Chicago.

But in New York, where it had been an important device in the twenties, it had fallen into relative disuse in more recent decades. Riklis was to become its proponent and to influence others, notably those with whom he was to become joined, to emulate him.

Suspicion and cynicism greeted the young Israeli. The word had gone out from Minneapolis of a brash, new empire-builder who taught Hebrew at night and was a brokerage's customer's man by day. Wall Street regarded him from the outset as an unreliable upstart. So did most of the mercantile entrepreneurs in New York who by then were already important and affluent figures. They did not know if he had any substance to him. They did not like his reputation. And they did not care at all for the unfavorable publicity he was getting.

As most of them were Jewish, they were hypersensitive to any Jew who seemed to flaunt his Jewish traits, especially when it was obvious that a certain amount of anti-Semitism was behind the rancor he was stirring up.

Riklis seemed to have come at the wrong time. The financial community was wary of anyone who didn't follow the normal channels, much less one who openly espoused pyramiding companies on a rickety substructure. If one block (company) collapsed, if its creditors called their loans without much notice, what would happen to the pyramid? Collapse, like a house of cards, of course, they reasoned.

Besides, Wall Street had had its knocks with a coterie of financial wizards—Insull, Gilbert, Wolfson, Ditisheim, and others. Was the smooth-talking security analyst from Israel by way of Minneapolis simply another one? A prominent financial columnist for a New York newspaper thought so and said so endlessly, scathingly. Barron's, the respected financial weekly, published a highly critical article on Riklis and that seemed to set the tone for a generally unfavorable appraisal of him that lasted for years.

Throughout this period, Riklis moved ahead with his plan to build a big entity, buying McCrory–McLellan–Green, a combination of several variety store chains which he had helped to develop as a group by various purchases and sales. He added this large group of stores to the fold of Rapid–American, a holding company that he put together from the former Rapid Electrotype Company, a maker of electrotype plates and stereotype mats, and American Colortype, a printing, toy, and metal-sign making company. Somewhat earlier, he had made passes at Balcrank, Inc., and the Gruen Watch Company (both unsuccessful efforts) and then at Smith–Corona and Butler Bros. (also unsuccessful from a control standpoint but financially remunerative). He retained the Butler corporate shell, now known as BTL, and he maintained a complex ownership of MMG through United Corporation, a holding company, which was in turn controlled by H.L. Green, a variety store chain.

"At this point," noted a 1962 article in Fortune, "Riklis's situation could be summarized as follows: He controlled Rapid; Rapid controlled BTL; BTL controlled United; and United controlled McCrory–McLellan."

In July, 1960, however, the jerry-built structure was modernized and propped up. A merger plan involving BTL, United, and McCrory-McLellan, was approved, with McCrory Corporation emerging as the parent company, and with Rapid–American still in control of it all.

Encouraged by his empire-building progress, if not by his favorable publicity, Riklis continued on his peripatetic way, closely watched by all, including the merchant princes and industrialists in the same field. It is not hard to envision them with wide eyes and mouths agape at this wonder boy from the West and the Mideast. In 1960, McCrory bought the Oklahoma

Tire & Supply store chain for $28 million, and the Economy
Auto Stores the same year, following it up the next year with
the purchase of the Lerner Stores, the country's largest
ready-to-wear chain, for $60 million.

Later, Riklis was also to acquire control of S. Klein Depart-
ment Stores and Best & Co., two leading New York-based
retail chains, as part of McCrory; then operating control of
Glen Alden Corporation through Rapid–American, with
Glen Alden under the Riklis streamroller then acquiring
BVD Corporation, the Philip Carey Manufacturing Company,
building materials, the Stanley Warner Company, owners of
a large chain of movie houses, and the International Latex
Company, and Schenley Industries, the large distiller. Rapid–
American, spurred by Riklis, of course, pushed ahead with
its own acquisition program, acquiring Joseph H. Cohen &
Sons, the largest domestic producer of men's clothing, and
Leeds Travelwear, which made luggage and sporting goods.

By then, reluctantly but pulled toward him as though
magnetized, the others in the ruling tier of New York's merchandising world became generally sold on him. It had become
a matter of (1) defending him for his earnestness and co-
religionism; (2) the sheer, animal excitement he created in
the markets; and (3) he had presented a new way of life for
them in which affluence could be furthered without the pressures on their part of finance and insecurity.

In short, he had convinced them that he was an honest
gambler, an admitted wheeler-dealer, and literally a wizard at
using "paper" to build a business empire.

But, ironically, at a time when he had won important adherents, the incessant flow of unhappy publicity took its toll.
When *Barron's* ripped into him, at least two of the group
bolstered his stock by buying about 200,000 shares at a time
when the price was fluctuating. It helped, of course, but it
was not enough. For by that time, it was clear that he had
wheeled and dealed himself beyond his capacity to consolidate.

His new troubles struck home when McCrory's shareholders late in 1963 stunningly turned him back on a pet plan to sell Lerner's to Glen Alden for $56 million to raise cash. This was two years before McCrory was to obtain control of Glen Alden, but, at that time, Rapid–American had had losses and so had McCrory, and a transfusion of money was vital. Riklis had counted on the sale. Now the whole structure shook perilously in the ill wind.

The thirty-nine-year-old financier drove home in a daze from York, Pa., where the special stockholders' meeting had convened, and on arrival could barely lift himself out of his Cadillac. The press now ripped into Riklis and the word that he was through reverberated through the canyons of Wall Street.

Some weeks later, in a synagogue in Great Neck, L.I., where Bas Mitzvah (confirmation) services were being held for his daughter, Riklis sat silently, tears rolling down his cheeks. He was dollar-poor at this point and was unaccountably shaken because a creditor was threatening legal action unless he promptly received $8,000 due him. It was a sorry, humiliating moment for a tycoon who headed a company with annual sales then of about $600 million.

Unkind critics revived the appellation that had first greeted him in New York—"Reckless Riklis, the Rapid–American."

His plight was roundly discussed and weighed by the group. There were mixed feelings, even among those who were already working for him as division chiefs. He was getting what he deserved; he had overextended himself; he had brought disgrace to his race and his calling; and so on and on, the argument went. But in the final analysis, all these points were submerged in a majority opinion that the unfortunate empire-builder should be helped, if it could possibly be done. He had too much to offer; his example would be used against others of his religion; he had already accomplished much for himself and for them; and the members of the hierarchy themselves had too much invested in the various stocks of his complex to let him go down the drain. That was the new argument and it was the prevailing one.

Three things happened at this stage which raised Riklis out of his seemingly bottomless pit and sent him on to new heights.

First, discreet calls were made on the banks that held the big loans on the Riklis enterprises. While none of this debt was immediately callable, an expression of confidence by the lenders who held $55 million in Riklis debts would go a long way. They listened to the entreaties and decided to go along. Their feelings about Riklis's probity and long-range ability to come out on the plus side were communicated to the right people on Wall Street. The point of this was to bolster confidence in the plummeting value of the Riklis stocks.

Secondly, Riklis, who has a propensity for drawing a series of interlocking circles that grow in circumference ("A small investment can eventually control an enormous business") forgot this principle temporarily and set about rehabilitating his empire. If he planned to build a merchandising complex, he would have to operate as a merchant, and he did. A new plan calling for a crash program was put into effect. It included the closing of many unprofitable McCrory–McLellan–Green stores, cutting unproductive store space by increasing selling space, slashing idle stock, and generally reducing inventories. A sixteen-store Long Island group was tested first and when it proved successful the move was extended to other store groups. And greater freedom was given to regional managers and store managers and sizable incentives were offered to them if earnings reached 3½ per cent to 4 per cent on sales.

Thirdly, Riklis gave an increasing latitude of operations to Samuel Neaman, the operating vice president of McCrory. Riklis made him president of MMG. Neaman, also a native Palestinian who became a British subject, is a management expert, a believer in helping people to "do what they are

capable of," and a stern believer that good management principles apply equally well regardless of the specialty of the
business. Neaman rose in the British army during the Second
World War from private to major (surely an unusual feat in
that class-prone force) and met Riklis when the future empire-
builder was a chaplain's assistant, driving a jeep in the same
military area. Despite the difference in rank, they found much
in common and had long discussions. The long friendship was
evident about twenty years later when Neaman flatly told
Riklis immediately after the debacle of the Lerner sale, "Now
comes the *chochma* [the trick] that you have to put over."

However, probably as important as any step that the turn-
about involved was Riklis's acquisition only a year later of
List's well-heeled ($42 million in cash and cashable assets)
Glen Alden Corporation, entirely without cash and without
requiring the aid of banks. Wily, bluff Abe List had been
among the first to register confidence in Riklis. When some
of the big lenders tried to dump Riklis during the worst
time and offered his post as head of the complex to List, the
Glen Alden chairman refused and insisted that Riklis was still
the best man. The distraught bankers had offered the post, too,
to Harold Lane, Sr., the chairman of Lerner Stores, but he had
also backed Riklis. But, to keep the record straight, both List
and Lane were already in their sixties and had met their
greatest challenges. Nonetheless, they were sincere in expressing their confidence in the younger Riklis.

Of course, List's willingness to sell his company to Riklis
was not altruistic, since, if anything, the old "liquidator" was
a shrewd businessman. If Riklis could not have delivered the
necessary payments to seal the acquisition, List would still
have had his company. But, if Riklis met the obligations,
List could take his equity plus and spend much more time on
his philanthropic and cultural activities.

Looking back several years later on Riklis's emergence from
his most serious troubles, one of his most articulate critics

believes that the money lenders failed to use "normal prudence" in going along with the embattled financier.

"Riklis was the recipient of the banks' avarice and greed," declares this critic. He adds, "Why should banks be allowed to use funds imprudently that belong to depositors? Evidently, environmental influences can sway even the judgment of a bank's president.

"But, how can a small business competitor fight back when the giant firms have access to so much money?" he asked.

Jealousy, or justified criticism? Riklis has faced much of both in his career, as have all the others in the New York group, if to a somewhat lesser extent. The entrepreneur hardly becomes less of a target as he deepens his penetration and widens his sphere.

11. "YOU WANT A MILLION? TWO MILLION?"

IF Riklis emerged as a focal point of a great deal of the activities of the big New York enterprisers, Charles Bassine simultaneously assumed an increasingly important role on the same stage. He became a chaperon, a catalyst, a marriage broker (corporate), and a molder of events.

Few on the scene had his combination of individual power, dynamic personality, and winning affability. His great affluence helped, too. While a dominant temperament and a vibrant way of getting things done count heavily in the commercial skyscrapers of Manhattan (and in Chicago and Los Angeles, too), nothing seems to be quite as impressive as money. Even the best-heeled in the New York group often describe Bassine as "a very wealthy man."

No matter what he is doing at the moment, the hirsute, now dour, now grinning Bassine exhudes the same aura of power and good nature. He is like a coiled spring of ambition and perhaps avarice, heavily covered by an insulation of heartwarming affection for all. But those who have crossed him or failed to measure up to his demands have long remembered the whip of his resentment.

The paradox of his nature is his great desire to help, to develop new enterprises for others and to straighten out the problems of those he likes or admires. When the youthful Jack Schwadron left as merchandising vice president of Alexander's, he was not yet certain that he wanted to join Ferkauf's Korvette. He went to see Bassine, an old friend, much as most in or around the ruling circle eventually go to Bassine when troubled.

Said Bassine to Schwadron: "You want a million? Two million? Do you want to go into business? Ask me whatever you want but don't ask me to buy your Alexander's stock."

Bassine was the one who originally brought Ferkauf and Schwadron together for the first time. It took place in his own kitchen in Great Neck, L.I. Bassine and Ferkauf were not only friends, but the brilliant, moody Ferkauf was also a customer of Bassine's Spartans' apparel business. Bassine had a natural, vested interest in seeing Korvette thrive, to solve its problems, and to forge ahead.

Riklis and Bassine also became close. Each advised the other on the merits and demerits of a deal in which either was interested. Riklis told Bassine how he could buy the forty-five-store Atlantic-Thrift Centers chain through use of a debenture deal and thus almost immediately obtain Atlantic's earnings. And, later, when Ferkauf turned in desperation to Bassine to take over the control and supervision of the ailing Korvette business, Bassine and Riklis talked it out and so Bassine agreed, as long as it would be entirely on his terms.

But there is another, important element in Bassine's life and power-packed success. It is Arthur Cohen, Bassine's very boyish-looking son-in-law, who heads Arlen Properties, a real estate developer. Arlen's under Arthur Cohen has built and owns all the Spartan discount stores, as well as many of the

Korvette store properties and some that are controlled by the Riklis complex. Thus, Cohen and indirectly Bassine have a great personal interest in seeing that Korvette and McCrory remain in good shape. Both Bassine and Cohen are good-sized shareholders in both Korvette, or Spartans, as the parent company is now named and Rapid–American, which is Riklis's original entity. In 1969, Spartans purchased most of its store properties from Arlen and Cohen became a vice-president of Spartans. But he still retained his own company.

"It may not involve any formally interlocking arrangements as directorships," comments one source close to the group, "but look what it amounts to. Charley Bassine and Arthur Cohen really control Riklis, who in turn controls Rapid–American, which controls McCrory, which controls McCrory–McLellan–Green, Lerner Stores, S. Klein Department Stores, as well as Glen Alden, which controls the BVD Corporation, Philip Carey Manufacturing Company, the RKO Theatres, the Stanley Warner Company, and now much of Schenley Industries. . . ."

Interlocking interests are scarcely relegated only to the New York hierarchy, but it is a prominent element in its make-up. It is also a prominent trait of American business today and scarcely any important industry is without it, despite government efforts to curb it. The problem is that anyone, including heads of a company, can buy into another company's securities. There are no laws against an individual's purchases.

Perhaps if Bassine had not lent money to Riklis, as he has, or if Bassine had not befriended Ferkauf, or if List were not happy to see the potential in Riklis of taking Glen Alden on to new heights so that List could indulge his charitable endeavors, or if Kittay were not happy to take his equity now by selling BVD to Riklis, etc., etc., all their paths would not have crossed in the important way they did.

So, intentionally or accidentally, the mutual benefits or

the financial or other help most provided to each other had the effect of creating at least token obligation among two, three, or more individuals in the group.

For a while, a Bassine son and a Ferkauf daughter were also engaged to be married, but this social alliance was broken off. It was not to quietly terminate, however, as many youthful engagements do. A bevy of overindignant Korvette shareholders complained at a meeting convened to consider the Spartans–Korvette merger that such a corporate marriage was arranged to cement the children's nuptials.

Redfaced, mortified, openly disgusted, the sensitive Ferkauf whispered up to the meeting's chairman, "Tell them— tell them the engagement has been broken off."

But there are other ways of looking at the reasons for the homogeneous nature of the New York rulers. One is that circumstances, as the maxim goes, brings together strange bedfellows. Another is that the arena of contest for the quick and the acquisitive ultimately becomes tight and narrow as each reaches greater heights of success and power, so that the arena can become a harmonious place at times and a site of fray at other times. Thus, a competitor can become a friend and a rival and a partner and an adviser and a competitor again, all in the same person.

If Riklis may be the wheeler-dealer par excellence in the group, if Bassine has the de Gaulle-like strength and emotional power, if Chester Roth is the smartest, if Ferkauf has the best merchandising skill, who is the sharpest of the lot?

"Abe List is probably the shrewdest, hardest guy I know," declares an associate.

"He got stuck with the RKO Theatres—he wanted to get his stock back up again and so he let Riklis catch up with him. List originally bought the RKO stock at $4 a share. Riklis was then given control and List was just delighted when Riklis parlayed it all into buying Philip Carey, BVD, and then Stanley Warner. So who was the shrewd one? You tell me."

But the strange thing is that Riklis confided, shortly after McCrory acquired its big and controlling interest in Glen Alden, "Abe List is my great friend and a wonderful gentleman. I couldn't be luckier."

12. THE TANGLED WEB

So goes the complex relationship among these men, beginning so often with egotistical and selfish goals and ending paradoxically in mutual interests and successes. "When one is in trouble the others help out, but the game keeps changing," reports a long-time, inside source. "If it's not Riklis and Bassine, it's List and Riklis. Or Bassine and Ferkauf. Or Roth and Berger. Or Riklis and Kittay. Or Bassine and Farkas."

The friendship does not only show in times when one of them is in trouble. It will flower when one is on the prowl, too. Riklis, after spending millions of Glen Alden's assets to acquire an approximate 20 per cent interest in Schenley Industries, a very profitable distiller with sales of about $550 million a year, bested the P. Lorillard Tobacco Company as suitor for Schenley, but found that he needed considerably more funds to increase his holdings in the big liquor company. It was to be the biggest acquisition of his career.

Earlier in 1967, bouncing back from disappointment that Schenley and Lorillard were talking merger, he had decided to buy 200,000 shares of Schenley at $50 a share, $8 a share off the market price, as a company investment. He was fortunate in being able to get them and he did because a large shareholder had heard rumors that the Schenley–Lorillard deal was off. But the next day, when the two potential merger partners denied the rumor, Schenley's stock shot up to 61, and Riklis quickly sold out at a profit of $2 million. The coup startled and electrified the financial world both for its dramatic success and its neat risk.

In mid-1968, when Lorillard decided to quit the race for

Schenley against a Glen Alden offer, Riklis's friends rallied to his need for help. A half dozen or more bought Schenley stock in their own names to the tune of many millions of dollars which they either immediately turned over to Riklis or held onto until he would need them. These purchases were a big ace in the hole for Riklis until his proposed tender offer for most of the Schenley shares from shareholders would be approved by the Securities and Exchange Commission.

It proved again that "friends"—in this case, his old friends in the group—do help.

Of the eight, Roth and Farkas are the most removed. But power and affluence, which move its owners into the same narrow circle, tend to naturally flow in a pattern of mutual interests. It would be hard for such as these two to be altogether remote from the activities and interests of the rest. Self-protection and the challenge of staying in power by remaining in touch and by occasionally participating preclude a genuine independence.

That is also why others come in and out of the New York hierarchy, in its fluxing nature or "changing game." So, broadly, the group includes in its periphery such as Harold Lane, Sr., the chairman of Lerner Stores; David Schwartz, the chairman of Jonathan Logan; Seymour J. Phillips, the chairman of Phillips-Van Heusen; Michael Daroff, the president-chairman of Botany Industries; Ira Guilden, the chairman of the Trade Bank & Trust Company; Sol W. Cantor, the president of Interstate Department Stores; and Stanley Feldberg, the president of the Zayre Corporation; and others.

It does not include W. Maxey Jarman, the retired chairman of Genesco, Inc., formerly the General Shoe Company, a company which has become the largest diversified producer and retailer of apparel in the country. Jarman, a complex, highly-skilled entrepreneur, developed a sizable family shoe company into a $1 billion complex of manufacturing and retailing. He is a loner and unorthodox by nature. His fiercely independent and restless nature would probably have never permitted him to penetrate or to remain in its inner circle. He remains independent even of other non-Jewish businessmen in the New York's big mercantile industry.

The fact of their Jewishness is a source of concern among the group's members, for they fear that it will denote that Jews run their industry, or, in effect, since it is New York's biggest commercial and industrial business, that they run New York. While this point may be moot, it is a fact that in New York, at least, businessmen and entrepreneurs of the Hebrew faith seem to fill most of the leading slots in the mercantile sector.

But this is not unusual, for ethnic alliances or similarities are common in more than one field of endeavor. The white Anglo-Protestant dominates the banking and insurance fields in the United States. Italians operate many companies in the building and contracting fields. Americans of German descent who own delicatessens buy from primarily German–American suppliers. Chinese–American restaurateurs and owners of hand laundries adhere to such entrepreneurial activities and give their business, as well, to Chinese service companies.

Much of the ethnic dominance in any one field has to do with the opportunities open to each racial strain and to the opportunities in a particular field. Intolerance often limits such opportunities. And sometimes the flow of immigration changes the national texture of an industry. In New York's bustling garment industry, for example, the Scotch were the ownership group in the late nineteenth century and early twentieth centuries. But, as the Russian and Polish Jewish immigrants arrived, their natural tailoring and handicraft talents led them into the clothing shops, and then they eventually emerged as the new owners. Italians came in and succeeded to production and ownership opportunities. Now, it is possible that Negroes and Puerto Ricans ultimately will become prominent not only as workers but as owners in that industry.

13. THE FUTURE NOT AS THE PAST

WHERE will the New York hierarchy be five, ten, and twenty years from now? All the companies represented are strong and their future seems secure, if contingent on the well being and prosperity of the nation's economy and consumer population. Much will depend on the entrepreneurs' ability to capitalize on the opportunities that lie ahead, but their track record is already a remarkable one.

Riklis has privately said that he is determined to build the biggest Jewish company in America. He has also become increasingly occupied with image, both personal and corporate. Roth, shooting for $500 million in sales and then $1 billion, lined up his successor as president years ago but confesses "there will always be Chester Roth, the chief executive." In the meantime, he carefully studied Penn Central's proposals for a merger, but that deal, like an earlier one with the American Tobacco Company, also fell through. Bassine, who is fighting the battle of his charmed, successful life, is fighting mightily to digest the big portion he has bitten off in the marriage between Spartans and Korvette. The sweet power and the awesome responsibilities of running a $1-billion company were more than he bargained for.

Ferkauf retired from Spartans–Korvette early in 1968 and has started a new chain of specialty stores in an obvious attempt to prove to himself (and to others) that he can do it all over again. List, Kittay, and Berger have assured themselves of financial security by giving up their entrepreneurial roles. But that is not so easily done—one can't throw over the habits of a lifetime—and so they remain flexible, open-eyed and open-eared, still opportunistic.

Are they all happy, everything considered? Often, the push for more power disappears when one's affluence reaches great heights, for then the drives of a lifetime seem to have given up their edge. And, not infrequently, one's stamina runs thin after long, long battle. Today, a number of multi-millionaires in their senior years work for the younger Riklis, who, despite his great success and the $2 billion-in-sales proportion of his empire, is not yet personally wealthy. And while they sometimes wonder about the justice of it, they like the promise, if not the security, of having an unfettered, uninhibited entrepreneur running things. All in the New York group unquestionably feel a great sense of personal accomplishment. But are they contented? One of them answered the question by quoting an old Talmudic proverb: "Who is rich but he who is satisfied with his lot?"

Their game will continue changing as the hierarchy gives way to the inexorable turns of fate, fortune, and fortitude. Some of the older members will die, and as fresh opportunities arise, newer entrepreneurs will grope and push their way to the top rung. But these, despite any great accomplishments that they might make, will be hard put to emulate the particular skills, the dynamism, and the entrepreneurial legerdemain of their predecessors. Nor will they probably be as controversial.

Eight

————— ◆ —————

THE IMMIGRANT
ENTREPRENEURS

1. THROUGH THE GOLDEN PORTALS

"ARE Americans always sick?" Stephen Klein asked himself. Wandering along the streets of Manhattan in 1939, the Viennese, immigrant, candy-maker was surprised to see that drug stores occupied almost every street corner. How could it be in this land of honey, butter, and cream, he wondered, that its people were so frail that they required such ready access to medicine and drugs?

In Vienna and other European cities, Klein knew, instead of pharmacies there was a fancy chocolate shop on practically every corner. Pursuing his curiosity, young Klein learned that New Yorkers were hardly that sickly. They might, in fact, he learned, take to the Viennese corner candy shop. And so the 1,200 Barton's candy shops were launched.

Just a few years ago, Arthur B. Belfer, a Polish immigrant who had arrived here penniless in 1939 and who had never gone beyond high school gave $2 million to Yeshiva University's Graduate School of Science. The token down payment was a stock certificate for 30,000 shares of Belco Petroleum Corporation, the company Belfer had founded.

Twenty years after he arrived here in 1947 from Poland, David T. Chase held the deeds to numerous shopping centers around the United States. The forty-year-old Chase, after being liberated from a concentration camp and settling in Hartford, Conn., where he became interested in real estate, had accomplished quite a feat in business. He had accumulated an average of one shopping center a year in the United States since he had entered the country.

Since 1820, when the United States Immigration Department began to keep records, a human torrent of more than 40 million from other countries has poured into the United States.

The heaviest decade of immigration was from 1901 to 1910, when 8,795,386 came to this country. And out of that many-tongued, polyglot, tattered mass emerged many of America's greatest citizens of the twentieth century, statesmen, educators, scientists, businessmen, artists, and others.

But, only three decades later, or just before, during and after World War II, an entirely new wave of immigrants streamed here from Europe, fleeing the Nazi persecution, the confiscation of their homes, and the theft of their futures in the homeland.

Between 1941 and 1960, 3,550,518 immigrants, refugees, and displaced persons were admitted. And out of these millions have come a new wave of eager-eyed, self-made men. They contain a surprising number of today's most successful, most daring men of enterprise.

Debarking at the John F. Kennedy International Airport, in New York, the new, principal port-of-entry, succeeding Ellis Island, the new arrivals, like their predecessors, found fertility and promise in the new country. Only this time, it was in an environment where there was already at least a superficial cynicism about opportunity for the individual. Whether from malaise, or from the enervation that comes from high wartime earnings and even higher postwar living or from the temporary security of adjustment pay for returning soldiers and subsidized education for war veterans, many native and naturalized citizens, including many young men, did not appear to be bitten by the bug of entrepreneurship.

This probably had a great deal to do with the eagerness of war veterans to return to the sweet calm of civilian life. And, once having done that, their primary attention turned to the challenges and pressures of an education and a career.

A good many Americans, of course, took advantage of the opportunities of an economy turning full circle from a wartime to a civilian state.

But the astonishing success of many new refugees only a few short years after their arrival is indicative of an unusual perspicacity combined with great ambition. There is nothing quite as revealing as a fresh viewpoint fixed on a situation wherein other viewpoints are just a bit jaded. An opportunity gap was created and quickly filled by the new immigrants.

There is no element quite as vital as motivation. It is clearly the moving force in American economic history, from the time that the first settlers put down their first timbers in rocky New England or in the loamy Virginia soil, or when they were compelled to exploit their own borders after the embargoes of a bitter Britain after the War of 1812, or when the nineteenth-century tycoons pushed west for rail-lines, lumber, and land. And it was no less the spur that opened new vistas for successive waves of immigrants to America.

From Ellis Island, they spewed forth in the late nineteenth and early twentieth centuries into the sweatshops, the tenements, and the stores of the cities and to the farms and the plants of the American plains. From the instant of their arrival, they strove to plumb any opportunities that the new land might unfold. Their success was so great that one could

easily believe that there could be no new opportunities awaiting still newer arrivals.

The later emigrants of the forties, fifties, and sixties had
two major motivations. One was poverty and its accompanying, burning frustration, leading to a yearning never again
to be poor.

Americans who were only too happy to see the Second
World War end and to enjoy the fruits of an increasingly
affluent civilian life could hardly accept with equanimity
the unbelievable zeal of the European displaced persons
after they arrived here. Much as they may have preferred not
to, Americans were dismayed, even offended by the scrab-
bling, the scrambling, the street-corner peddling and the
door-to-door selling, and the endless dedication to their work
of many refugees. This resentment was often abetted by the
foreigners' obvious arrogance, spurred in part by the belief
that the United States had been spared much of the horrors
that their countries had experienced. But Americans were
sobered when, inadvertently or not, they saw the concentration camp numbers permanently inscribed on the arms of
many of the new arrivals.

That, of course, denotes the second major motivation—the
great desire for tolerance, for freedom to pursue their lives
without the terror of the midnight rapping on the door, the
insane, criminal behavior that had turned Europe into a
nightmare. They wanted for themselves and for their children
a new, nonpolitical, nonideological environment in which to
grow and thrive.

What did the foreigner need in the postwar years to find
a niche? Some used the money they came with to open stores,
small plants, or service businesses (laundries, shoe repair,
watch repair, floral shops, etc.). Others applied specific skills
they had attained and found that there was a great demand
in this country for engineers, scientists, mechanics, draftsmen,
medical, and electronics technicians.

There was another group that had neither money or particular skills. Instead, these newcomers had a speculative instinct and a vast ambition to apply it. After a variety of menial jobs, which served in a sense to educate them to the ways of the land, many of these immigrants searched out the entrepreneurial vacuums, the economic gaps, the hidden opportunities that Americans seemed to be overlooking.

A childlike directness is evident in the particular opportunistic efforts of some. In others, the hereditary instincts of an Old World shrewdness and remarkable ability to concentrate on money-making are clearly visible.

In any event, the most spectacularly successful new immigrants exhibited a freshness of approach that offers cogent lessons, and perhaps a reason for some self-searching for thoughtful Americans who may be convinced that they live in a narrowing environment for opportunity.

2. BLUHDORN: RIDER OF THE GULF & WESTERN PLAINS

OF the three leading proponents of the sixties' greatest business trend—the development of the big, corporate, conglomerates—two are foreigners who came to the United States in the forties.

All three are among the most successful, modern practitioners of financial leverage, the practice of buying companies so that their assets, cash, securities, or other equity can be used to buy other companies. Their growth is based on the number of revolutions of this cycle.

James Ling, the high-school dropout who built Ling–Temco–Vought into one of America's fastest-growing companies, was born in Texas.

Meshulam Riklis, the peripatetic chairman of the McCrory Corporation, was born to Palestinian parents while they were traveling through Istanbul.

And Charles G. Bluhdorn, the excitable, endlessly energetic chairman of Gulf & Western Industries, was born in Vienna. He was sent by his father, a Czech-born importer, to study in England when he was eleven so that he could behave himself better in school. The "bad boy" then came to the United States in 1942 when he was sixteen.

At that early age, he became a $15-a-week clerk in a cotton brokerage house. He had several other jobs, became a U.S. citizen, and joined the U.S. Air Force. Discharged from the armed services in 1946, he worked as an order clerk for a plate-glass distributor and took night courses at Columbia University. A year later, Bluhdorn, even then intense and restless, dreamed of possessing his own business empire. He took another job as a $60-a-week clerk in a tiny, one-room, export-import house. It was the break that the ambitious, twenty-one-year-old needed, for it opened up to him the world of commodities, of dealing in tremendous lots of foodstuffs.

He was left in charge of the business when its owner went to Europe on a brief trip. Within days, young Bluhdorn had shifted the operation from a minor one to a dealer in international trade, buying from one country to sell to another. When the astonished proprietor returned, he couldn't believe what he saw—invoices, bills-of-lading, and receipts for sales of large quantities of lard to Brazil and Yugoslavia, coffee to America, malt and sphagetti to Italy. But, that first year, his business rose to $1 million. He was delighted, but it was not to last. By then, his youthful, if overzealous protégé had a faraway look in his eye.

When he was twenty-three, Bluhdorn invested $3,000 to open his own export-import business in Manhattan. It became obvious to him that a fortune could be made on a tiny stake in the international commodities game where prices rose and fell many times in a day. Soon, he was importing as much as $1 million of coffee a day.

He began speculating, especially in coffee, a risky but rewarding commodity because of its frequent price changes. But, by 1956 when he was thirty, he had made his first million, and all in the frenzied world of coffee. Recalling those years, he declared in 1965 in an interview in *The New York Times:*

"It was a very hectic business. Tremendously erratic. A Palisades Amusement Park—sometimes amusing, sometimes not, but always a roller-coaster."

If he found pursuing a one-product market nerve-racking, Bluhdorn's eventual turn to operating a conglomerate, wherein many products or divisions are involved, proved more to his liking. Obviously, unlike most people, businessmen or otherwise, who find their security in a simple pursuit of their destiny in a narrow channel, Bluhdorn was of a different stripe.

Yet, it was in a quest for a more stable business that he quit the percolating world of coffee trading. He was looking for a new vehicle to mount. When he found it, it was to become a springboard for a complex of automobile parts, manufacturing, mining, chemicals, and tobacco.

Looking for a "public locomotive to hang an idea on," as he told the *Wall Street Journal,* he selected the Michigan Bumper Corporation, which became the nucleus of his budding conglomerate. Gradually, he bought a majority of the stock of Michigan Bumper. It was a small firm but it had a listing on the American Stock Exchange and its stock was cheap.

He merged it into a Houston auto parts distributor that he acquired and he continued to add similar small companies to the group, now renamed Gulf & Western. Auto parts had the stability the budding entrepreneur wanted. They didn't rise or fall along with economic changes. In bad times, drivers hold on to their cars and use even more replacement parts than in good times. And, when car sales pick up and production rises, parts business gains both from supplying new cars and from furnishing replacement parts when the new cars are running a year or more.

Seeking to weld a national network of auto parts manufacturers, distributors, and warehouse facilities, Bluhdorn accumulated mostly by acquisition thirty-three auto parts warehouses and 150 auto parts distributors by 1966. He also branched out into the manufacturing of jet-engine parts and survival equipment for astronauts. Along the way, he acquired late in 1965 the New Jersey Zinc Company, a large mining and chemical company, which by the following year boosted G & W's annual sales to about $300 million.

Now, however, Bluhdorn, an emotional, brash, gesticulating collector of companies ran into the same stiff-lipped, hardnosed lack of affection with which Wall Street always greets financial upstarts. The fear cycle that such an attitude seems to generate stuffs itself on the food of cynicism and on a doubt about a new personality. If holders of large blocks of stock in a company start dumping their shares, with or without justification, a selling bath may quickly follow. The result is usually a severe drop in the company's securities and a strategic loss of its bargaining power in dealing with lenders and potential merger partners.

Bluhdorn realized that he had to bolster Wall Street's confidence. But, it was mainly because his antennae jangled meaningfully at the prospect that Bluhdorn set about acquiring Hollywood's old-established Paramount Pictures Corporation. Wall Street liked it and so did many investors, as Bluhdorn suspected. G & W's stock, now prestigiously listed on the "big board," the New York Stock Exchange, became one of the most active, reaching a new high in value on the announcement of the Paramount Pictures acquisition.

He had really arrived. But, now sitting on a high, open perch, he had become a target and there were times he didn't like it. He bitterly resented *Life* magazine's 1967 article, headlined, "Multimillion Reach of Wall Street's 'Mad Austrian,'" because he felt it caricatured him.

Bluhdorn's unusual way of going about his business arouses comment, both pro and con. To some extent, like that of Riklis, it has not been American in nature, or, at least, not twentieth-century American. It is European and perhaps even reminiscent of the free-wheeling, open nature typical of nineteenth-century America. "You're crazy!" he is likely to tell the head of a merger-company prospect, who expresses doubt on the wisdom of tieing up with Bluhdorn. But, eager to clinch a deal and to convince the prospective seller that he is doing the right thing, Bluhdorn will exhort him to "stop being a little company when by letting us give you everything you need, you can be a big company."

What financial men and a good many native-born Americans have trouble about accepting in the Bluhdorn–Riklis type of new entrepreneur is their openness, the fresh, eager face that they present of wanting to do business for the sake of all involved. Of course, what the skeptics accurately suspect or sense behind the surface sincerity, which is so easily dismayed by cynical disbelief, is that there is much that has gone on before the approach was made. What it amounts to, they later find, is an opportunistic chicanery, or, at the very least, a strong effort of having done the homework beforehand so well, to have searched into every nook and cranny of the potential deal, that the opponent is caught off guard and probably will not prove a match. And so, to keep it all in balance, many haven't.

As, in the case of New Jersey Zinc, the largest U.S. producer of zinc, Bluhdorn so persisted in hounding the head of a group of dissident shareholders to buy his block of stock that the man gave in mainly to get the zealous G & W chairman off his back. He curtly informed Bluhdorn that he had only five days in which to come up with the cash for a higher offer. But the not-so-mad Austrian was already a step or two ahead. He had scouted the financing possibilities. The day he was extended the deadline, he prevailed on the Chase Manhattan Bank to give him a loan of $83 million, or almost triple the net worth of Gulf & Western. By then, Bluhdorn already had management's holdings in his pocket, too, as well as the funds to buy the shares of the dissident group. He had won both the battle and the war.

So, perhaps if speed and persistence are classic American entrepreneurial traits, Bluhdorn is indeed a native. In seeking to acquire control of Paramount Pictures, he similarly kept after a pair of unhappy shareholders, flattered them for having a "sacred mission" in wanting to modernize the staid, unprofitable movie company and warned them that their ideas had created so much bitterness on the Paramount board that they would never be able to put them across. Only he, Bluhdorn, could be their champion, he told them, and even make them look good to their backers by buying their shares at a profit.

He got their approval at lunch. That night, not wanting to give anyone a chance to reflect and back out, he consummated the deal by hammering out all the details. A second, contending group now also gave in and offered Bluhdorn their shares.

What did such persistence gain Bluhdorn's company? A library of recent movies, which could be rented to television for about $200 million, and total assets of $300 million. The price: $165 million.

Not content only to spearhead G & W's growth by all this to well over $600 million in annual sales, Bluhdorn made a number of personal investments. He became an important shareholder in the H. C. Bohack Company, the venerable supermarket chain, and in Ward Foods Company, a bakery products company.

His deals for G & W marched on, almost stumbling over each other. Early in 1967, he bought for $60 million the

South Puerto Rico Sugar Company, which numbers among its assets three hundred thousand undeveloped acres in the Dominican Republic. A day later, G & W also bought a block of stock for $4 million in E. W. Bliss, a large machinery manufacturer. A few months later, Bluhdorn paid $17 million for Desilu Productions, a television show producer headed by Lucille Ball. And late in the summer of 1967, he acquired the Consolidated Cigar Company.

What makes Bluhdorn hop, skip, and jump? A quest for bigness, for getting there ahead of anyone else. Most of his deals involve "paper," as well as cash—either a dilution of G & W's stock or of its subsidiaries, or the floating of new issues, in a snow of "confetti," thus "paper." This is typical of the other proponents of conglomerates, who find this method of payment (sometimes called "counterfeit" by their most acid critics) the most convenient way of buying other companies.

Bluhdorn, whose aim was to reach $1 billion in sales by 1969 (an easy goal, as it turned out) on his way to reaching $2 billion in much less time than the first stage took, once attempted to explain what stimulated him. It was a classic case of understatement. "My parents didn't have any money to speak of and this creates a tremendous ambition," he said. "I had in mind to go into business and be successful."

3. THE SIMPLE WORLD OF ONE IMMIGRANT

Paul Baumer is the fictitious name of a real but improbable man.

As a teen-ager, he saw almost his entire family down to second and third cousins hauled off by the Nazis in Hungary to be exterminated, including his own father. The proud, dignified parent, however, had taught his son to be self-sufficient, partly by his own example. By the time Paul had reached the age of eighteen he had had great need to be self-sufficient. He had seen many deaths, was forced to move hundreds of bodies to mass graves, and had lived literally on the edge of survival in ten concentration and displaced persons camps.

Today he is the head of a small but rapidly growing business empire in America. The improbability of the emaciated, twenty-one-year-old youth who emigrated here in 1948 with $5 in his pocket turning it into several million dollars is one thing, but the manner in which he did it, violating some of the most precious American business tenets, demonstrating a courage, even a *chutzpah,* in an alien environment, is something else again. The little, chunky multimillionaire who is now fond of $300 suits and $35 ties is unorthodox in his thinking and his methods are unusual. And while his criticisms of American methods are probably largely defensive, they offer an interesting outside look at some of our business mores.

Although a relative helped bring him to the United States, Paul was immediately on his own. He lived in a New York ghetto on exactly a dime a day, eating a few pieces of bread and perhaps a bowl of soup. He would walk around the crowded, dirty streets in confusion and dismay. Wasn't there a job somewhere that he could have to keep himself alive?

Eventually, he found one, many of them, in fact. In eighteen months he held some fifteen positions. On one factory job, where he earned $30 a week, he asked the owner what time he opened the plant. The next morning when the boss opened up at 7:30, Paul was there. He remained until the factory closed at nine. "I did this for a week, much to the owner's surprise," Paul recalled, "and then I told him I could run the place."

Baumer was given his chance and two weeks later was indeed put in charge of the plant, rising in salary from $30 to $175.

Still searching for something that would interest him, he sold door-to-door and peddled for two years. He seemed to outgrow the job all the time, but something kept him at it. Perhaps it was an instinctive feeling that this contact with the people would teach him more quickly than anything else what America was all about. But, after two years, he sold his goods and route.

He used the money he got from that experience and others to buy a series of businesses, each one a bit larger than the previous one. But all the time he kept seeking "something that would work for me twenty-four hours a day."

Finally, the business opportunity that he had been looking for appeared. By sheer persistence, he wore down the reluctant seller and obtained control. As Paul recalled, "The business had quality, its statements seemed legitimate (my greatest fear in acquisitions is untrue statements) and it was beautiful—beautifully mismanaged."

The owner held more than half of the shares outstanding and wanted $1 a share to sell out. Baumer decided that for all practical purposes his offer hid the real problems. Actually, he realized, the owner had nothing to sell, because he had an immense amount of debt outstanding. So, Paul made an unusual offer and it was accepted. He would pay $1 for a 90 per cent interest in the company.

It worked this way: the owner guaranteed to pay the debts to the banks, which he had personally guaranteed, for four years. After that, the successor corporation would assume the new debts. But the owner was now happily relieved of the burden of continuing a lagging business.

Paul's new business was a large plant manufacturing art objects. Pursuing a policy he had followed since he became an entrepreneur, he decided to ferret out mismanagement immediately by totally immersing himself in the problems of the business. He spent thirty-six hours awake, studying everything that went on. He particularly scrutinized the price-cost, inventory-to-sales, and overhead-to-quality relationships.

Then he made a series of rapid-fire decisions. He cut the large staff substantially and made several executives double their functions. A key executive was earning a small salary and supervising people who made only a little less. "How could he feel the proper sense of responsibility?" Paul asked himself. So he fired the man and brought in a replacement at a much higher salary, who earned it by being efficient and cutting costs.

Also, Paul felt that the prices that the concern was getting for its products were low. To analyze his move in this regard, he asked himself if the business was to be a quality one. He decided that the distribution system didn't call for it, but there was a need to improve quality and the service so that "the good customers would stay with us." And then, after taking steps to see that this was done, he raised his prices.

What were the results of these moves? For the first time in many years, the business was put on a profitable footing.

Now quite well off and gratified by his attainment in getting a business that worked for him "while I sleep," Paul retired. But this lasted only two years. He had become very bored. "You can't retire at thirty in a country where everybody works," he said.

The answer, of course, was to buy another business. He went to his bank and told a vice president that he wanted to acquire another company. "What kind of business do you have for sale?" Paul asked. The banker answered, "What kind of business do you want to buy?" Paul said, "It doesn't matter—I'll take anything." The banker had evidently never heard anything like that and he was quite confused. Paul finally left after an hour, realizing that he would have to tell the bank what kind of business he wanted. A few days later, he returned, told them what he wanted and the bank found it for him.

Happy, eager, and filled with a sense of challenge, he once again threw himself into his total inspection regimen. He studied every aspect of the new company, a producer of quality toys, for two months, and then in a matter of another six weeks made all the changes.

They involved a total reorganization of the business. Nothing that cost $1 or more escaped the glare of the hot-eyed entrepreneur. He cut the staff in half, simplified the manufacturing process, and found that he could produce 100 per cent more merchandise. Without adding any new equipment but by resetting the machinery and altering the flow of materials, everything could be delivered to production workers without loss of time. He also launched an advertising campaign, a new, direct mail, packaging, and trade show program, and distributed a new catalog. He also enlarged the sales staff.

How did it all work out? Within two years, sales rose sharply and a loss was turned into a profit. Also, Paul achieved a full reversal in the ratio of current assets to current liabilities. He had transformed the toymaker into a solvent and profitable company.

Now involved in adding to his thriving little empire, Baumer is convinced that there are two main principles in business—simplicity and the elimination of waste. Profits come when one concentrates on those two things.

Why do most new businesses fail? Mostly, he believes, because by the time a person starts his own business his mind is too habit-formed to function effectively. In each person's life something is needed, some compulsion, some stimuli to build a habit of crystallizing one's thinking. Why are things being done as they are? one has to ask himself. What should be done to correct a situation that is obviously wrong? A high degree of objectivity is needed.

Paul does not employ attorneys or accountants, except to fulfill legal requirements. He doesn't ask friends for business advice. Why? "I don't generally value people's opinions. Business is like chess, its moves are different every time."

A lawyer is not supposed to be a businessman, Baumer adds, but to give advice only for legal problems so that he can protect his client and so he must be spurred by his client.

Nor does Paul read much or place much confidence in what he reads. "By not reading, I allow myself to accumulate knowledge through listening, observing, and thinking things through," he said. "When I do read, such as the different opinions of professionals on Wall Street in the financial pages, I don't take them seriously because most have a diplomatic, built-in, self-protection in their remarks. But in all these and other statements and stories, I try to gather the sense behind the concocted articles. And, out of that, a certain figure is being formed like out of clay. If you are a realist, you can do it. You can see the sense of it. People believe what they want to believe—very few think clearly."

Paul Baumer is convinced that his own case and others prove that it is still possible to "make it" in this country. So few Americans appreciate the freedom and opportunities that they have. "How many have the United States Constitution framed in their offices? I do."

Security is one thing that Baumer says he learned a long time ago. It has something to do with being self-sufficient. Security is not the fear of doing something to get out of a rut. Paul believes that there is no real security. The only security is within yourself, the ability to think and to act. Security is not the savings that a hard-working man accumulates in his lifetime.

Why not? A man saves money all his life, he said, and chances are that he uses only a small portion of it. What happens to it? It obtains a small amount of interest and is passed on to his family, but the use of it is ignored during his entire lifetime. Money, Baumer emphasizes, is a commodity to be used, while the mind and the ability to use it objectively are all the security one needs.

The habit of saving for the future is what keeps men working for employers and in jobs that they don't like, chained to "desk monsters." In the intervening years, he concluded, the individual has forfeited "his freedom of thought and his freedom of action."

4. AND OTHERS WHO GRABBED THE RING

THERE were others, many others, who came here in those years, who looked for, found, and seized opportunities.

. . . Working twenty hours a day, with his flashlight in his mouth to give him light in the dark, Janis Risbergs became the most productive carpenter working for Levitt & Sons, the big Long Island builder. Soon, the smiling, burly Latvian, who wanted no more of either Russia or Germany and emigrated to the United States in 1947, became a Levitt subcontractor, hiring and coordinating the efforts of all the Latvian craftsmen he could find. In 1959, he bought control of General Builders Corporation, a real estate developer hovering on bankruptcy. By employing zealous Latvians like him who were anxious to make good in the new country, applying the most effective mass construction techniques and giving all his greatest devotion, Risbergs within a few years was operating a company with assets over $30 million.

. . . Henry A. Federman was manager of a bank in Germany but had to leave it in 1939 because of religious persecution. After a year in England, he came to New York and became sales agent for mahogany bowls being manufactured for a friend in Haiti. He also began exporting watches and soon took a good look at the American watch market. It occurred to him that the mass customer might respond to low-priced watches that had colorful bands. "Why not a fashion wardrobe of watches for a woman like her wardrobe of shoes or handbags?" he asked a friend. He formed the Sheffield Watch Corporation, developed a number of European supply sources, and tried out his ideas on the public. The response was good. It became especially good when he used a new color process to anodize aluminum watch cases—four thousand of them selling in one store in a week. Diversifying his line, offering as many as six hundred watch-and-band variations on a handful of watch movements, he raised Sheffield into a public company in twenty years with sales of $17 million.

. . . Leon Jolson, also a DP, who came to America in 1947, with his wife and $8 in his pocket. A third-generation member of a family that had been in the sewing-machine business in Warsaw, Jolson started a repair shop in the Bronx. He recalled the quality and workmanship of the Italian-made Necchi machines from his experience with them in Europe and wrote to the company, seeking to represent it in the United States. The Jolsons prepared samples of what the versatile Necchi machines could do, sent out a large mailing, and within weeks, were flooded with orders for thousands of machines. A new corporation was formed, The House of Necchi, and the Swiss Elna portable sewing machines were added. When he celebrated his first anniversary of American citizenship, Jolson was already the head of an American firm with annual sales of $25 million.

. . . Hans Fischer, who obtained his engineering education in Vienna, entered the United States in 1939 and worked as an engineer for a number of large companies. In 1951, he started his own engineering consulting concern, H. Fischer & Associates, Cleveland, and touched off a hard-sell promotion campaign that threw staid professional engineering groups into a tizzy. Ignoring the complaints, offering a fresh, hardheaded service at lower costs than others, Fischer developed his company into one with 150 mechanical engineers, started several side businesses, and became a millionaire shortly after he reached forty.

. . . Julian J. Studley, a Belgian refugee who came to the United States in 1946, turned from diamond polishing to real estate and decided that tenants needed more attention than landlords. Specializing in office leasing because he smelled large commissions in Manhattan's giant office building boom, he started his own office to carry the torch for the tenant. His pitch was that the company that leased the space determined the value of an office building (the tenant's credit as represented by the lease obligation determines the structure's mortgagable value) and that a lease represented a major capital outlay (a 10,000 sq. ft. lease at $6 a sq. ft. for twenty years equals $1.2 million). He offered a multi-faceted service, including a research study, often running to three hundred pages containing detailed real estate analysis. An affiliated architecture-design company supplied environment analysis and proposed suitable space. The results of his efforts on behalf of tenants, which created a mixed feeling among landlords, was the establishment of offices in seven major U.S. cities and in seven foreign cities. A millionaire before he was forty, Studley employs sixty salesmen who earn $2.5 million in commissions. Like the other immigrants, he had detected a current market need and filled it.

5. "WE WILL PROSPER HERE"

THE New York Association for New Americans is only one of a half dozen social assistance organizations that have sprung up since World War II to foster emigration of Jews to various parts of the world. Most are organized along ethnic lines, Protestant, Catholic, Jewish, Lutheran.

The NYANA has systematically surveyed the successes and

failures of those it assisted to come to the United States. Its purpose was to determine the nature of their adjustment to the community.

"In the almost two decades of our existence, we have served over 115,000 men, women, and children from various parts of the world," said Philip Soskis, executive director. "From 1949 to the middle fifties, we worked with displaced persons primarily from Eastern Europe. Then came the Egyptian and Hungarian refugees.

"When those numbers declined by 1961, we began to deal with the Cuban and Rumanian refugees. The binding thread among all these thousands of individuals has been the strong desire to live in freedom, to live as Jews, and to lead normal lives."

The organization, assisted by the United HIAS Service, the United Jewish Appeal, and contributions by many Americans, conducted studies of the experiences of three distinct groups of new immigrants which it had aided.

These included surveys of 100 families of some 9,000 families of European displaced who emigrated in 1949; a survey of 200 Hungarian families of 1,100 such families which entered the United States in 1957; and one of 100 of the 600 families aided in the Cuban Refugee Program and brought in between 1961 and 1965.

Of the original one hundred European families that settled here in 1949, the social organization issued a report on their progress after ten years in this country. In part, the report read:

> NYANA was astonished to learn that 45 among the 100 family heads surveyed currently own and operate their own business. We have no ways of knowing, of course, whether this percentage would be applicable to the other 9,000 families settled in 1949, since it seems extraordinarily high. On the other hand, we know from the survey interviews that several others tried their hands at businesses and failed, and that at least an-

other five are presently saving up to go into business for themselves eventually. A few of these businesses—about five—were started with small loans from NYANA.

The others were started either with loans from friends or relatives or with money that they had amounting to a few thousand dollars on the average from German indemnification funds given to them for the loss of freedom and health during the war.

Twenty-two of these businesses are small family enterprises employing no outside help. The other twenty-three employ approximately 130 workers. Considering the fact that one of the arguments often used against liberalizing our immigration laws is that newcomers take jobs away from American citizens, it is noteworthy that in this group more than one hundred jobs were actually created for others.

Among the types of businesses started by the 1949 refugees, aside from the small retail groceries, bakeries, delicatessens, laundry, shoe repair, tailoring establishments and other stores— mainly family-operated—were four manufacturing establishments and seven contractors in such diverse fields as plastics, construction, heating equipment, electrical fixtures, women's raincoats, etc.

Of the Hungarian families, the organization reported ten years after they had arrived that "as in previous surveys, the newcomer's drive to be independent is very compelling. There is a strong drive toward being one's boss."

Thirty-eight of the forty-three men and women who came from Hungary reestablished themselves in their original professions or crafts and forty new businesses were started. These ranged from an art gallery to a knitting mill to a mountain resort.

"Some own small family enterprises and others employ from one to forty additional persons," the NYANA said. "These newcomers are not only supporting themselves, but have also created job opportunities for others. If we include family members also employed in the business, two hundred

people owe their jobs to these forty Hungarian refugees who
arrived here penniless ten years ago."

The Cuban group was unusual because most of its members
had already emigrated to a Western hemisphere country
after fleeing from persecution in Europe. After several years
in Cuba, they had left it "not because there was any anti-
Semitism there," as the NYANA put it, "but because they did
not want to live under a Communist regime."

On the Cuban families' progress here five to six years after
their arrival, Mr. Soskis said:

"Their economic adjustment is also reflected in a beginning
trend toward acquiring small business. This has always been
one of the ways that we can test the upward economic
mobility of our clients. Business ownership was fairly common
in the Jewish community in Cuba. Many had small, family-
operated shops and stores; others carried on fairly large
manufacturing establishments employing sixty to eighty persons, which did business in the hundreds of thousands of
dollars. The efforts of twenty to thirty years to build up many
of these businesses ended in the confiscation of the property
and assets as the individuals fled the country.

"This, however, merely spurred on some of the former
businessmen: thirteen of the hundred families interviewed
have already reestablished themselves in some business venture; some in small retail shops, a shoe store, a costume
jewelry shop; some in manufacturing on a small scale. While
most of these businesses are still solely family-operated at this
time, three of them are already employing four additional
persons."

These newest immigrants, now on the third phase of their
search to find a compatible home, seem as bright-eyed and
undaunted as their predecessors.

"We escaped from Poland years ago with nothing and

prospered in Cuba," one former Havana businessman observed. "We came to the United States with nothing and we know that we will prosper here because we are in a free land with many opportunities."

In addition to the New Americans organization, similar groups have worked valiantly to bring homeless people here. The Church World Service, for example, assisted 113,000 to emigrate to the United States from the end of the Second World War through 1960. The Lutheran Immigration Refugee Service brought in about 60,000.

Zealous, conscientious, and responsible, the newcomers returned a surprisingly high percentage of the travel loans extended to them by the assistance groups. In less than five years, those aided by Church World Service repaid $1,413,468, or 69.7 per cent of the net collectible amount of $2,026,235. Of the loans granted by the Lutheran group mostly to Esthonians and Latvians 90 per cent was repaid.

Facing language barriers, adjustment to a strange environment, and frequently unable to qualify by American professional or academic standards, a good many of the new immigrants were not able to thrive to the extent they had hoped for in the new land. Among them were such professionals as lawyers, doctors, and engineers. Their problem, which often proved insurmountable, included age, academic degrees not acceptable here, and specialized experience which seemed to have no practical parallel or market in the land of promise.

In such cases compromise had to be made by the immigrant, and it was often accompanied by bitterness and disappointment.

Against this background of some startling successes, and struggles by others, as well as frustrations, new opportunites beckon once again.

These are expected to emerge from the cessation of the United States national origins quotas system on July 1, 1968.

That system, which had set the immigration pattern since 1929, was based on preserving the ethnic balance that existed in the United States when the 1920 census was taken. In October, 1965, the program was revised to provide that no foreign country would have its quota of potential immigrants to the U.S. reduced. However, each quota's unused portion would be assigned to a pool from which potential immigrants everywhere could be selected.

The method used for selection in the revised system was a preference plan that gave most of the new visas to relatives of U.S. residents. A smaller number was distributed based on talents and skills needed in the U.S. This dual distribution concept will continue.

Already, the revised system has allowed the entry of many immigrants from countries whose quotas had been very small. These include Italy, Loyalist China, Greece, Portugal, the Philippines, and India. Those countries with a declining number of visas are England and North Ireland, Germany, and Poland. In other words, Southern Europe and Asia stand to receive more emigration opportunities to the United States and Northern Europe less.

Total immigration here is gaining probably because of the freeing of unused quota segments and their transfer to other nationals eager to take advantage of them. In 1967, for example, total immigration here was 361,972, the highest yearly figure in more than forty years. The results of this new flow of immigrants on entrepreneurial activity will be worth watching.

6. THE TRAUMA RUNS DEEP

WHAT type of people emerged from the terrible experiences that were suffered by the refugees from Nazi tyranny and by the human flotsam that floated from one European displaced persons camp to another? Obviously, it is difficult to generalize. Yet, it is safe to say that those who survived that travail can scarcely be as normal in their psychological makeup or in their outward behavior as those who never had such experiences.

Discussions with past and present associates of a number of the self-made American businessmen who came out of the war-born terrors frequently reveal that they have a deeply-rooted distrust and uneasiness. Some fear that American politics and its practitioners are so naive that there is an ever-present possibility that a dictatorship of right or left may develop as it did in their own countries. It is not so much a matter of contempt for those who never experienced the terrors of genocide and persecution as it is a permanent disbelief that the world can ever be right again—anywhere.

The lack of humanity so starkly directed against many of the new immigrants, businessmen or otherwise in the land of their origins, has had the effect of dehumanizing some of them in various ways. While some are almost pathetically grateful on the surface for the kindness and success they found here, underneath it all the loss of their families and of their ideals will never allow them to feel secure again.

And a few have reacted with deeply psychoneurotic tendencies. One was bitterly described by an ex-employee as being "unhuman," demanding "more than total loyalty." He was further described as being unable to sympathize with the fears and problems of his staff because he is either unconscious of them or considers them insignificant. Such a businessman spoke sharply to his secretary on one occasion. When she took dictation with tears streaming down her cheeks, he appeared to take no notice and continued dictating until he was finished.

Another was termed "coldly superior" and "supremely egotistical" in evaluating his great success in this country, which he did often. At one point, recalls a close associate, one businessman commented, "To me, the whole world is just a shmuck [Jewish slang for penis, in the most derogatory sense] and I'm the only smart one."

It cannot be overstressed that extremes such as this particular case are exceptions. In many more cases, the distrust of others, the lack of sensitivity, and the megalomania are more subconscious than they are evident.

Nine

———•———

SONS OF THE SELF-MADE

1. THE COMPLEX RELATIONSHIP

YOUNG, eager, bright-eyed, he spoke glibly and confidently for a minute of his future prospects. Suddenly, he paused, and resumed, or tried to, his tongue and breath caught in a pathological stammer that brought the blood high to his smooth face and acute embarrassment to his listeners. One by one, they turned their eyes away until, quite suddenly again, he was speaking quickly, glibly, confidently.

He never referred to his stammer during the hour-long conversation. But he didn't have to, for it was frequently repeated before his companions left, sympathetic and even saddened at this singular and dramatic flaw in an otherwise composed and assured son of a wealthy father.

They didn't understand why until a close friend of the family explained it simply. "Harvey's father is a man who has succeeded at everything he tried to do from the day he was born. Today, he's one of the big men in American industry—sharp, tough, a hard man and a demanding man.

"But he has one problem," the family friend added. "He

has two happily married daughters and his son, who is his youngest, is the apple of his eye. But, somehow, he can't tell him so or show him how he feels. All he can seem to do is be brusque with him. Once the father told me, 'I wish to God I could talk to my boy and tell him what a fine kid he is and praise him when he does something especially good. But I can't—I guess I've been a perfectionist toward everyone too long.'"

Perhaps that is why the twenty-three-year-old son has told so many people, "I'd like to make out on my own. I just don't know what I would do if Dad wanted to help me. I'm just not sure that I could ever measure up to him. But I hope he never asks me if he could help."

This particular real-life situation is not typical of the relationship between the average enterpriser and his son. But it has several elements that are typical of the effects many self-made men have on their sons.

These include the inhibition caused by overwhelming accomplishment on the immature and untried; a serious gap in communications not merely in minor but in major matters, as well; and, perhaps most important, a dichotomy of objectives created by a lack of mutual understanding which, in turn, comes from the different circumstances in which both father and son grew up.

But there are two sides to the question. The fathers are not always responsible for the situation. They are not always in control of the unhappy relationship, and, therefore they are not always the causative factor of it.

"Anything a rich father does is wrong," asserts Dr. Milton R. Sapirstein, the New York psychiatrist. "When his wealth reaches well beyond a certain point, the father has a rough time raising his children. The thing that most people would like to believe is that the father crushes the son and he ends up a spineless idiot.

"That is not the case at all," adds Dr. Sapirstein. "It happens, of course, that a powerfully motivated father by his very nature becomes an example of achievement that the son cannot hope to emulate. How many successes can there be in one or two generations? Sometimes, it is a pathetic situation for the second generation. They have no place to go. But it is not because the father wants to hold his son down. He wants to be proud of him but he is usually disappointed."

His remarks generally sum up those of other psychiatrists. A more detailed approach to this is contained in Chapter Six, under "The Family Relationship." But, suffice it to say here that the father-son relationship is a delicate and complex one when the parent attains important stature in his field. This is hardly a situation relegated only to business, but includes the arts, education, science, and politics.

The son's attitude toward the father hovers between pride and envy, between gratitude and compulsion to succeed on his own, and between hope that heredity will help him and a sense of rejection because strong fathers traditionally have weak sons.

Why do some sons make it while others don't?

The question presupposes that the son of the self-made man always either feels under duress that he must also succeed in business or have his own, self-propelled drive to succeed. That is not so. Some neither want to repeat the father's success or simply are interested in other pursuits having nothing to do with the same type of achievement that the father made or the recognition he obtained.

Other young men feel driven to imitate the father's success and even to surpass it. A third type is not sure what he wants but feels pressured to be successful, too, in some manner or degree.

Exceptions though they may be, Howard Hughes and J. Paul Getty, America's two richest men, are sons of self-made men who were able to tremendously expand their inheritances.

Hughes did it by a furious acceleration of his aircraft and

tool companies and by investments in other aircraft concerns and real estate. Getty's means was to seek out the big oil gushers, adding oil to real estate and aircraft stock. Their individual fortunes have been estimated at more than $1 billion each.

Both had the motivation to accomplish what they wanted on a grand scale. Getty, in his book *How to Be Rich*, describes what it takes: "Luck, knowledge, hard work—especially hard work—a man needs them all to become a millionaire. But, above all, he needs what can be called 'the millionaire mentality': that vitally aware state of mind which harnesses all of an individual's skills and intelligence to the tasks and goals of his business. . . ."

Many other sons are altogether different. They enjoy the affluence of their environment and share joyfully in their father's fame or importance. But they seek neither to repeat his example or to live any more constructively than to enjoy a constant round of the hedonistic life—to travel the wine, women, and song circuit. These are the most disappointing to their fathers, especially those who came up from nothing and hoped they were erecting a dynasty in their own image.

One such eternally hopeful businessman, for example, has two sons, neither of whom has followed his own dedicated lead. The younger became a teacher, and a sincere and devoted one. The older agreed to come into his father's business but soon showed himself to be a playboy. In ten years he was married and divorced several times, tried often to apply himself to his aging father's business problems and failed, consoling himself in sabbaticals at night clubs, ski lodges, resorts, and brothels.

The father was disappointed in both. He became philosophical in time over his younger son, but turned increasingly bitter over the older one. It resulted in the frequent exchange of harsh words, the pleasure-loving son usually ending his part of the argument with a contrite admission of resignation.

"What can I do, Pop, that's the way I am," was the gist of it. His father's several heart attacks in his latter years were ascribed by friends to the older son's exploits.

Sometimes, the sons try and try hard but they can't quite accomplish what their parents did. In one case, the parent to be emulated was the mother of two sons. She was a strong-willed, creative, and vigorous executive with a flair for making money. For over two decades, she built an important whole-saling concern which, by the time she suddenly died, had annual sales of more than $10 million. Both young men, taking the place of the father who had died early in their lives, had worked closely with their mother. When she died, they took control and did well for a time.

Fortunately, when they ran into their first serious troubles, help appeared in the form of a large diversified company that wanted to buy their firm. The troubles the sons faced were the result of inept management and were deeply rooted but the purchaser did not know precisely what it was buying. The price was a very good one, making the two young men rich for life. They were retained in major capacities to run their former company for the new owners. But the weakness of their operation gradually became evident. Both were finally let go in terms that were not at all friendly.

Today, both are trying again but in a different field. Their new interests are entrepreneurial and they have the inde-pendence that comes from substantial personal assets. They do not feel a sense of failure but they and those close to them know one thing for sure: Their affluence and position are the direct result of their mother's efforts, rather than of their own.

In the United States, there are about half a dozen major companies in which the original family holdings still pre-dominate. Among them are DuPont, Gulf Oil, and General Tire & Rubber. The latter, founded in 1915 by William F. O'Neil, is an unusual example of what can happen when a successful father has sons, in O'Neil's case, five, and when those sons, three at any rate, take over the business and like it.

William F. was himself not particularly anxious to follow his father's footsteps. Michael Augustine O'Neil had left County Cork in 1877 to settle in Akron, where he had started the M. O'Neil Company, a dry goods store. That business today, now owned by the May Department Stores Company, remains Akron's largest department store.

But Michael's son stayed away from his father's store and, after graduating from college, started a Firestone tire distributorship in Kansas City and seven years later formed the General Tire Company. While Michael O'Neil reluctantly became one of William's backers, he remained nervous about his son's prospects since the bankruptcy rate among the many Akron tire companies was unusually high.

General Tire became a big success, despite the newspaper clippings of continuing business failures that Mike O'Neil would casually drop on William's desk. Although the firm was slow to diversify, it made its first move in that direction in 1942. It acquired a New England radio network and then two years later Aerojet Engineering, which became Aerojet General and eventually one of the largest suppliers of spacecraft and rocketry.

The O'Neil investment of $1.2 million in Aerojet soared to something like $150 million two decades later. Under General's direction, Aerojet's sales catapulted from $2.5 million in the year it was acquired to $703 million in 1963.

Before his death in 1960, William pushed a variety of other acquisition moves. For years, he had worked to interest his boisterous sons in the business. Three responded positively and, after World War II, came into the company. The father's interest became channeled more and more toward acquisitions. The sons were trying to learn the business at the same time that they were jockeying for position as the heir apparent. In the family, there was competition on two levels—the father with the sons and the young men among themselves. The hectic, boisterous pushing and shoving continued into their home but the interplay always resolved itself short of dissension.

Today, the three sons, Tom, John, and Jerry occupy the company's top posts, supervising a very successful operation. Annual volume is now over the $1 billion a year mark and the earnings return on shareholder's equity is the best of any major tire and rubber company.

As competitive as ever, the three O'Neils have come to terms with each other. They decided several years ago to have equal authority and complete autonomy. Each is responsible for a different function and has complete responsibility for it. And to keep out of each other's hair, Tom, the board chairman, operates from New York; Jerry, the president, from Akron; and John, chairman of the finance committee, out of the nation's capital.

Once in a while, a young man teaches his successful father a few tricks. One such situation involved three generations of a leading merchandising family. The founder, an innovator, with a keen sense for store location, customer service, and promotion, left an important business to his son. The company then entered into a period of four decades when every thing the founder had started was implemented, strengthened, and updated. But essentially the son's regime was more that of an enlightened caretaker, than that of a creative man.

Then, his own son took over at the father's retirement and within months uprooted policies laid down by the two previous generations. He cast aside the traditional retailing molds and announced daring changes in store hours, advertising, and merchandising. His father was horrified as were other old-time executives. "Why tamper with proven, successful methods?" they demanded. But the son pushed on.

The customers, however, were delighted. They responded

almost immediately in positive terms, even though some recoiled with displeasure at the changes. Within two years, the store's volume had jumped 25 per cent and its earnings a like percentage. At the end of four years, the youthful president opened two new stores, both of which did well from the moment they opened their doors. The skeptic, his father, then became his most vociferous adherent. He let it be known that his son was nothing less than a throwback to his own father, both having a strong strain of "the genius."

However, just to make sure that he was not being over-optimistic, the far-sighted but noncreative father arranged for the company to be merged into a larger, publicly held firm and exchanged his own equity for the shares of the new owner.

Another father whose experience made him sensitive to the future took a bold step, too. He had operated a small company of his own for some years and had no great aspirations. When his two sons came out of the Marines, however, he encouraged them to start their own business and loaned them $40,000 to do so. He had confidence that they could succeed in getting off the ground for they had worked for him for several years prior to World War II.

Two years after they started in on their own, he sold his own business and joined them. The company moved steadily ahead, helped by his calm coaching in the back room. He rarely came into the main office, but spent most of his time in the field either in the growing number of plants or dropping in for social but helpful chats with customers and suppliers.

Like his sons, he was surprised by the success of their venture and by the rewards all obtained from it. As the country's economy boomed and the concern assumed the proportions of a budding giant, he began to notice that there were several important areas of the company's operations that were weak and unrealized. His experience in running his own company for many years and his instinct for circumnavigating imminent problems convinced him that action of a firm type was needed to protect the valuable enterprise his sons had built with his help.

So he urged them to hire an outside executive, a highly accomplished management expert, and to bring him in at the very top rung. They protested, especially at the suggestion that he would get $110,000 a year in salary (they were only drawing $85,000 a year) and with substantial stock options. They also feared the competition that his arrival would represent. But the father won them over, as he had in many other ways since the sons had started the company. The new executive's qualities and value became immediately apparent. And it also quickly became apparent that he would soon supplant one of the sons as president and become more important than either of them, facts that the father had anticipated. He knew his sons, after all.

Occasionally, a father will take a long step over the years to safeguard his legacy. A bizarre example was William Randolph Hearst. The autocratic chief of the publishing empire created a family trust which controls all the voting stock of the immensely wealthy Hearst Corporation and terminates on the death of the last surviving son/or grandchild who was alive at the time of Hearst's death.

The effect of this controlling hand from the grave is to severely limit the management of the company by Hearst's two sons, grandchildren, and several highly placed company executives, who constitute the trust's board of trustees.

As a result, as William Randolph Hearst, Jr., told *Forbes* magazine, "That's what makes this business of acquisitions, say, or of developments of our resources like the land at San Simeon so difficult. Because we can't act the way the executives at, say, General Electric can act. They can concern themselves with things like profit margins and earnings in one year as opposed to a previous year. We're trustees for the future generations, rather than people interested in getting something for ourselves. Why develop the San Simeon land right at this moment when we expect it to be worth double or triple its value in the next fifteen or twenty years?"

The Hearst empire had its start in funds given to W. R. Hearst, Sr., by his parents. George Hearst, a California senator left $1 million to his son, after striking it rich in the Comstock lode. Young Hearst also received another $7.5 million from his mother, Phoebe Apperson Hearst, who sold the family interests in Anaconda Copper to stake her son.

The only child of vibrant, outgoing personalities, William Randolph Hearst was a striking example of a son who greatly exceeded his parents in his accomplishments, impact on the national scene, and sheer force of his temperament. He had an exuberant and dominant personality, which often turned baleful toward friends and employees or toward any opponent of his main life-thrust which was to express his own, often bizarre longings for success, at any cost.

In a sixty-year career, he was charged not only with starting circulation wars but military conflagrations, as well. By continuous blasts of his journalistic guns, he helped fan a spark, the Cuban insurrection of 1895, into the fire of the Spanish–American War of 1898. Learning from the sensational, melodramatic technique of Joseph Pulitzer, he outdid Pulitzer to become the arch-proponent of "yellow journalism."

The publishing-broadcasting-landholding complex that Hearst left had tangible assets which, in 1968 or seventeen years after his death, was estimated to be worth more than $500 million. It encompassed not only major metropolitan newspapers (now reduced in number from thirty to nine in such cities as San Francisco, Los Angeles, and Albany, N.Y.), but a chain of fourteen magazines, such as *Good Housekeeping, Cosmopolitan, Harper's Bazaar,* and *House Beautiful;*

258 The Self-Made Man

Avon Pocket-Sized Books, a leading paperback book publisher; the King Features Syndicate; and a sprawling land, mining and timberland, and real estate empire.

Still a privately held corporation, one of the two or three largest in America, the Hearst company will probably have a value of several billion dollars when the trust's provisions run out about the year 2000.

Hearst's objective in creating the family trust was to avoid onerous estate taxes. But, as long as the trust remains in effect its limiting of the use of vast funds seems an ironic twist in an era when money usage through investment or plowing earnings back into modernization or expansion represent an invigorating, synergistic practice. Hearst's posthumous control until the year 2000 will exert an increasingly restraining tug on his family as other corporations flex their muscles and as money management becomes more sophisticated and effective.

2. TRACING AMERICA'S DYNASTIC LIFELINES

How did the sons of the most famous American tycoons fare under the combined challenges or the onslaught of their fathers' success, personality, and public condemnation or approval? And what of their own sons? And grandsons?

Nine of the most durable American dynasties are examined from this standpoint. The conclusions bear an interesting and compatible relationship to the views of the modern-day psychiatrists in Chapters Five and Six on their own experiences with the current father-son situations.

THE ASTORS. William Backhouse Astor, who succeeded his father, John Jacob Astor, as America's richest man, neither dressed the part, or needed his forebear's wealth, which he largely inherited anyway, or lived magnanimously. He was clearly cast in his father's mold, but his edges were not as decisive. However, starting with an immense base, he quintupled the fortune that the old fur trapper had left. The son took over his father's role well qualified, having already been familiar with the varied, far-flung Astor activities.

He lived eighty-three years, two less than his father, and was eulogized almost as widely as his father, and his exploits, not unlike the parent's, were controversial but not nearly as condemned. But, by common consent among historians, he was only a pale reflection of John Jacob.

William B. left an estate more or less equally to his sons, John Jacob II and William B. Astor, both of whom were already wealthy in their own right. The older, John Jacob, received a good education at Columbia College and Harvard Law School. He served during the Civil War as a colonel on the staff of General George B. McClellan and spent his life managing the family estate and taking a minor part in New York's civic and political life. His brother, William B., was a shy man, whose greatest fame lay in his great wealth and in his marriage to Caroline Schermerhorn, of the important land-holding Schermerhorn family. As Mrs. William Astor, she became a famous hostess, the queen of New York's society of the era.

John Jacob II and William B. together left estates worth $225 million. John Jacob bequeathed the bulk of his $150 million to his son, William Waldorf Astor. After inheriting this large fortune, part of which he used to build the Waldorf section of the old Waldorf-Astoria Hotel, the son developed a dislike for American life. He moved to London where he bought a magazine and a newspaper, owned two vast estates, and generally and lavishly used his great wealth to wrest a place in English society. He was rewarded for his contributions to Britain's war effort in World War I with a peerage, a recognition that pleased him greatly. His estate was valued at $90 million.

His older son, Waldorf Astor, succeeded him as a viscount, also becoming a member of Parliament. He was named publisher of the London *Observer*, which his father had acquired in 1911. The younger son, John Jacob Astor, lost a foot while in combat in France, bought the London *Times* and became its publisher. He, too, served in Parliament.

The American limb of the Astor tree continued with William B.'s son, also known as John Jacob Astor, the fourth Astor to bear the name. He went to Harvard and assumed management of the family's fortune. Just before the turn of the century, he built the Astoria Hotel alongside his cousin's (William Waldorf Astor) Waldorf Hotel. The two buildings were later combined as the Waldorf-Astoria Hotel.

The fourth J. J. Astor was also an inventor, responsible for such diverse developments as a turbine engine and a bicycle brake. He fought in the Spanish–American War but was drowned in the wreck of the *Titanic,* leaving an estate of $87 million.

His children by a first wife were William Vincent Astor and Alice Muriel Astor. A few months after he died, his second wife gave birth to the fifth John Jacob Astor. Vincent, who broke out of the family's conservative mold by selling many of his slum properties to New York City on easy terms and by espousing the early New Deal, had inherited the bulk of his father's estate, or about $69 million. Alice Muriel received a $5 million trust fund. And the baby, born after his father's death, was given a fund of $3 million.

THE VANDERBILTS. Just as did the patriarchal John Jacob Astor, whose older, feeble-minded son was pathetically removed from any consideration in the dynasty's succession, Cornelius Vanderbilt, the molder of the New York Central Railroad, shunted one of his two sons aside in his immense legacy but for an entirely different reason.

Almost all of the $100 million estate went to William Henry Vanderbilt, the plodding, parsimonious, money-loving older son. Cornelius Jeremiah Vanderbilt, the younger son, a lover of the gambling tables and an enthusiastic visitor to the better brothels of the time, had been in his father's disfavor for years. His share of the fortune was a puny $200,000 in government bonds, a trust fund conditioned on his future behavior.

The old man went even further. He added ridicule to Cornelius's inheritance by ruling that if the profligate tried to draw in advance on the trust fund, he would lose it altogether. The fund's income was, instead, to be doled out to Cornelius solely to maintain and support him during his life. And, on his death, it was to revert to his older brother.

Seldom had a sane son of an enormously wealthy father been so sorely treated. However, in the wake of a trial brought by members of the family (the Commodore also had eight daughters who were given token inheritances), Cornelius Jeremiah received an additional trust fund of $400,000 and about $200,000 in cash, as a settlement. Less than three years later, however, he committed suicide. Unlike his father and brother, he had always been troubled by a feeling that making money was futile and therefore he had neither interest in nor talent for its techniques. His frustration was encouraged by his father's keeping him on such a pitiable allowance (for his fun-loving ways) that the son of America's richest man often borrowed money from friends and strangers.

The Commodore felt proud of his vast financial attainments and unquestionably settled most of it on his older son because he knew that in him his own name and efforts would be perpetuated. So the old man left nothing to chance. Six months after his will was read, it was found that there was a codicil. Approximately $11 million in stock was removed from William Henry's inheritance and written over to the older son's four sons.

One was Cornelius Vanderbilt, who ultimately took over the family holdings and became chairman of the New York Central. He bequeathed large sums to educational and religious institutions and left a $70 million fortune. Another was William

K. Vanderbilt, who, with his brother, Cornelius, helped to establish the Vanderbilt Clinic, was a well-known yachtsman, and whose wife was a leader in New York's society. A third son was George Washington Vanderbilt, who established a 100,000-acre private park near Asheville, N.C., and engaged in many philanthropies.

Alfred Gwynne Vanderbilt, a son of Cornelius the younger, became a famous breeder of horses. He went down with the *Lusitania* in 1915. Harold Sterling Vanderbilt, a son of William K., achieved fame as a sportsman, taking the America's Cup yachting races several times.

Motivation toward business was generally lacking in the Commodore's descendants. Their inheritances were so great, multiplying from generation to generation, that most of them felt little of the spur that had so driven Cornelius the older. It was to prove a characteristic of many of the offspring of the tycoons.

THE ROCKEFELLERS. The founder of perhaps the penultimate American business dynasty (perhaps greater than or equal to the DuPonts), John D. Rockefeller, Sr., lived so long that his great philanthropies almost, but not quite overshadowed the controversial exploits of a lifetime. For the last forty-two of his ninety-seven years, he concentrated on giving money away as systematically as he could.

He had only one son, who, surprisingly enough considering his forebear's lean issue, had five sons, as well as a daughter.

John D. Rockefeller, Jr., spent most of his life in recognition of the social responsibilities that came with the $1 billion accumulated by his father. Between them, the two gave away about $1 billion to civic and charitable projects. The increasing value of the stocks that they turned over to foundations eventually raised their contributions to about $3 billion.

The young Rockefeller worked intimately with his father

starting immediately after his graduation at twenty-three from Brown University. He tried to learn every detail of both the business and the philanthropic activities. His greatest wish was to please his ascetic, demanding parent and there are incidents on record to show that he did. For example, he confidently and coldly withstood a direct demand from J. P. Morgan to sell the Rockefeller ore lands in Minnesota. It could well have been a test of his mettle from his own father, who had directed Morgan's question to his son. When the old man heard that his son had politely demurred from even a remote possibility of a sale and then excused himself, he told John D., Jr., that he would have done precisely the same.

The son's activities were full and diverse in the contrasting worlds of making money and giving it away. But, as the Rockefeller millions multiplied through appreciation and investment, John D., Jr., applied himself zealously to philanthropy and to its caretaking. He helped his father to develop the Rockefeller Foundation, formed various social research organizations, and made gifts to Protestant, Catholic, and Jewish institutions.

He contributed the library building to the League of Nations in Geneva and the land for the United Nations headquarters in New York. During the depression of the thirties, he visualized vast changes in urban development and established the Rockefeller Center in Manhattan, a fourteen-building complex almost completely built by 1939. He died in 1960 at eighty-six, a son who had served both his father and society well.

His own sons were raised with the same feeling of social responsibility for their great inheritance. The eldest, John D., III, involved himself in many of his father's activities, both business and philanthropic. He, too, served as chairman of the Rockefeller Foundation and aided in the development of the Lincoln Center of the Performing Arts.

The second son, Nelson A. Rockefeller, became interested in international affairs while a student at Dartmouth College. He was appointed coordinator of inter-American affairs in 1940 by President Franklin Roosevelt, held a variety of governmental posts in subsequent years and was elected governor of New York on the Republican ticket in 1958. He was a presidential aspirant in the 1960 and 1964 Republican nominating conventions, a glamorous and popular personality in spite of his great wealth.

Laurence S. Rockefeller, the third son, concentrated on business. He became a member of the New York Stock Exchange and headed Rockefeller Center. While Nelson's philanthropic activities centered on cultural projects and foreign economic aid, Laurence's were in cancer research and wild life conservation.

The fourth son, Winthrop Rockefeller, worked for a number of years in the petroleum industry and, in 1953, settled in Arkansas, where he bred prize cattle. He held office in many of the family enterprises, was chairman of Arkansas' industrial development commission, and became governor of the state in 1966.

David Rockefeller, the youngest who was born in 1915, turned to banking after brief government service and became president of the Chase Manhattan Bank. Like the others, he was active in philanthropy. However, because of his position and an ability to articulate his convictions, he became a leading spokesman for American business in the sixties.

THE MORGANS.   If John Pierpont Morgan evaded the control and possessiveness of his father, Junius Spencer Morgan, to emerge as the greatest financier of his era, the swath he cut in his turbulent seventy-six years bequeathed forces that effectively held down his own son.

That son, also known as John Pierpont Morgan, found that his father's success in erecting a great financial structure generated considerable antipathy in the marketplace and in government against power concentration. The result was legislation and restrictions that hampered his efforts to emulate his father's exploits.

He attended Harvard University and after a stint at Drexel, Morgan & Company's London branch, he became a partner in that banking house, which was substantially owned by the elder Morgan.

His father's death in 1913 left him, as the only son, most of the financier's fortune and he also succeeded to the control of the family's main banking house, J. P. Morgan & Co. He, too, then became the country's most important financier, but he had neither the dominant personality of the swashbuckler or the environment in which to assume the parent's stellar role.

His accomplishments included raising large funds to aid the Allied during World War I, one issue totaling $500 million, and financing $1.5 billion of Allied military purchases in the United States. After the 1929 stock market crash, he spearheaded the formation of a banking pool of almost $250 million to support stock prices. But, unlike his father's success in dominating and halting the 1907 panic, the efforts of the son failed.

However, until his death in 1943, he remained an important figure in domestic and international banking, promoting many mergers and floating billions of dollars worth of American and foreign stock issues. He was a pale version of his father, without much of the other's tremendous verve for aggrandizement. Yet, he was a more upright, wholesome individual.

Like his father, he intensely disliked publicity and used much of his wealth for charity and public works.

THE FORDS. Edsel Ford was the only son of Henry Ford and surely one of the most mistreated sons of any tycoon. At Edsel's early death at the age of fifty in 1943, his elderly father, ill himself and pathetically confused by a world he no longer understood, a war he hated, and a President he despised, was griefstricken and remorseful. He had every right to be in such a state for he had harassed and persecuted Edsel for years.

In any relationship between father and son, one looks for normal tenderness and indulgence that a fond parent usually extends, especially to an only son. But, in the case of the Fords, all that was missing. Yet, on Edsel's part, there was what one might expect. He was a calm, thoughtful, and reasonable type and it is easy to picture him reacting in constant awe of his monumentally-famous but irascible and explosive parent.

Edsel was never more than the nominal head of the Ford Company, even though he was president for a quarter century. In 1918, when the elder Ford had his attention diverted to other interests, such as an ill-fated venture in making Ford tractors, he resigned the presidency in favor of his son. He continued, however, to fully exert his control despite the change in titles.

Henry Ford used Harry Bennett, who ultimately became a Ford vice president and a director, to keep Edsel in line. Bennett was Ford's chief labor-relations lieutenant, a former prize fighter and sailor. He had been employed to organize within Ford's factories a team of muscular men to control the vast work force. It was known as "Ford Service" and operated in the Ford plants as an internal espionage and security system, its true nature welling to the surface in the roughhousing of troublesome workers, among other practices.

Bennett was directed to "influence" Edsel, whose quietly expressed views were in sharp contrast with his father's. The ex-fighter's role vis-à-vis Edsel was definitely a bullying one and he continued to perform it with the full consent of the elder Ford.

But, if the retribution could not take place in Edsel's tragically short life, it came during his own son's. Henry Ford, II, was named executive vice president of the company in 1944 when he was twenty-seven. His father had died the year before and his ill, unhappy grandfather had taken up the company's reins again but was unable to cope with a creeping decline in its fortunes. Then, in 1945, the young man became president and he began a process of removing deadwood and political and ideological hangers-on that had accumulated around the founder for decades.

Bennett was one of the first of about one thousand managerial executives to be discharged in short order. The young president, who within the next two decades became widely respected for his hardheaded honesty and administrative skills, then began a long-term program to return the company to the competitive sharpness it needed. He used the example of the peerless General Motors corporate structure and keen marketing techniques as his guide. Eventually, he even acquired some of GM's most talented executives to help him.

THE MELLONS. Andrew W. Mellon, like J. P. Morgan, was one of those rare sons of enterprising businessmen whose accomplishments so far outstripped their parents' that the family name is remembered almost entirely for what the son, rather than the father, did. Yet, in Andrew Mellon's case, Thomas Mellon had an important, perhaps inspirational bearing on the son's progress. A Pittsburgh lawyer and judge, the older Mellon became a successful banker who shared substantially in the burgeoning industry of that smoky metropolis. Judge Mellon, for example, backed Henry Frick, the coke king, loaning him money (at 10 per cent interest) and advancing him credits of $100,000 during the 1873 panic.

Andrew left college at seventeen to open a lumber business with his brother, Richard. The success of their enterprise surprised the father, who, from that point on, saw in Andrew an unusual talent for finance. The two young men shortly afterward came into the elder Mellon's bank, and when Thomas Mellon retired in 1886 they assumed control of Thomas Mellon and Sons.

Four years earlier, however, the father had shown his deep respect for Andrew by transferring to him the ownership of the family bank. Andrew was then thirty-four.

In 1889, with the brothers operating the bank together, Andrew exhibited the mark of his entrepreneurship. With Frick as a supporter, he organized the Union Trust Company of Pittsburgh and became its president. Two arms of it emerged fullgrown as the Union Savings Bank of Pittsburgh and Thomas Mellon and Sons, now incorporated under a new name as the Mellon National Bank. Union Trust had an initial capital of $100,000, its assets swelling in time to $300 million. It was to become one of the country's largest financial institutions.

But, ambitious as this move was, it was only the beginning, only a chapter in the Mellon saga. Not only did Andrew expand his already large holdings in the American Locomotive Company, Gulf Oil Company, the Pittsburgh Coal Company, and in a variety of public utility, hydroelectric, steel, insurance, and traction companies, but he helped to found the Aluminum Company of America, the Carborundum Company, and capitalized on Heinrich Koppers' new system of coke ovens.

The Mellons invested about $100,000 in the fledgling Aluminum Company. The concern made tremendous strides, paying the Mellons in excess of $8 million in dividends before it was sold in 1931 to the Bethlehem Steel Company. Their dividends and their share of the purchase price gave them a return on their investment of $17 million.

As Andrew Mellon's interests became ever more varied, his wealth accumulated and he emerged as one of the four wealthiest Americans of the day. In 1921, he resigned as the Mellon Bank's president to become Secretary of the Treasury under

President Warren G. Harding. He also held that post under two succeeding Republican Presidents, Coolidge and Hoover. His cabinet tenure was marked by a plus and a minus. He reduced the war-inflated national debt from $26 billion in 1921 to about $16 billion in 1930. However, in negotiating agreements with European governments to pay their war debts to the United States, he failed to pin down the debtor nations so that all but one defaulted.

He became ambassador to Great Britain just before President Franklin Roosevelt brought in his Democratic administration. When that happened, Mellon withdrew to private life. His great reputation, which had slipped during the Depression, received a hard shock when his 1931 income tax return came under investigation in 1935 on a charge of a $3 million deficiency. The issue was over a rule that he himself had approved in 1929, a provision requiring taxpayers to report holdings of tax-exempt securities.

He was exonerated of the charges four months after he died in 1937 and four years after Richard had passed on.

THE HARRIMANS.   Strange are the differences between father and son. Even stranger are the differences in the motivations, the *raison d'etre,* between the generations. One of the best examples in American business history is that of the Harrimans. Edward Henry Harriman became one of the most important railroad tycoons of his time and one of the country's sharpest financiers. His son, W. Averell Harriman, inherited a great American fortune but devoted the major portion of his life to a career of devoted, often frustrated government service.

The father was born in 1848 in Hempstead, N.Y., the son of an embittered, itinerant minister who became rector of an Episcopal church in that Long Island community. Edward received virtually no schooling, and, at fourteen, during the Civil War, he went to work on Wall Street as a broker's clerk. Precocious and eager to learn all he could in his seven years in the financial center, he closely observed all that was going on around him—and there was plenty. Giant manipulators bestrode the scene, such as Vanderbilt and Gould, and the small, bright-eyed youngster learned well.

In 1869, while he was chief clerk in the broker's office, he invested his tiny funds to sell the market short. By the time he was twenty-two, he had already acquired the $3,000 to buy a seat on the stock exchange. Now he represented others and he speculated in his own right. In one day, by a daring foray in coal stocks, he earned a profit of $150,000. Although he overreached himself at times, he became known to professionals as a brilliant new force on Wall Street. He also showed that he had enormous talents—the ability to transform seeming defeats into triumphs, skirting the traps that lurked everywhere in the raw jungle of the emerging financial market, and a sense of the shape of the future.

But his direction was to change radically. It came in the pert form of the daughter of William J. Averill, owner of the tiny Ogdensburg & Lake Champlain Railroad. In marrying Miss Averill, Edward's attention was turned to his father-in-law's little rail-line, tucked away in the northeastern corner of New York State. His sensitive, acquisitive nature reacted. He quickly saw in the unprepossessing sprawl of track a strategic obstacle that could be used to advantage to harass or thrwart Vanderbilt's plans to expand the New York Central.

To capitalize on the plan, he rebuilt the little line, forced the other stockholders to sell out to him, and generated a bidding contest between the New York Central and the Pennsylvania Railroad. He finally sold out at a profit to the Pennsylvania.

Emboldened by this feat, he launched a series of maneuvers on an ever-increasing scale that netted him eventual control of the Illinois Central, the Union Pacific, the Central and Southern Pacific Railroads, and the Oregon Railroad and

Navigation Company. By use of his intricate knowledge of the securities market and his undeniably great administrative skills, he had succeeded in taking command of the rail-lines from Chicago to the Pacific Coast.

It was a stunning performance. From nowhere, he had come to dominate the railroad landscape, even outwitting such giant manipulators as J. P. Morgan. The latter never forgave Harriman for this humiliation, forever after snortingly describing him as "that little fellow." However, they were not always to remain rivals, not when it was convenient to become allies. After Harriman's 1901 defeat by James J. Hill, another contemporary railroad collector, Harriman, Hill, and Morgan teamed up to form the Northern Securities Company, a holding company created to stifle railroad competition. But it was ordered dissolved by the U.S. Supreme Court.

Harriman's tactics were controversial. He would often issue bonds on one of his roads in order to acquire control of another, leaving a stream of such paper in his wake. His exploits were investigated and censured by the Interstate Commerce Commission in 1907, two years before Harriman's death at sixty-one. In his amazing, acquisitive life, his sole interest was to continue to constantly expand his control of property, or so it seemed. However, he also organized a scientific expedition to Alaska, sponsored boys' clubs, and gave $1 million and ten thousand acres of forest land to New York State for park acreage in the Palisades Interstate Park.

Harriman, who left a $100 million estate directly to his wife, bequeathing nothing to his sons and daughters, was a slight but highly charged man. Only a few months before his death, he was plotting to acquire the Vanderbilt holdings in the New York Central.

His older son, Averell, was tall, rather stoop-shouldered, bemused, and outwardly phlegmatic. He graduated from Yale four years after his father's death and succeeded to a series of the elder Harriman's posts and directorships. He also founded the Merchant Shipping Corporation in 1917 and the private bank of W. A. Harriman and Company. In 1932, he became chairman of the board of the vast Union Pacific.

But, strangely, considering his father and his background, the sensitive Averell Harriman had a keen feeling of social obligation. In the early days of Franklin Roosevelt's New Deal, Harriman became administrator of the National Recovery Act. He was a staunch Democrat and took numerous posts under Presidents Roosevelt and Truman. He became ambassador to Moscow, where he had a protracted interview with Stalin, and in various diplomatic capacities participated in most major international conferences during World War II.

Back in the U.S., he was named Secretary of Commerce under Truman. In 1954, he was elected governor of New York but was beaten by Nelson A. Rockefeller in a reelection bid. Shy and sincere without pose, Harriman was not an effective speaker or campaigner. His articulation was defeated by a mumbling honesty, so that listening to him campaigning on a street corner was a painful affair. His audience usually melted away to a few indigents. Since candidates are usually chosen for their personality and volubility, his 1956 unsuccessful candidacy for the Democratic presidental nomination and his defeat by Rockefeller in New York surprised no one.

In 1961, the nonetheless well-respected Harriman became President Kennedy's special roving ambassador and, in 1963, he was appointed Undersecretary of State for political affairs. His own disappointments appeared to have been submerged in a deeply felt desire to serve the public. From that standpoint, Edward H. Harriman would have had some difficulty understanding his son.

THE DU PONTS. America's most populous business dynasty, and one of its most important, the du Ponts of Wilmington, Del., came from an unusual antecedent.

Pierre Samuel du Pont de Nemours was a French economist

and public servant who became president of the Constituent Assembly during the French Revolution. He was a key spokesman on financial matters among the revolutionaries, a publisher of economic and political tracts, and would unquestionably have remained in France if matters hadn't taken an adverse turn for him.

As the Revolution's course became more radical, more wayward, and more violent, the idealistic revolutionary fell into disfavor. He went into hiding for a time and published pamphlets opposing the extremists. In 1792, he was jailed for reactionary views. Seven years later, he emigrated to the United States to escape further persecution.

Pierre had two sons. The older, Victor Marie, had preceded his father to America in 1787 as attaché to the French legation to the United States. A year before Pierre arrived, Victor had been appointed France's consul general in New York. After his father's emigration, he decided to settle in the U.S. and became a businessman, subsequently failing in two enterprises.

Accompanying his father to America was a young son, Éleuthère Irénée du Pont, who, at that time, was twenty-eight. At seventeen, Éleuthère had become an apprentice in the royal powder works where he learned under the famous chemist, Antoine Lavoisier, how to formulate and manufacture gunpowder. When he came to America, he saw an opportunity because of the poor quality of the domestically produced gunpowder. He decided to make it himself and, in 1802, began manufacturing in a plant he had set up on the Brandywine River near Wilmington.

Two years later, the concern of E. I. du Pont de Nemours & Co., sold its first batch of gunpowder. Its sales in that first full year of 1804 totaled $10,000. Éleuthère was joined by his older brother, Victor Marie. Their father, Pierre, kept journeying back and forth between the United States and France, playing a sort of cat-and-mouse game with the changing regimes. On Napoleon's return to France in 1815, the elder du Pont fled again from France and finally settled in the new country with his two sons.

A resourceful, patient man, Éleuthère kept improving his product and his manufacturing process. Despite a lack of funds, the piling up of large debts and both benefiting from and being plagued by his family relationships, Éleuthère's business grew. The War of 1812 brought him heavy orders from the U.S. Government. The brothers became directors of the Bank of the United States. Éleuthère's counsel was highly sought on business opportunities and Victor became a director of the Delaware legislature.

When Éleuthère died in 1834 at sixty-three, Antoine Bidermann, his son-in-law, served as the company's president until 1837 when he was succeeded by Éleuthère's oldest son, Alfred Victor. Alfred promptly drew up a partnership agreement with his two brothers and four sisters which lasted until 1899. He retired from the presidency in 1850.

His brother, Henry, then took over the firm's management and justified his father's faith in him by becoming perhaps the most outstanding member of the family. He had graduated from West Point in 1833, but relinquished his commission when Éleuthère asked him to come back to Delaware and become an expert in black powder manufacturing.

Under Henry's rein, an energetic and creative supervision led to four decades of great progress. The DuPont company built a large sales organization, diversified its gunpowder production to include blasting powder and dynamite, and decentralized its manufacturing.

Henry's son, Henry Algernon, also went to West Point, graduating in the second year of the Civil War at the head of his class and became an artillery officer in the Union forces. He won a Congressional Medal of Honor for his services in an 1864 engagement. He then entered into a business career during which he was also associated with the family business.

He quit his business activities in 1902 and was elected to two terms as the U.S. senator from Delaware.

After Henry DuPont's death in 1889, events multiplied as more du Ponts crowded on the scene.

There was Eugene du Pont, Henry's successor as president and a grandson of Alfred Victor; and another grandson, Alfred Irénée. Just prior to Eugene's death in 1902, when the old partnership arrangement ran out, Alfred urged two other grandsons, Thomas Coleman and Pierre Samuel, to join with him in buying and controlling the company. There was an urgent need to do this since a competing group was attempting to buy the company.

In the 1902 reorganization, Thomas became president and the same year bought out DuPont's principal competitor. In the next few years, through a series of financial moves, the company became the country's largest manufacturer of explosives. The federal government in 1907 filed an antitrust suit against it and succeeded in 1912 in dividing DuPont's industrial powder-making facilities. Pierre Samuel organized a syndicate in 1915 to acquire Thomas's holdings and assumed the DuPont presidency.

The purchase of Thomas's shares by the syndicate headed by Pierre created a family rift that lasted for years. Alfred Irénée, who had been a vice-president and director, found himself forced into an inactive role with Thomas's sellout. He brought suit against Pierre for breach of contract but lost the decision.

He purchased several Delaware newspapers and editorially opposed the election of both Thomas Coleman and Henry Algernon du Pont to the U.S. Senate. Alfred's efforts were effective, at least for a while, before both of his relatives managed to wend their way to the capital.

World War I brought a tremendous boom to the DuPont Company. In 1914, DuPont had a smokeless powder manufacturing capacity of 8.4 million pounds a year. In 1918, the figure had zoomed to 455 million pounds. In the thirties, a special Senate investigating committees found that DuPont's munitions sales gross totaled $1,245,000,000 to various nations from 1915 to 1918. During the same period, six du Ponts had incomes of at least $1 million a year.

DuPont's greatest strides, its great diversification, came initially from the seizure of German patents by the U.S. in 1917. This permitted the company to enter the big dyestuffs market. Later, DuPont expanded its scope by manufacturing rayon, paint, cellophane, and a variety of chemicals.

In 1920, Pierre du Pont came to the assistance of the General Motors Corporation and invested $49 million in the then troubled auto maker. In 1936, it was revealed in a report of the Securities and Exchange Commission that DuPont directly owned 9.8 million shares of GM stock, worth then about $690 million. Some two decades later, however, the government ordered the company to divest itself of these GM shares.

The populous family produced other du Ponts to head the company. Irénée du Pont, Pierre Samuel's brother, served as president from 1919 to 1926, ushering in yet a further era of diversification. Another brother of Pierre, Lammot, succeeded Irénée as president and remained in that post until 1940 when he became chairman of the board.

After World War II, DuPont entered into its greatest expansionist era through important and successful research and development efforts. These resulted in the creation of a family of synthetic fibers, nylon being the one with the most widespread applications.

Despite the fact that DuPont has more than 200,000 outside shareholders, family control still is predominant. But, while the family continues to be prolific, operating management in recent years has been given for the first time to non-du Pont's. However, major decisions remain vested in a du Pont-controlled executive committee.

One hundred and sixty-five years after its founding, the

Du .'ont company was earning $390 million in income on sales that exceeded $3.2 billion. The vast du Pont success is marked by a patriarch whose unusual combination of idealism and economic philosophy probably imparted a flexibility of thinking to his early descendants; by his son, Éleuthère, who had the entrepreneurial instinct and market sense to found the company; and a grandson, Henry, who was generally credited with being the most outstanding of the long line; and by many weak family members who left little impact.

The family, through its company, also benefited from being able to satisfy a paradoxical pair of instincts on the part of its customers—the desire to blow themselves into destruction and the desire to live better in order to enjoy life.

THE KENNEDYS. One of the most frequently published stories in recent years is that of Joseph Patrick Kennedy, who emerged from a modest Boston background to become one of America's classic self-made men, siring nine children including one who became the President of the United States. The assassination of John F. Kennedy, and five years later, that of his brother, Senator Robert F. Kennedy, puts the family apart in American political history as an indigenous dynasty over which tragedy hovered as it did with the Gracchi family, the Roman statesmen and social reformers, more than two thousand years earlier.

Although Joseph Kennedy's sons followed political rather than business careers, the saga of America's leading business dynasties would be incomplete without a brief retelling of how the father's drives and ambitions became expressed in his sons.

The Kennedy forebears were Irishmen who emigrated to Boston. Patrick J. Kennedy, father of Joseph Kennedy, was a saloon-keeper who became a Boston political chief. His son was a thin, intensely ambitious twenty-four-year-old when he graduated from Harvard in 1912. He told his family and friends that he would be a millionaire by the time he was thirty-five.

After serving briefly as a state bank examiner, he became president of the Columbia Trust Company, a small, East Boston bank, at twenty-five. That same year, 1914, he married the daughter of the mayor of Boston, John F. (Honey Fitz) Fitzgerald.

During the First World War, he was an assistant general manager of a Quincy, Mass., plant of the Bethlehem Shipbuilding Corporation, and after the war was for five years Boston manager of Hayden, Stone & Co., an investment-banking firm. While there, he developed skills for speculating in the gyrating stock market of the twenties.

He developed an interest in the motion picture industry, both in connection with managing theaters and in producing films. He went to Hollywood and became one of its major financiers. He returned east in 1935, with a fortune of about $5 million.

By then, he and Rose Kennedy had had all their sons. The oldest was Joseph, Jr., a brilliant student and personable young man, fated to die in the Second World War. The second, born in 1917, was John Fitzgerald, a wiry, thin boy, who seemed overshadowed by his older brother's ability as a student and his leadership qualities. Robert F. Kennedy, born in 1925, was short and slight, also brilliant and ambitious but introverted. A family friend recalled that "Bobby" in his teens and as a young man often sat somberly in a corner, a bit away from the family, and was inclined at times to temperamental outbursts. The youngest son, Edward M., was only three when his father returned from California. He developed into a handsome, athletic youth, much in the image of the oldest, Joe, Jr.

As a father, the elder Kennedy urged and even demanded that his four sons "play hard and study hard." But John, who tried mightily, seemed to have trouble with both. He played in half a dozen sports at school, for example, but never made the varsity. And, when he graduated from Choate in 1935, he placed only sixty-fourth in a class of 112. Yet, he was voted by his classmates as "the most likely to succeed."

Throughout the Depression, Joe Kennedy was not dismayed by the poor economic conditions and was successful in numerous financial ventures. Some of them showed his starkly opportunistic nature. When President Franklin Roosevelt surprisingly named Kennedy, who had supported him in the 1932 campaign, to the important position of chairman of the new watchdog agency, the Securities and Exchange Commission, there was an outcry from many in the securities markets. But Kennedy assumed direction of the SEC with firmness and efficiency and convinced most critics that they were wrong.

The President showed his respect for Kennedy by later naming him chairman of the United States Maritime Commission and then quickly appointed him to the most important American diplomatic post, that of ambassador to Britain. Kennedy's naturally controversial nature showed itself. He supported the appeasement policy of the Chamberlain government toward Hitler and backed nonintervention by his own country.

In November, 1940, he resigned his ambassadorial post. Later, he returned to business, already quite rich and he then became immensely wealthy from a series of real estate ventures.

He had raised his sons to think of a career in public service. The possibility that not only a senatorial post but even the Presidency might be open to a Catholic was raised in the Kennedy homes in Brookline and in New York not in questioning but in ringing terms. The fact that, after World War II, all three surviving sons became U.S. senators may be directly traced to the father's ambitions for them and the direction in which he pointed them.

John F. Kennedy's singular attainment through illness, convalescence, extreme youth, and religious prejudice to become America's thirty-fifth President, its youngest and first Catholic Chief Executive, denotes, of course, considerable courage. It is unusual, as has been mentioned previously, for a son to attain not only the hopes a father has for him but to far exceed the parent's accomplishments. And President Kennedy's shocking death in November, 1963, at the hands of an assassin added the somber mantle of martyrdom to the grace, honesty, and idealism that made him the outstanding symbol of his time.

"I grew up in a very strict house," he said, two months before he was elected President, "and one where there . . . were no free riders, and everyone was expected to . . . give their best to what they did. . . . There is no sense in trying to do anything unless you give it your maximum effort. You may not succeed but at least the effort and dedication and interest should be there."

One can only guess what surged through Joseph Kennedy's mind, only partly recovered from a serious stroke, when he learned in June, 1968, that a second son, Robert, had been struck down by an assassin's gun. Regret at the family's urge to expose itself through ambition and public service to danger? Personal guilt and remorse? Pride in what his sons accomplished in their all too short lives? Only the family knows.

3. CHANGING OBJECTIVES

I⊤ is obvious from these accounts of the most important bloodlines of America's industry and commerce that the main difference among fathers, sons, and grandsons was their varying life goals. And that, quite obviously, too, reflected the differences in the environments in which each generation matured.

To these conclusions, one could raise some interesting suppositions. For example, would William Waldorf Astor, the great-grandson of the original John Jacob Astor, have developed his aversion to American life and transplanted himself to English society, if his forebears hadn't been so immensely wealthy? Or was it over ennui with the "crassness" of American culture? Why did Cornelius Jeremiah Vanderbilt pursue the fast life when he knew for certain that it meant he would get only the leavings of the Commodore's fabulous estate? Would some measure of self-respect inspired by more confidence from his father have straightened him out?

If Edsel Ford had rebelled, would his father have realized while his son lived the error of the persecution that he inflicted on him? Did the pioneering entrepreneurial genius of John D. Rockefeller, Sr., run out in succeeding generations because the grandsons were robbed of their empire-building motivation as a result of the great inheritance? Why did Averell Harriman respond so spontaneously to the social implications of the New Deal? And what if Joe Kennedy had compelled his sons to strike out boldly for themselves in the business, rather than in the political arena?

These questions, of course, may be aimless, since people do not respond to hypothetical but only to actual stimuli. But far-fetched as their premises may be, they point up the fact that motivations reflect the different human reactions to varying environments. Thus, the "generation gap."

There are "generation gaps," however, and generation differences. Let's consider a prominent example of each.

Huntington Hartford is a grandson of the man who built the world's largest chain of supermarkets and food stores. George Huntington Hartford, then twenty-six, started The Great Atlantic & Pacific Tea Company in 1859, as a cut-price seller of tea, added food, and expanded across the country. His sons, George L. Hartford and John Hartford, came into the business in their teens and grew up in it. Each made significant contributions.

George, for example, learned that baking powder, which was high-priced in the 1880's, consisted only of alum and bicarbonate of soda. He hired a chemist to make the baking powder in a curtained-off back section of the main New York store. The company then put it out under its own name and sold it at a fraction of the market price. It was the beginning of A & P's entry into other foods and into manufacturing of its own products.

John, seven years younger, was responsible for the most important decision in A & P's history. He suggested to the family that big savings could be gotten on overhead and lower prices could be offered if the selling process were simplified. But his father and brother refused to listen to such ideas that they drop all unnecessary services, sell over the counter, and only for cash. Finally, Mr. Hartford gave in. "Open up one store along the lines you describe," he told John, "and see what happens."

So John opened an "economy store," without even a sign on its front, around the corner from the main store in Jersey City, which was A & P's greatest money-maker. Within six months, the old A & P was forced out of business by the new store.

The heir to the A & P empire, Huntington Hartford, has veered away from it for many years. The handsome, flamboyant Hartford (he is named after his grandfather, the "George" being dropped) inherited in 1922 10 per cent of the founder's fortune. He proceeded to dispose of it piecemeal. One of the biggest sales was in 1959 when he sold 700,000 shares for $31 million and another big block for about $22 million. His holdings of the 24.8 million shares outstanding by 1966 had been whittled down to about 1 million shares, worth about $20 million.

In the interim, he had been engaged in two unsuccessful marriages and in a series of business disasters. One was *Show* magazine, a glossy, inflated journal of the entertainment world (which he sold at a $7 million loss) and in which he later bought back a 30 per cent interest. The Handwriting Institute, was begun because of Hartford's ardent belief that graphology indicates character, and it became defunct. He founded Manhattan's Gallery of Modern Art, which had an annual deficit for some years of $580,000.

His determined support of his art gallery in the face of its deficits brought him a good measure of respect. But not such other ventures as one for $30 million to build a five-hundred-room hotel on Paradise Island in the Bahamas in which he subsequently sold a 75 per cent interest for $12.5 million.

Despite his reluctance to become personally involved in the company his grandfather started, he is one of its most vociferous critics. His particular ire is addressed at the John A. Hartford Foundation, the owner of a 34 per cent interest in A & P, which he charged controlled the company and was hamstringing its management. Hartford held a press conference late in 1967 simultaneously to plug *Show* magazine and to promise that he would continue his battle with A & P.

Fred Morgan Kirby represents a completely different case. His father is Allan P. Kirby, who has one of America's greatest personal fortunes, estimated at more than $300 million. Fred Kirby is only eight years the junior of Huntington Hartford, but took a reverse course of action. He sold a company that he owned and successfully managed in order to go into his father's business.

His father's business is considerable. Before the elder Kirby became seriously ill in 1967, he had been chairman and president of the Alleghany Corporation, as well as its controlling stockholder. Alleghany is a vast holding company that owns the largest single stock interest in the New York Central and also owns the multi-billion-dollar Investors Diversified Services, which is probably the biggest group of American mutual funds. Allan Kirby also was at various times the premiere stockholder of F. W. Woolworth, the New York Central and the Manufacturers Hanover Trust Company.

The elder Kirby, an old, skilled proxy fighter who had joined with the late financier, Robert Young, to acquire tremendous holdings, had started from a good base. His own father had been a highly successful retailer, who had learned his profession from the pioneering Frank W. Woolworth. He left Allan Kirby $50 million.

Fred Kirby graduated from Lafayette College in 1942, and served in the U.S. Navy until 1946. He took further business study at the Harvard Graduate School, then joined Vicks Chemical Company as a production manager. In 1950, he heard of Filtration Engineers, Newark, which made rotary vacuum filters. It was a struggling, absentee-owned business headed downhill. He acquired it and in the next six years turned it around. In 1956, he sold it to take an active role in his family's business.

In September, 1967, after Allan Kirby had been taken ill, his son was named chairman of the board of Alleghany. He had had a decade of assisting his father in the management of the big holding company. If there was a generation difference between the Kirbys, it was probably hinted in the fact that Fred Kirby had preferred first to make it on his own before joining his father's business.

But, between many successful entrepreneurs and their sons, a generation gap does exist, of varying proportions. In no other circumstances is this as dramatic as in the case of the hippie sons of some self-made men. The sons' waywardness from the social establishment strikes hard at the very core of the fathers' yearning for a great measure of respect from that society.

In one such situation, an unhappy father complained bitterly to his wife, "All right, he doesn't want to dress like a human being. He doesn't want to see me. He doesn't want my money—he just wants to be one of those flower people. But can't he do at least one little thing for me—can't he just change his name?"

Ten

———— ◆ ————

WOMEN WHO MADE IT

1. DOES IT MATTER IF SHE'S A WOMAN?

MANY of the noon-hour onlookers at the windows of the Park Avenue branch of Hornblower & Weeks-Hemphill Noyes would probably be surprised if they knew the identity of one of the registered reps who sit at the series of desks inside.

Some of the women among the spectators wear a lipstick that she created, a long-lasting type allowing only a minimal color transfer which helped to spark the boom in the cosmetics industry. Others are investors in the company that she founded in the midforties.

At her desk, a pert, trim Hazel Bishop deftly juggles a sandwich and a cup of coffee with her papers and her telephone, glancing often over her shoulder at the moving quotations on the board. The noon hour is her busy time, for that is when the biggest number of buy-and-sell orders come in.

In 1954, the industrial chemist-entrepreneuress, who started out to be a doctor, sold her interest in Hazel Bishop, Inc., for a handsome sum. She then took a job as a registered representative with Bache & Co. Several years later, she switched to Hornblower & Weeks, in furtherance of her "second career," after a considerable success with her first.

The air travelers who stream across airports every day to board the cream-lime-vermillion jetliners of Braniff Airlines and relax into the couturelike decor of the interiors also might not suspect the origin of these palliatives to taste, color, and feel. Perhaps when the stewardesses would appear during the trip in successive changes of wardrobe designed by Emilio Pucci, clothes ranging from the outercoat for ground-wear to harem-style culottes when they serve coffee, the travelers might just be titillated enough to wonder how it all came about.

But only those who read widely and retain some of it might know. It is all the creative handiwork of Mary Wells, the fragile-looking blonde founder of Wells, Rich, Greene, Inc., one of the most dynamically successful new advertising agencies in years.

In one of the most startling flurries of publicity in memory, the combination of Miss Wells' beauty and her impact on the advertising world have been repeatedly cited to demonstrate a yet further new wrinkle in the changing socio-economic pattern of America.

And, in New York City's lonely newspaper scene, where three daily journals have departed to leave only the New York *Post* to satisfy homegoing commuters, a woman, Mrs. Dorothy Schiff, has succeeded to a role as the only publisher of an afternoon newspaper. How many of the growing number of readers of the *Post* know that it is being operated by a woman?

How many care?

The answer to these questions is that few people, whether they wear Hazel Bishop lipstick, or invest in the successor company, Bishop Industries, or travel via Braniff, or buy the *Post,* know that a woman is the creative and/or the entrepreneurial spark behind them. And, more important, even fewer would care.

Sex may be the big difference between men and women, but in corporate life, notwithstanding some of its anti-female prejudices, ability counts a good deal. This, of course, is not to say that, other things being equal, a man will not be given preference for advancement by other men over a woman. But demonstrated talent has a way of coming to the fore regardless of the sex of its exhibitor.

On the entrepreneurial scene, where the financier, banker, or backer must base his decision on an idea and a person, sometimes in the reverse order, the prejudice against women is correspondingly less than in the command levels of corporations. The quality of leadership and of an inexorable drive to a goal—hence, entrepreneurship—rates prime consideration at the big investment banking houses in New York and other big cities, which often provide that essential lifeline to new and existing businesses—money.

So, in April, 1966, when petite Mary Wells departed the Jack Tinker & Partners subsidiary of Interpublic, Inc., with two colleagues to start her own agency, the three entrepreneurs needed something more than the $30,000 each was putting into the kitty. Gustave Levy, a senior partner of Goldman Sachs and a director of Braniff, an account that left Tinker to join Wells, Rich, Greene, arranged for a $100,000 loan. Harding Lawrence, Braniff's president, used his influence to obtain the loan for Miss Wells, whom he admired.

The fact that Lawrence admired her so much that he married her the next year is probably beside the point. Goldman Sachs, which is not known to throw money around, was sold on more than the limpid brown eyes and cool self-confidence of Mary Wells. After all, she already had had a fantastic career on Madison Avenue, climaxed by a partnership at Jack Tinker at $80,000 a year. When she said, "We would like to be the best creative agency in the world," Levy of Goldman Sachs reached into his corporate pocket.

Does the entrepreneuress need the same qualities as her male counterpart? Yes, of course, but she must also have at least one other singular trait.

Greatly suspect as she is of always being a woman, with all of the gender's classic, mercurial nature and characteristic emotionalism, the female corporate chief must also have the ability to carefully steer a course midway between cold judgment and the passionate drive that a company aiming for the heights, or, at least, for a good measure of success, inevitably requires in its leader.

So carefully is she watched for this sensitive quality, or, conversely, for the manifestation that she is, in fact, a woman, that she will not easily be forgiven for the weakness, the indulgence that many a male entrepreneur will be. Oddly enough, we smile understandingly at the willful emotional behavior of some of our tycoons ("he has to be tough to be where he is, doesn't he?"). But, when it comes to women we insist that they display their emotionalism only in the privacy of the home. And when they carry on outside it, we sadly attribute it to their sex. ("God, aren't they emotional!")

A woman simply has to act like a man in business to stay on top.

That is to say, she must act decisively, judiciously, and be coldly analytical, albeit as gracious as she can manage. If she is head of her own company, her ownership removes much of the onus of needing to be a female-seeming-a-male, but, even in such cases, she must pass the muster of her board of directors, her bankers, and even of her investors.

As a leader of men (and of women, too, who seem to be even more critical of a woman boss than men), the entrepreneuress must inevitably have the quality of success by generating better efforts on the part of her staff. Dorothy

Schiff may write some gushy, impulsive, even silly notes of suggestion to her colleagues among others that are pointed and well taken, but the fact remains that the New York *Post* has been in the black since 1949, or for about twenty of the approximate thirty years since she personally assumed its command.

Perhaps the most successful women in business are those whose style—which they exhibit in personality, mode of living, creativity, or manner of administration—is compatible with the company's objectives. Vera Neumann, the founder of Vera Industries division of the Manhattan Industries, Inc., is basically an artist. But the $15 million a year fabric printing company revolves around her ideas and spews forth a flood of Vera-designed scarves, blouses, table linens, and sportswear. She was able to adapt her talents to commerical use and to run a company that makes products designed on her Japanese *sumi-e*-style drawings.

Another but somewhat different example is Ida Rosenthal, who, with her late husband, William, founded in 1922 Maidenform, Inc., now the world's largest manufacturer of brassieres. Rosenthal concentrated on design whereas the four-foot, ten-inch Ida handled the financial and sales functions primarily. After his death in 1958, Ida took over all functions, no less immensely entrepreneurial then than at the outset thirty-six years before. A member of her family described it:

"She always had an ambition. First, it was to get into business, then to be successful, then to be the biggest in the industry, then . . ."

So, the widowed Ida became chairman of the board. Each morning, she now inspects personally the new orders that come in from the men on the road, explaining, "I want to see if the salesmen are working or playing golf." In her eighties, she travels across the country, dropping in at brassiere departments wherever she is to see how her goods are selling.

Although Dorothy Shaver was not a self-made business-woman in the sense that she founded a company, the late president of Lord & Taylor had a style that made the famous Fifth Avenue store a much more striking and appealing one than it had been. She gave it topically unique status as a vice president when she challenged Parisian domination of international fashion by promoting and publicizing the clothes of sixty young unknown American designers between 1932 and 1940. As a result, some, such as Claire McCardell and Lilly Dache became cornerstones of the American couture. Such efforts, as well as the taste of her offerings and presentation, brought great prestige to the store and honors to Dorothy Shaver. In 1946 and 1947, she was voted the outstanding woman in business by the Associated Press. And many national and foreign awards were bestowed on her.

A paragon of sophistication in the most sophisticated of cities, Miss Shaver was, however, not the product of such a city. She was born in Center Point, Ark., population three hundred.

Such women, as did the infinitely greater number of their male contemporaries in the top executive offices, emerged from a variety of backgrounds. Their early lives pointed little toward their ultimate skills in entrepreneurship. But they became dominant in the fields that they had ventured into, much for the same individual traits as the men. Their stories are as inspiring as those of the self-made men; and perhaps more so, considering their attainments in the face of the oft-mentioned complaint that each one was, after all, "only a woman."

2. HAZEL BISHOP: CHEMICALS TO LIPSTICKS TO STOCKS

It is rare for women, or men, for that matter, to have had as many careers in one lifetime as Hazel Bishop, born in Hoboken, N.J., in 1906. Perhaps some of it was due to her family background. Her father loved to start new enterprises and her mother loved to run them—after Henry Bishop was off on the next one. He once had seven going at one time.

Despite the fact that talk around the dinner table was frequently about business, Hazel decided that she wanted to be a doctor. She completed premedical studies but the 1929 crash prevented her from going on to medical school, so she became instead a chemical technician in a hospital. At night, she pursued bio-chemical research studies. After five years, she was appointed technical assistant to a dermatologist, working in his laboratory until 1942.

She spoke to patients during that seven-year assignment, seeking to learn whether they had come to see the skin specialist because of using soaps, cosmetics, perfume, or shave creams. And she used the knowledge she gained on experiments, for she had developed some new concepts, including one for a nonallergic but retensive lipstick.

Again, circumstances prevented her pursuing her research on cosmetics. This time, it was World War II, but it gave the curious-minded, zealous chemist a chance to extend her research to other fields. As a senior organic chemist for Standard Oil Company, concentrating on studies of aviation fuels, she helped develop a special gasoline for bombers. In 1945, while at Sacony Vacuum Oil Company, she furthered her research work in petroleum and was later credited by the American Chemical Society for "notable research" in that field.

In the meantime, she was busy in her kitchen with her double-boiler. She had no facilities for laboratory work at home, but there were always the pots in the kitchen and that was enough. After more than three hundred experiments over two years, she was ready. Her lipstick was introduced in November, 1949, at a fashion show by the alumni club of her alma mater, Barnard, where she had been a premedical student.

The "Lasting Lipstick" had a strong consumer impact, especially after Consumer Reports, which independently tests products and compares them with their manufacturer's claims, concluded that it did have a long-staying quality. Within five years, fifty other companies had come out with competitive lipsticks. Sales of Hazel Bishop, however, mushroomed from less than $50,000 in 1950 to more than $10 million in 1953.

But, after only two years, Miss Bishop resigned as president of the company, and three years later sold her full interest in it, realizing a substantial profit for all her efforts. Between 1954 and 1962, she founded three other companies (none of which used her name in the title, according to an arrangement with the purchasers of Hazel Bishop, Inc), all producing or marketing consumer end-use chemicals. She also became prominent in chemical industry activities and as a lecturer.

Once again, however, in November, 1962, she switched careers. It seemed to her that she had a good deal to offer as a "customer's woman" in a stock brokerage—lots of energy, technical know-how, a great liking for personal contact, and a wide business knowledge. After a brief training period, she joined Bache & Co. She was right about her capacity to help people buy stocks. According to Bache, women make the best registered reps because they are more patient and take pains in researching securities.

She still concocts her own lipstick and make-up. It's only a hobby, of course, but while she thrives on selling stocks, Hazel Bishop has held on to her double-boiler.

3. MARY WELLS: THE "NOW" ADVERTISING WOMAN

THERE may be more grim spectacles, but the aspect of a roomful of automotive company top brass staring steely-eyed and coldly skeptical is a gauntlet that most men would run with their insides hot and churning. Only it wasn't a man who faced the board of the American Motors Company that day in 1967 in a room filled with the hard gloom of declining sales and plummeting earnings. It was a slim, lightly made-up, soft-spoken woman of just under forty.

She completely disarmed the directors. You won't, she told them in effect, be able to compete on sex, shape, or image on a direct basis with Ford cars. But you can by showing the car buyer that you care more for him by giving him more, she said. "Lovely things that show that you care," she added, "like the carpeting that you've put on the rear deck of your stationwagon."

They agreed, not that they didn't resist Mary Wells' later implementation of her idea. But they gave in enough to let her get across her theme that once you make the customer feel you love him, he'll love you in return.

Actually, there's more than one way to do this. Showing that you care is one way, but doing it in indirect ways made Mary Wells extremely successful. This is the technique of humanizing advertising with the touch, the feel, and the self-recognition of the target himself. People respond warmly when they realize with a glow of surprise that they are observing a reflection of themselves and of their own behavior. Or they are pleased by a soothing welcome to their senses, as in the case of the Braniff jetliners, presenting a rainbow splash of pastel colors so appealing against the silver, gold, and bright contrasts of the other airliners.

Unquestionably, Mary Wells has an instinct for rapport with people, demonstrated in terms of how she expresses an abstract idea in its most pragmatic form. This gift, part of the weaponry of the best salesmen and of the most successful entrepreneurs, has been shown in most of the Wells, Rich, Greene campaigns.

Within a half year after the three partners opened up shop in April, 1966, they had obtained six clients with billings of $30 million, were employing forty-five people, and had taken sparkling new space in one of the new Madison Avenue buildings. Without a public relations department of their own, they had obtained more publicity in more important media than had any agency in years. And, more significantly, Miss Wells and her partners were already planning ambitious new projects on top of successful ones for the same clients.

"We are completely geared to our times—terribly aware of the current sounds and fears and smells and attitudes," she told *Newsweek* magazine at the time. "We are the agency of today." Competitors sniped away at Mary's humorous, piquant, frank advertising. It was cute, they admitted, and, added snortingly, "but it won't sell."

But it did sell. Braniff, in a remarkably short time, began to show the fastest growth rate in the airlines industry. However, it dropped "Operation Strip," as the wardrobe changes of its stewardesses was called, about the time in 1968 that Mary also dropped the Braniff account for a bigger client, Trans World Airways. But Braniff's Harding Lawrence, her husband, didn't seem to mind by then.

Philip Morris, whose then new, long cigarettes got Mary's wry, self-knocking kind of approach showing the unexpected effects of the Bensen & Hedges 100s cigarettes, crowed that it had never obtained such an immediate sales result.

The Youngstown, Ohio, girl who made it so big and so controversially in New York was kept eternally busy and outgoing by her mother in elocution, dancing, singing, music, and acting lessons. At eighteen, she entered a leading New York dramatic school, decided that acting was not for her and went to Carnegie Technical Institute. She met her first husband there, Burt Wells.

Back in New York, Mary became a Macy's copywriter, then

Macy's fashion ad manager at twenty-three, a copywriting group head at McCann-Erickson at twenty-four, and then one of two copy chiefs at Doyle Dane Bernbach at thirty-one. From there, Interpublic got her at a high salary multiple to become a partner in its Jack Tinker group.

Like many of the entrepreneurially-minded men and women who had already made it, she long had had the drive to be on her own. But neither she or her partners expected their success to come as suddenly and as fully as it did.

Just as she had disarmed the American Motors board, she has captivated many other people by eschewing the obvious and courting the simple off-beat. Her plans are ambitious and her modesty admittedly small, and perhaps justifiably. The agency's motto, only semi-facetious in nature, is, "If we were modest, we'd be perfect."

4. DOROTHY SCHIFF: DURABLE AMATEUR ON NEWSPAPER ROW

FOR many years, the prevailing attitude in New York's newspaper industry was to regard the publisher of the New York *Post* as a bumbling, vacuous amateur. The afternoon tabloid seemed to be going nowhere, despite the continuing reports that it was operating on a profitable footing. A succession of editors had diffused its long-time and once sincere liberal news coverage, tilting it more toward sensationalism and an overabundance of columnists.

But, suddenly in 1966 and 1967, all the critics were treated to a rude awakening. After the New York *Mirror* left the morning field, the once-powerful New York *Herald Tribune* folded. Then, shortly afterward, the owners of the *Tribune*, the Whitney Communications Corporation, the Scripps-Howard Newspapers, which operated the New York *World Telegram and Sun*, and the Hearst Corporation, which published the New York *Journal American,* combined their efforts by starting a new afternoon newspaper, the *World-Journal-Tribune,* to succeed all three of their papers. But, in less than eight months, that journal ceased publication.

So, Dorothy Schiff had the afternoon field to herself, but it was apparently not to be for long. At least six other newspaper and publishing companies indicated that they were considering starting a competitive product. But, some months later, the two most likely entrants, *The New York Times* and the New York *Daily News,* announced that their studies showed that there simply was not a big enough market to warrant the effort.

What enabled the "amateur" to survive against the efforts of such smooth professionals as Scripps-Howard, Hearst, and Whitney? As eager-eyed, idealistic, and yet down-to-earth in her economics in her midsixties as she was in her teens at Manhattan's Brearley School, Dorothy Schiff herself is the answer.

The granddaughter of Jacob H. Schiff, an early partner in the banking house of Kuhn, Loeb & Co. and the banker for the Union Pacific in its formative years, Dorothy Schiff was reared in the world of the affluent New York society. As did many well-bred young women and matrons of the day, she was active in social welfare activities. She made her debut in society in 1921, married a stockbroker in 1923 at twenty, and divorced him in 1931. She married George Backer the following year.

As a board member of several social agencies in New York, she found herself confused between her family affiliation with the Republican party and the suffering and privation of the unemployed during the Depression. She resolved the internal conflict by converting to the Democratic party and backing among her own class the welfare issues championed by President Franklin Roosevelt.

It was during a trip to Albany, in 1939, where the Backers had gone to help in social welfare lobbying, that she heard of the dire financial problems of the New York *Post*. The oldest newspaper in the United States, founded by Alexander Hamilton in 1801 and New York's only crusading liberal newspaper, the *Post* had passed through various hands until it came to a troubled rest under the ownership of a Philadelphia publisher, J. David Stern.

When Stern responded to the Backers' inquiries about the rumors with a plea for financing help, Dorothy countered, "I don't finance what I can't run." Stern then agreed to sell. To buy the *Post*, she invested more than half of the $9 million she had inherited from her father, Mortimer L. Schiff, who had also been a Kuhn, Loeb partner.

The first year under her ownership, the paper lost $1,250,-000, and ran for a decade in and out of the red. As a member of the *Post*'s board, vice president, and treasurer, she used her control to continue a liberal policy but maintained an independent stand politically. In 1942, the year she divorced Backer, Dorothy Schiff succeeded him as president and publisher. The following year, she remarried, this time to Theodore O. Thackrey, an able editor who had risen from the *Post*'s ranks. He became its editor and publisher the same year, contributing much to its performance until he left in 1949. Later, the couple decided to end their marriage.

Now, Dorothy Schiff was running things again. She raised the paper's price from three to five cents and changed the *Post* from a full-size newspaper to a tabloid because she felt it could be more easily handled by the readers. In earlier years, she had also shown a venturesome spirit. In 1945, she had the *Post* publish a special San Francisco edition, during the United Nations Conference, to show the delegates that there was a newspaper representing American liberalism. Also, that year, she launched a Paris edition of the *Post*, but it was dropped after 177 issues because it was too costly.

And, in 1948, she purchased the *Bronx Home News*, merging it into her own paper.

About that time, the *Post* had almost fifty columnists, a fact that was a subject of derision to her professional competitors but which seemed to build reader loyalty. For a while, she wrote a column herself, but ended it when the task became onerous. In 1961, James A. Wechsler, whom she had named editor of the *Post* twelve years before, became a columnist and editor of the editorial page. Mrs. Schiff took the occasion to assume the news control, becoming editor-in-chief, as well as publisher, in 1962.

Her fierce independence was evident when she was able to win an apology from Walter Winchell in 1952 on a libel charge that he had called the *Post* a "pinko-stinko" sheet. It was evident again in 1957 when she won a "freedom-of-the-press" suit to obtain a transcript of a judge's charge to the jury in a manslaughter case of a policeman who had killed a boy. That independence flared up once more when Mrs. Schiff withdrew from the New York Publishers Association during the 1962–63 New York newspaper strike and resumed publishing after eighty-six days. The others remained out for another twenty-eight days, leaving only the *Post* to satisfy the city's newspaper readers and, incidentally, to pick up considerable available advertising.

Alone in the afternoon after the *World-Journal-Tribune* had ceased, Mrs. Schiff immediately raised advertising rates and picked up more columnists. But she didn't do much to improve the *Post*'s editorial qualities. Nonetheless, within a year, circulation had jumped from 425,000 to over 800,000.

So, the amateur, and a woman, at that, had won out against the pros. What she had done was hard for them to take, but she was very nice about it. She didn't crow, but her demeanor had a regal confidence. Few people after a while begrudged it. One intriguing thing about graciousness is that the natural reaction to it is—graciousness.

5. VERA NEUMANN: "I START EVERYTHING AS A PAINTING"

WHEN Vera Salaff was a little girl going to public school in Stamford, Conn., her father paid her fifty cents every time she filled an art book with drawings of her own. A sign painter who did some work for Meyer Salaff's tea-and-coffee importing house gave her her first art lessons. Her father encouraged her to try all types of graphic media. A progressive, idealistic man, he ran repeatedly in the Stamford city elections on the Eugene Debs ticket for city treasurer but never won.

After high school, Vera went to New York and attended night classes in art at Cooper Union and then took life-drawing, history of fashion, and illustration at the Traphagen School of Design. Days, Vera worked in various art studios, drawing fashion illustrations. Briefly, she was a designer in a Seventh Avenue fashion house, then became involved in home furnishings design.

In the midthirties, she met George Neumann, an ambitious young management expert working at Republic Aviation Company. An artistically minded man who had come from an old textile printing family in Hungary, he had graduated with a degree of doctor of business administration from the University of Vienna, an academic attainment roughly equivalent to that of a doctor of philosophy.

A harmonious pair, they were married in 1938. "One day," recalls Vera Neumann, "we just decided we ought to work together in some way."

They had not only similar interests but also complemented one another. Together, that first year of their marriage, they built a silk-screen frame, prepared the paint, and ran off some table linens and place mats from drawings that Vera made. Soon, the couple saw that they needed some experienced selling help and capital. Werner Hamm, a textile merchandising man whom they knew, became their partner and they started business in 1946 with a capital of $2,000.

Hamm showed samples to B. Altman, the Fifth Avenue department store, and hurried back with a surprisingly large order. The Neumanns managed to fill part of it and then sought something more adequate than the kitchen table on which they were operating the silk-screen frame. They rented a second-floor studio at 17th Street and Irving Place in Manhattan.

"I remember it so well for many reasons," Vera said, "because, for one thing, it was the building that Henry Luce, the founder of *Time* magazine, had lived in and the landlady kept telling us that we, too, would move out as soon as we became successful. She was right."

Other orders came in from several New York department stores and everything looked promising indeed, except for one small but devastating item. Reorders could not be met because of a post-World War II shortage of gray or unfinished fabrics. The bright future that the trio had looked forward to looked suddenly very dim. But Werner Hamm, anxious to keep the operation going, took a representative sampling of Vera's designs to Schumacher & Co., a home furnishings supplier to the affluent. The reaction was excellent and Schumacher gave the little company an order for ten thousand yards for which it supplied the fabric and committed itself to more.

Over the next decade, Vera's designs began to appear in a variety of items, scarves, blouses, and other types of linens. Her designs became distinctive, abstract in the form of Japanese *sumi-e* brush strokes, and the colors were vivid and pure. Design pirates paid Vera Neumann the dubious honor of knocking off her work with fascinating verisimilitude. The company found itself hauling the copyists into the courts and successfully restricting them at the price of high litigation costs.

As the demands for more production grew, the Neumanns found an abandoned mansion at Ossining, N.Y., on a ridge overlooking the Hudson River, and installed their operations there. Not long after, spurred by the technology-minded George Neumann, the company added a wing housing two highly efficient, automatic screen-printing machines.

During the ensuing years, Vera Neumann became simply, "Vera," an internationally known designer whose name was emblazoned by a number of leading American stores on "Vera Boutiques," little, instore shops containing a variety of her products.

The technique of combining Vera's unusual designs with mass production methods to sell to a mass audience proved to be one of the outstanding examples of a wedding between art and technology. It was one of the first important realizations in America of the philosophy of the famous German school of design known as Bauhaus. This was a post-World War I thesis that insisted that art and engineering did not have to go separate ways. The artist, the theory insisted, could learn to create his work within complex technological and economic capabilities, with important benefits to the total effort. It was "synergism" before the term was coined.

George Neumann died in 1960, but by then his engineering-artistic skills had helped greatly to build a company with substantial staying power. "I was more than lucky," Vera Neumann said in a candid interview. "We had the right combination of principals. My lucky break was the two men I worked with from the very outset—they didn't restrict me to last year's best-selling designs to play safe, and we all realized that to be a leader we had to stick our necks out."

She added, "I start everything as a painting and we try our utmost to see that it is produced authentically. It was a wonderful feeling to see the working girl, as well as a wide audience, taking to our free-form abstract designs."

Why *sumi-e*? "I like it because it allows me to leave out

everything extraneous," she said. "With one brush stroke, I can be both impressionistic and graphic—you could *potchka* it up with a lot of brush strokes—but it would add nothing and detract much."

Today, Vera has twenty artists in her company to project her ideas, but she wants them all to be creative. One day a month, she gives her art department a "museum day off," when its members can renew their creative instincts and return refreshed and eager.

6. IDA ROSENTHAL: BRASSIERES FROM PARIS TO PAPUA

"Nature made woman with a bosom, so nature thought it was important," Ida Rosenthal said, a few years ago. "Who am I to argue with nature?"

Not, one might add, that she would want to. Anymore than this tiny, bright-eyed matriarch of the American foundations industry would approve of the topless dress. After all, Maidenform, Inc., the company she founded with her late husband, William, produces in excess of 125,000 brassieres a week on five continents and sells them in one hundred countries.

Ida Rosenthal, born Ida Cohen in 1886, the eldest of six children, in a small *shtetl* (village) outside Minsk, built the largest company of its kind in the world from a reverse reaction to the fact that dress firms in the twenties would advise women to "look like your brother." The upshot of this was that American women in the first few decades of the twentieth century looked tightly bound, flat-chested, and, obviously, unnatural.

The Russian immigrant, pursuing William Rosenthal, who fled to the United States to escape being drafted into the Czar's army, caught up with him and married him in 1905. Ida set up a dress shop first in Hoboken, then in New York.

She noticed that frequently, because of the era's restrictive bind on the bosom, her dresses did not look well on her customers. To correct this, Ida and a woman partner created a "little bra with two pockets but not too accentuated." The accessory, which radically provided both form and uplift, was given away with each dress.

Less than five years later, the success of this innovation caused Ida to decide to concentrate on it and to give up selling dresses. The business that she and her husband founded grew quickly. During the thirties, when fashion became feminine, Maidenform leaped forward, even though those were the years of the Depression. In the war years, the company obtained priorities for materials, partially, as Ida Rosenthal repeatedly observed afterwards, since it was in the national interest. It seemed that a wartime study of employee productivity showed that women who "wore uplifts, bras, or girdles, were less tired than others at the end of a day."

Expanding its output, Maidenform took pioneering steps in mass production, time-motion studies, and in the development of specialized equipment.

As the pipelines swelled, a large sales organization was set up and subsidiary companies were established to manufacture abroad. By the late fifties, Ida was producing and selling almost 10 per cent of all the American-made bras. But the fastest-growing market was in other countries, Europe and other continents. Accounts were being opened even in the topless-attired tropical islands, such as Papua and Pago-Pago. By 1959, annual sales of Maidenform had climbed to $34 million and the original staff of only ten employees had grown to four thousand.

By then, the company had benefited from more than a decade of its whimsical, catchy advertising theme, "I Dreamed I went Shopping [and endless variations thereof] in my Maidenform Bra. . . ." The idea was to show the versatility, the verve, and the active lives of women who wore Ida's bras. Her products were subsequently expanded to include a line of undergarments, sleepwear, and swimwear.

In 1963, when she was seventy-seven, Ida returned to Russia for a visit, the first American woman to go there as a member of an industrial exchange team. She found Russian bra and girdle trends a throwback to the U.S. style circa 1923 and it fired her ambition to ignite a bra "revolution" there.

She travels around the world today, visiting accounts everywhere, paving the way for new business—a tiny, energetic businesswoman whose "Maidenform dream" was solidly rooted in a woman's knowledge about other women and practical innovations. Her daughter runs the business today as Ida performs the role of elder stateswoman and sales ambassadress. "Quality we give them," she said, referring to her customers. "Delivery we give them. I add the personality."

7. OLIVE ANN BEECH: UP, UP, UP FROM SECRETARY TO AIRCRAFT CHIEF

In the summer of 1925, Olive Ann Mellor, a blonde, pleasant, cool-eyed Kansan girl, applied for a job as a secretary and bookkeeper at the Travel Air Company, in Wichita.

The owner, Walter Beech, was a maverick in the aircraft industry, an untrained designer with an infallible instinct for aerodynamics and an inclination toward whiskey and pretty women. He studied her with a seeming casualness, commented favorably on her legs, hired her, and then warned her not to bother the married men among the company's twelve employees.

Olive, five years later, was to become his wife. But on the occasion of her employment interview, she replied, coolly, "Don't worry. I'm not going to bother you, either."

By 1929, Olive had filled more than one job in the shoe-string airplane manufacturing company, including, besides secretary, receptionist, switchboard operator, bill collector, and paymaster. Beech himself was wrapped up in winning airplane races and designing new models. Just before the big stock market crash, when Curtiss-Wright offered him $3,250,000 for Travel Air and a vice-presidency, Olive successfully nudged him into accepting. Walter came out of the deal with $1 million net and a job in New York.

The next year, he found himself lonely in the big city and began courting Olive in earnest. Two years after they were married, Walter tired of being entangled in the red tape of a big corporation and the couple returned to Wichita to start their own airplane company. Walter became president of Beech Aircraft; Olive was secretary-treasurer. She assumed the same role of managing the pursestrings and keeping the dreamy-eyed designer on his feet, as she had earlier at Travel Air.

But, from the outset, Olive made it clear to Walter that she wanted to be paid for her efforts. She meant to work hard, to give all her energies to the business, but she was to be compensated. And, once she was paid, the money was her own and she invested it. It represented her claim to independence, as well as her personal security for her little girl, born in 1937.

The week that Olive gave birth to her second child in 1940, Walter lay critically ill in the same hospital. It was encephalitis and he was to be hospitalized for a year.

This blow turned out to be not only a personal but almost a business disaster. The company was engaged in producing training planes for the war that was sure to come and had an $82 million backlog of orders. The Reconstruction Finance Corporation, which had issued the concern large war-work loans, and the military procurement authorities, became very concerned over the company's ability to deliver without its chief.

Fresh from her own hospital bed, Olive took command of

the situation. She quickly dismissed a new executive who was foisting himself as a replacement for the sick boss and also asked thirteen others who had recently joined to leave the company. She appointed as a general manager a qualified mechanical engineer who had been with the company for several years. After the inquisitors withdrew and the Beech production-line hit a good stride, Olive negotiated a $50 million line of credit with thirty-six different banks.

The erratic pattern of the aircraft industry, up with defense contracts and down with a return to peace, brought back the bankers and other professional worriers several more times. And it was Olive who soothed them and sent them away, partially assuaged if not relieved.

Perhaps the stoic calm and the icy resolution of Olive Beech were most needed when her husband died in 1950. More than ever, work became an obsession, particularly when she then became the corporation's president. Some years later, she told an interviewer of the *Saturday Evening Post,* "The majority of people today don't know what the joy of work is."

The private plane craze brought big dividends to Beech Aircraft. Walter Beech's design and engineering principles gave the company an excellent reputation which has grown in the years since his death.

After Olive steadfastly refused to allow her engineers to come out with a low-priced (under $15,000) aircraft that would only emulate those of competitors, they devised one with a number of novel features that could sell for $13,300. Olive was jubilant. Even her critics admitted that her stubbornness had paid off.

Much respected and honored, Olive Beech is today the austere, only successful woman chief executive of an aircraft company. Some cynics claim that she is no more than an ambitious secretary who made it big by marrying the boss. Others say her unusual combination of talents put Beech where it is today. And still others, including those perhaps closest to her, observe that she is a lonely, distant figure, not merely because this reflects her nature, but because she is a woman who also happens to be the head of an important company.

And what of Olive Beech as a person? She never smoked, or drank (perhaps champagne on a special occasion), or used nail polish, or dyed the gray out of her hair. The sign on her door and the signature on her letterhead read simply, serenely, sexlessly, "O. A. Beech."

8. THINKING WOMEN, ALL

THE tally of other self-made businesswomen is not long, but it has others who left an edifice (lace-trimmed) in the form of an enterprise that they started or one in which they molded a concept in their image. Or, if their initiative did not quite yield those results, they invaded a world almost exclusively dominated by men and competed with them most effectively.

If the stories of such women are basically simple, it is mainly because their efforts thrived from a "good idea" and these must be basically simple.

For example, Catherine T. Clark, a Wisconsin housewife, who had more than the normal share of amibition for a woman also liked to bake bread for her husband and two daughters. She savored the whole-wheat bread made by a small baker in a nearby town and convinced her husband, a minor bank official, to mortgage their home for $7,000 to buy the recipe and open a small bakery. This was in 1943. Brownberry Ovens, as she called her firm, grew rapidly with the addition of new products, all aimed at the family that liked quality baked goods that are several cuts above those on supermarket shelves. The company made a profit from the first day. Sales rose from $23,000 the first year to almost $4 million by 1960 and have mounted steadily since.

Carole Stupell's big idea hit her after she got fired. As an ambitious, young assistant buyer in a New York department store, she aroused the ire of her superior, the buyer, who thought that Carole was after her job. In 1929, Carole opened a glassware shop in a hotel, latched on to a vase and sold it in large numbers as a zombie (tall drink) glass. After relocating in another hotel, she operated a successful glassware-gift shop on Madison Avenue for twenty-five years and then went "big-time" on 57th Street, one of New York's plush shopping lanes. Her greatest boon was her realization that women have trouble assembling an attractive, correlated table setting. Carole created her own collections, calling them "Carolated," and she has been selling them for as high as $10,000.

While Olive Beech may prefer to make aircraft and aerospace equipment, Muriel F. Siebert, a petite securities analyst, would rather deal in their stocks. In fact, she made her greatest coup in 1967 when she represented both buyer and seller in a $16 million turnover of 182,000 shares of Beech Aircraft stock. Deals like these earn her in excess of $500,000 a year. Her entrepreneurial drive reached dramatic levels when in 1968 she became the first woman member in the history of the New York Stock Exchange, paying $445,000 for the privilege.

Estée Lauder, an attractive, gracious woman with an instinct for imparting elegance into cosmetics—its fragrance, shade, texture, and packaging—founded her successful company in 1946, with the help of her husband, Joseph. During the thirties, she had begun work with an uncle in Vienna, a dermatology professor, who had developed skin-care preparations. She inherited the formulae and began her business in New York. Sensing the advantages of a complete line with understated but implicit taste, she built a quality name in all areas of cosmetics. Today, the Lauders, relaxed and affluent, with their son, Leonard, running the company and its twelve foreign subsidiaries, partake of the heady international life in their homes in Palm Beach, a town house in New York, and a villa in southern France.

And, of course, the ladies, the mesdames couturieres, of Seventh Avenue. In no other major facet of American business have the finest female characteristics of esthetic flair, intensity of motion and application, and emotion translated into pragmatism had such an opportunity to flourish. The collapse of France under the Nazi invasion gave American designers a needed thrust forward. And even though the great Paris couture was later resuscitated under the creations of Christian Dior, his disciple, Yves St. Laurent, Chanel, Balenciaga, and others, the Americans were able to capitalize on their opportunity for both national and international emergence.

Each came out of her chrysallis with an idea, a bright, blazing single idea or a many-faceted one. Claire McCardell, for example, may have been the prophet of the beatnik way of life, at least as far as their mode of dress is concerned. She believed in comfort at all times and on all occasions. Her designs were freely representative of the independence of the American woman—not regal but relaxed, not statuesque but feminine in a somewhat masculine manner.

Bonnie Cashin took the opposite stance. She designed clothes for the fast pace, even for women who didn't travel much but yearned to feel mobile in body and mind. She introduced boots as an accessory to an ensemble in 1942, twenty years before Paris discovered it to world acclaim. Miss Cashin strove to combine the use of natural fabrics, rather than synthetics, with natural backgrounds, the city, the country, the sea.

Pauline Trigère, whose French tailor father had emigrated

here in 1937, followed yet another idea—styles that were feminine, highly sophisticated, made in a subtly simple manner, with underplayed colors and expert workmanship. The theme was high-fashion played in low decibels.

Many other women made the big time in the American couture. Jo Copeland, Adele Simpson, Hannah Troy, Mollie Parnis, and others. All had modest beginnings, gained backing from bankers, family, or industry "angels," and succeeded. Most set up their own companies, geared to limited, quality manufacturing, rarely exceeding $3 million in annual volume, and mostly profitable.

Other, even more pioneering entrepreneuresses had preceded them on the American fashion scene.

Lena Himmelstein, a sixteen-year-old orphan, was brought from Lithuania to New York just before the turn of the century by relatives who wanted her to marry their son. But once she got a look at him, she wasn't interested. She became a seamstress, married David Bryant, a Brooklyn jeweler, who died two years later, leaving her with a baby son.

Lena pawned the only thing of value that David had left her, a pair of diamond earrings, to put a down payment on a sewing machine. By 1904, she had done well enough to open a store on Fifth Avenue, making quality lingerie and trousseau wear for both the retail and wholesale trade.

In those days, women were shy about their pregnancy. One day, a young matron customer of Lena's asked her to make three gowns, all exactly the same but consecutively larger in size. The young seamstress was horrified at such waste. She wished the woman well but told her, instead, "I'll make you a dress with an elasticized wasteband that will grow with you." And she did. The first maternity dress was made and Lane Bryant, the national chain that became synonymous with extra-size women's clothes, was launched.

"Lena" simply became "Lane" when a bank teller misread

her halting handwriting. Lena decided she liked the new name better, and adopted it as her own and as the name of her company.

Henrietta Kanengeiser, a bundle of energy who never grew taller than four feet, ten inches or weighed more than 104 pounds, was one of the major figures in the American fashion world between World War I and the fifties. She was born in Vienna in 1886 and came to New York's lower East Side to join her father about 1900. Even as a teen-ager, when she worked at Macy's as a messenger, she showed a flair for style and a personal taste that was on the flamboyant side.

Her first venture was a dress-and-millinery shop which she opened with a seamstress partner. Henrietta's focus was on the affluent society of New York and, although she herself never learned to sew or cut cloth or make a dress, she built an $8 million business by inspiring the talent of others. She sold her models to manufacturers to reproduce and freely adapted the best Parisian styles.

She became her own best advertisement—wearing her sophisticated, expensive clothes here and abroad in the world's great society showplaces. By the time she died at sixty-nine in 1956, she had dominated the emerging American dress-making world for well over a generation, under an assumed name with a wealthy connotation—Hattie Carnegie.

Florence Nightingale Graham, a Toronto-born cosmetician, worked for a beauty specialist in New York for two years before starting her own salon in 1910. She called it "Elizabeth Arden," combining the name from an early partner, Elizabeth Hubbard, and Tennyson's "Enoch Arden."

That first salon grew to fifty salons and plants in thirty countries, including the United States, Canada, France, England, and Spain. Custom-made clothes were added to a broad line of Arden beauty preparations. Two retreats, where women could revitalize themselves in hot- and cold-weather climates, have been successfully operated in Arizona and Maine.

Elizabeth Arden Graham, the name by which she was known through most of her career, built a large company by pragmatically insisting that better grooming was an important element in maintaining good health. When she died at eighty-one in 1966, her company had reached a sales level of $60 million a year. Her estate was valued between $30 and $40 million.

Overshadowing both Hattie Carnegie and Elizabeth Arden in personal flamboyance and attainment was a contemporary who was probably the most successful entrepreneuress of modern history. Helena Rubinstein, whose personal wealth was estimated at $100 million, was of the same elfin stature as Hattie Carnegie, four feet, ten inches. But she had a giant-sized personality and drive that were to dominate the international beauty world for decades until she died at ninety-four in 1965.

She showed a business sense as a young girl in Poland, helping her father in the wholesale food trade. Bored with medieval life in Crakow, she went to Australia to visit an uncle, taking with her twelve pots of cold cream formulated by a Hungarian doctor living in Poland. Helena's mother was an advocate of beauty care, insisting every night that her eight daughters apply the doctor's cream.

In Australia, women who were afflicted with rough, dry skin from the harsh sun and dry climate showed interest in the pots of cold cream owned by the tiny, striking Polish girl with the clear, white skin. Soon, Helena's mother was sending her another shipment. Helena borrowed £250, rented three rooms in Melbourne, and sent for the good doctor. Within a year, she had cleared £12,000 and within three years, she left for Europe with a kitty of about $100,000.

She set up salons in London, Paris, and then New York.

Expanding her line of cosmetics, she extended its use beyond the·then customary restriction to actresses and fast women to women of all types and degrees of beauty. She hired a doctor for each of her salons and donned a laboratory smock to give her merchandise a scientific look. She was the first to send saleswomen on the road to demonstrate to the average woman how to apply make-up. And she insisted on keeping prices high. "Some women won't buy anything unless they can pay a lot," she explained.

For fifty years after moving to America, she engaged in a business feud with Elizabeth Arden but never met her.

Her personal life was colorful and erratic. She lived in a twenty-six-room Park Avenue triplex, holding business conferences there while propped up in a theatrical, lucite bed in which the headboard and footboard were illuminated. She loved large, valuable exotic stones and beautiful copies. Her $1 million jewelry collection was filed in her bedroom in alphabetically-marked drawers, "D" for diamonds, "E" for emeralds, "R" for rubies. In other rooms hung an extensive art collection, including works by Renoir, Modigliani, Rouault, and Dali.

She left a $60 million business that employed thirty thousand people around the world. Her son, Roy Titus, now runs the fragrant empire that was built by the tiny, zestful cosmetician who convinced millions of women that beauties are made, not born.

9. SOMETIMES, IT'S HUSBAND AND WIFE TOGETHER

POPULAR opinion is that the battle of the sexes will be joined with particular impact if a married couple works as well as lives together. It's a safe assumption that the opportunity for conflict increases under the pressures of business tension. But, like any safe assumption, it is a generality. Much depends on the nature and the disposition of the individuals.

The generality is refuted by the fact that occasionally a husband-and-wife team achieves a dramatic success in business and is also at least reasonably compatible in private life.

Without any question, the most striking example of such a couple in modern American business are DeWitt and Lila Acheson Wallace, the co-founders and editors of *Reader's Digest*. The pocket-sized magazine, founded in 1922 in a Greenwich Village basement, has become a publishing industry wonder. About 27.5 million copies are sold each month, of which 16.5 million are circulated in the United States and more than 11 million are published in fourteen different languages abroad.

No other publication anywhere comes within fighting distance of that magnitude of circulation.

The sometimes evangelical approach of the *Digest* through its more than four decades of existence is not infrequently attributed to the fact that the Wallaces were both the children of ministers.

Wallace was a salesman of agricultural books for a St. Paul publishing company in 1915 when he got a bright idea after he had issued an entirely different kind of publication. He thought that it would be worthwhile to prepare a booklet listing free pamphlets that were available to farmers through state and federal experimental stations. The booklet was called, *Getting the Most Out of Farming*. As he traveled through the Northwest selling it to stores, banks, and feed companies for resale to farmers, the idea came to him that a digest of business-magazine articles might have a market. The concept was soon refined to that of a magazine containing a digest of pieces from general magazines.

Wallace was then twenty-one, tall, thin, with a selling flair. As a boy in St. Paul, he had always been enterprising. He had busied himself with raising chickens, tending a vegetable garden, and running his own electrical repair service.

After combat duty in France with the Army's 35th division, during which he was seriously wounded, he returned to St. Paul and studied magazine articles in the public library to determine which after a decade remained interesting and important. Early in 1920, he had his sample *Reader's Digest* ready.

Lila Acheson had encouraged him in the project. She was the sister of one of Wallace's college classmates, an English major who taught in high school, and who was later engaged in social service work.

Wallace now ran into a double disappointment. Not only did more than a dozen New York publishers refuse to buy his idea of *Reader's Digest* and publish it themselves, but he also lost a postwar publicity job at Westinghouse Electric in Pittsburgh.

His frustrations, however, flared into a decision to become a publisher himself. In 1921 he went to New York to get started. Lila was already working there. On October 15, they were married in Pleasantville, about thirty miles from New York.

Before leaving on their honeymoon, Wallace mailed circulars promoting his new magazine. When the couple returned, they found that they had 1,500 subscribers at $3 a year.

The Wallaces started by copying parts of selected magazine articles in the public library and found, when they requested permission to reprint, that editors were very agreeable, even though they would receive no reprint fees. At the end of the year, the couple moved to Pleasantville, occupying a rented garage and pony shed. Success came quickly, almost unbelievable in its scope. Within seven years, the Wallaces had 216,000 subscribers and a gross income of over $600,000.

Profits were so substantial that the couple began paying for their reprints and, in 1933, started publishing articles which either the Wallaces or their staff originated.

The venture's success, which in recent years has also included books digesting fiction and nonfiction, phonograph record and education services, indicates that the Wallaces truly have the touch of the people. Accused as they often are of publishing articles of sweetness and light, reduced to simple language and standard construction, stressing self-help, spiritual guidance, and all four-square maxims, even their critics, however, find it difficult not to admire their venturesome spirit and the carrying out of a concept to such remarkable proportions.

A four-story, $1.5 million headquarters and plant was put up in the thirties on an eighty-acre site near Chappaqua, N.Y. But the Wallaces insisted on retaining the cheerful-sounding Pleasantville mailing address. They also retained 90 per cent of the stock in the still privately held company, 10 per cent going to key executives who must sell it back to the company on retirement.

Profits were estimated in the "tens of millions" on sales that ran in 1968 of about $350 million. For the *Digest's* first thirty-three years, no advertisements were published. But after determining favorable reader reaction in a sampling, the Wallaces in 1955 permitted advertising to appear and it proved a boon. Within a decade, the *Digest* had the fourth largest revenue among American publications.

Now, in their late seventies, the Wallaces continue to run their business, with its more than eight thousand employees, displaying much of the same vigor and enthusiasm they have had for decades. Not infrequently, they will add a strong dash of candid sex or take a foray into political matters, the latter usually along conservative as opposed to liberal lines, in their articles. But their critics are not assuaged by these clear attempts to make the *Digest* more modern, more comprehensive, and to give it a point of view. After it became clear that their great momentum would continue, the Wallaces began to employ highly qualified personnel and to imbue them with their own philosophy. In fact, the views and decisions of the top *Digest* editorial and business executives are usually indistinguishable from those of the Wallaces, which incites their detractors, but helps to give the editorial product the consistency its many millions of readers expect.

If the world's most successful magazine was started by a married couple, it is worth noting that the world's largest toy company was also started by a husband-and-wife team. Elliott and Ruth Handler, of Los Angeles, founded Mattel, Inc., in 1945. Twenty-two years later, it had achieved annual sales of $123 million and net income of almost $3 million.

Actually, it was their second business effort. Married in 1938, Elliott studied to become an industrial designer and Ruth continued to work as a secretary in a movie studio. They lived in an apartment for $27.50 a month. Since they had no money for furniture, Elliott designed and constructed chairs and tables of plexiglas. The Handlers thought their furniture looked so good that they decided to make more of it and sell it.

They bought tools on credit and produced furniture in a vacant garage behind their apartment, then in a vacant Chinese laundry. They acquired some partners and also began making plastic jewelry. A disagreement with the partners resulted in the couple's selling out to them for $10,000.

Mattel was created by a partnership between the Handlers and Harold Matson, who had been the shop foreman in the earlier venture. Matson's last name and Elliott's first name were combined in the new company's name. But the partnership lasted briefly; Matson asked the Handlers to buy him out.

The first few years were a struggle. A brother-in-law invested $50,000 in the tiny company, in return for a stock interest. The new funds allowed them to further pursue their plan of making new products in the stiffly competitive toy industry. Then they came up with a winner—a modern version of the old music-box mechanism that could be stamped out mechanically for a few pennies. They installed the musical unit into a wide variety of items, from toy milk-shake machines to books. It brought them, by 1951, gross sales of $4 million.

After that, they registered strongly with one toy after another, having learned that originality of design idea coupled with strict cost-analysis could produce profitable high-volume sales. Elliott handled the research and development; Ruth handled the books. Each successful toy sold in the millions. The music-box unit, cutting across an ever-widening spectrum, was encased in some 60 million toys in a decade.

The Handlers took two steps that unquestionably catapulted them in a little over twenty years to the top of the heap. They adapted to the toy-making process the same precise production standards and manufacturing techniques that were used in heavy industry. They employed ten industrial engineers to refine the manufacturing processes and had twenty graduate engineers in their research and development section. The result of all this was a constant improvement in technology from the research function on out.

And, secondly, starting in 1955, when Mattel's sales were only $6 million, the Handlers began advertising on television, risking $500,000 to sponsor Walt Disney's *Mickey Mouse Club* for a year. If the response would only have been fair, Mattel would have been out of business. But so much impact did the TV show have on its tiny-tot and juvenile audience that, after a few weeks, orders and reorders literally filled the company's office.

The result was that Mattel increased its budget for local and network television, as well as for other media, to about 13 per cent of the company's annual sales. In 1966, for example, this promotion allotment amounted to about $14 million.

Naturally, their success made the Handlers rich, multimillionaires, in fact. Their combined stock holdings in Mattel totaled more than $45 million in value a few years ago and they own an estate in an exclusive Los Angeles suburb worth about $400,000.

Despite their astonishing accomplishment, there is one thing that the Handlers do not do: They never discuss business at home, where they enjoy a normal family life with their two children.

There are more than a few husband-and-wife teams that have been successful in the fashion business. Probably the most successful in more recent years are John and Arlene Meyer, whose company is John Meyer of Norwich, a Connecticut manufacturer of classically styled women's apparel, with sales of about $25 million. Their profits in the sixties ran in excess of 7.5 per cent of sales after taxes, or about at the very top performance of the American garment industry.

It was only after Arlene Meyer felt that she had gotten her three children more or less settled that she decided to give up her intense love of painting and join her husband full-time at the Norwich headquarters. John, who came from a family in the men's wear manufacturing business, had been progressing nicely, helped by his education which combined both textile engineering and business administration.

As an art major and painter, Arlene had up to that point contributed to the company styling suggestions and some ideas on advertising and promotion. In addition to her sense of color and form (she had had several one-woman shows of her paintings and shared in others), she was much involved in community affairs, in alumni activities at the Connecticut College for Women, and generally living the life of the suburban or country woman at whom the John Meyer lines were targeted.

The year Arlene Meyer came full-time into the business, 1964, or eight years after her husband had started the firm, the Meyers decided to plunge into the complete wardrobe approach. This meant coordinating or complementing colors and fabrics in all the items made and also producing a much greater variety. Their ambitious program led to a $7 million increase in sales between 1956 and 1966, their largest annual gain. With John running the company and Arlene operating as corporate secretary and as head of the design department, additional categories of apparel were put into the line in the next few years.

John Meyer is an exacting, precise type of executive whose knowledge of business and of apparel manufacturing in particular has enabled him to carve an enviable profit. Yet he attributes a big measure of the company's success to his wife. "Arlene," he says, with pride, "is a fashionable woman." What he means, by implication, is that Arlene Meyer, in selecting simple, natural colors and by adhering to traditional American design, submits each judgment to a testing process of her own intimate knowledge of the typical John Meyer customer.

Between John's skills and Arlene's talents and instincts, the company's success is hardly an accident.

10. PROSPECTS FOR THE LADIES

WHAT of the future of the American woman entrepreneur? Unquestionably it is bright. The same economic, demographic, and social factors that offer promise to business in general will tend to increase venture opportunities for women and permit their entry into more top corporate posts. It was never easy for women to climb high in the world of business but the barriers are gradually being lowered.

"It's harder for women to start businesses than it is for men," observes Vera Neumann. "I remember when we were looking for money—the bankers would wonder if I would return to private life when I had my children. And, if a woman is still unmarried, they wonder what she will do when she does marry and the babies come. But, all in all, I doubt that my being a woman hurt or helped. Other things counted more."

Mary Wells puts it a different way, which was actually not dissimilar at its core. "Being a woman probably helped me," she said, "because I can be direct and honest with a man, like his wife giving him the straight pitch." And, she adds, "If sales go up, the client doesn't care if you have green feathers and Swiss-cheese ears."

Characteristically, Olive Beech expresses it very simply and directly. "Women can be successful in any business," she declared, "if they are determined and are willing to work hard."

Sounds familiar, doesn't it? The same principles for success could even apply to men.

Eleven

———————◆———————

SHIFTING OPPORTUNITIES —TOMORROW'S ENTREPRENEUR

1. THE NEW BUSINESS CLIMATE

On a high ridge or in a broad valley, on a thousand highway crossroads outside major American cities, a singular cluster of buildings and industrial impedementa confronts the eye.

In the morning haze, before the highways become clogged with bumper-to-bumper traffic, lights flicker on in the hundreds of factory windows. They remain on all day, through the afternoon, the late evening fog, and the rural darkness, as the nearby highway blip-blop-blip-blop trickles to an occasional blip-blip. And then in the late night, many of the lights go out but some remain in the bigger structures and a few in the small. The third shift is on.

What the morning passerby sees is a large, sprawling building, with attached wings or free-standing annexes. This is the headquarters, or the executive office-distribution center, or a principal plant, of a larger or nationally known company. In its main office, its founder or his son or his successor sits, if it is a company headquarters. Most frequently, what the current company chief does is a far cry from what the original entrepreneur did. His function has been divided, and then subdivided, to meet the complexities of a changing age. The president, in short, has evolved into the "President's Office," or to a staff of as many as six.

But, just across the ridge or across the valley, surrounding the big building or its complex on almost all points of the compass are smaller buildings, less pretentious, and busy, too. The comings and goings from these are variously frenetic or doggedly practical. The principals or the executives of these concerns go about their work with a frequent anxious glance over their shoulders at the outlines of the big buildings. That is their customer and pleasing it is the constant rule.

These tiny firms, clamped virtually to the hide of the giant organism like barnacles, service and supply the big company. They are little machines shops, electronic parts makers, truckers, assembly points, data processing, or engineering consultants. They owe their business existence to the strange fact that bigness which breeds stability and massive output also breeds inflexibility. Suddenly, the big company finds that the intricacies of specialization and the opportunities of diversity prevent it from properly and economically supplying its own complete needs.

So an enterprising foreman or electronic data processing programmer or a warehouse chief or a master mechanic quits the big company and opens a little company just across the way. He supplies services and components to the giant more cheaply and perhaps more efficiently than it can do itself.

Perhaps the head of the big concern gets up from his desk occasionally to stretch and look out the window. There, from the height of his complex burdens, he sees the nearby landscape dotted by the industrial barnacles. A smile may crease his face, of nostalgic envy perhaps, as he recalls his own early years or a maxim like, "There's no salesman like a hungry salesman." Then, abruptly, he turns back to his desk to take up again the matter of the "President's Office," so different from what he or his predecessors have known.

These are two of the main entrepreneurial trends of the future—the fragmentation of the chief executive's duties and the rise of the small entrepreneur to supply the big one—but they are hardly the only two. What is most important about these two trends is that they point to the shape of the future, at least as far as the budding self-made man is concerned. Many other trends are also already visible in what are shaping up as the most important changes in the business climate in history during the next few decades.

The thrust of these changes comes to a certain extent from outside the corporation itself. There are first the demographic adjustments in the consumer market—higher population, income, employment, family formations, as well as a new age ratio and more discriminating, more sophisticated tastes in consumer preference.

These elements add up, of course, to a more affluent, younger, more demanding market with more time on its hands, more money in its pockets, and more dissatisfaction with tradition than any consumer market American business has faced. Moreover, all the socio-economic pluses are due to increase, whereas the minuses (unemployment, mortality, illness, illiteracy, minority group inequity, etc.) seem reasonably certain to decline.

So, the onus on business will be to cope with burgeoning affluence, literacy, sophistication, and demand for products of all kinds at the same time that it must adapt to a younger (and younger-thinking) customer, more impatient, more articulate, more whimsical, more liberal, and more knowledgeable, than any predecessors.

A second broad stimulus for change is the more stringent

pattern of the marketplace itself. Fired by two decades of unheralded prosperity and by its ability to produce an increasing growth rate of gross national product, business has nonetheless found itself gripped by a cost-price squeeze which has often hurt the competitive position of firms not anxious to surrender their traditional prices and profit margins. As a result, many companies made forays and then full-scale invasions into all manner of preserves heretofore staked out by others, including specialist companies, dominant ones, and diversified firms often protected from competition by their assets or skills or both.

This heightened competition has also been created by a conviction that management and shareholder equity must be hedged by avoiding economic turndowns through diversity of products or service. Hence, entry into new areas of endeavor, hence, more competition.

A third element in the changing business environment has come from the pressures of both government and consumer-protection forces zealous in their attempts to compel business to curb alleged abuses.

These pressures have mounted to an uncomfortable degree. The two Presidents Roosevelt may have had their serious confrontations with business but there was a generation between their administrations. However, there has not been a previous period when three Presidents in such a short span of years, as Truman, Kennedy, and Johnson, registered their opposition to certain business practices.

In addition, a consumer affairs assistant to the President appointed under Kennedy and Johnson became a focal point for direct complaints to the White House. Several congressmen and senators also took the consumer's problems to heart, seeking legislation that would protect her from abuses in lending, packaging, pricing, door-to-door selling. And vociferous housewives, picketing and boycotting supermarkets, added an aspect of a grass-roots movement against high food prices.

The willing cooperation of the federal government, if not its sponsorship, of all this railing against business ethics, was held by many businessmen to be perhaps the climactic act of government interference. But their ire had been raised by many other acts in Washington. Moves by such agencies as the Justice Department and the Federal Trade Commission in the past quarter century have curtailed business merger activities by either killing some outright or by imposing geographical or share-of-the-market restrictions on others. These had followed other onerous moves from Washington, such as on advertising allowances, the granting of franchises in distribution, and, in several decisions by the U.S. Supreme Court, the judgment that advertising dominance must not be allowed to create business monopolies.

None of it was so difficult that the businessman couldn't live with it, much as he protested its burdens. Sometimes, businessmen themselves can scarcely agree on what is best for them. The degree of selfish interest on curbing imports, for example, creates a major dichotomy in the business community.

One more reason for change is the difficult civil rights situation. Here, it has become increasingly apparent that business must take remedial steps to provide minority-group employment and advancement. This position represents an inescapable conclusion. That is, that the solution to the inequity, the civil riots, and the birth of the two-nation syndrome lies in the action that private citizenry mainly in the form of business must take, since governmental action has proven ineffective.

All these elements had developed in approximately two decades, but what they augur for business will probably last many decades. The close of the sixties clearly showed that the American business climate was filled with realities that were not only sobering but maturing in their nature. Out of the adjustment would come more sophisticated, more efficient, more self-reliant companies. Their attention would have to be fixed not only on the changing marketplace, but on the social, cultural, economic, and psychological considerations of the ghetto and the metropolitan (city, suburban, rural) area residents.

But what it would all mean to the entrepreneurial man who personally or whose progenitors had found the thirties, forties, fifties, and sixties a time to thrive is something else again.

2. THE CHANGING CORPORATE STRUCTURE

STRANGELY enough, the current and retired heads of the two largest business management associations in the United States have diametrically opposite viewpoints on the future opportunities for the small entrepreneur.

H. Bruce Palmer, president of the National Industrial Conference Board, believes that there will be continuing opportunities for the small entrepreneur in the next decade or two but is convinced that the future belongs to big business.

"The challenges will lead to bigness and complexity of organization," he says. "The features of the corporation through the rest of this century will be financial leverage, a team structure with checks and balances, and sophisticated marketing skills aimed to cope with a shorter life span for new products."

In Palmer's view, the realization that operational problems and the ability to capitalize on the complexities of the marketplace must inevitably give rise to bigger and bigger businesses has altered the motivation for the creation of new enterprises.

"For many years, the start of a new firm was broadly considered a life effort, or reasonably a lifetime career," he observes. "But that has changed. Today, the motivation is to build a business which can be made exciting enough to sell to a big, public company so that the founder and his top aides can become shareholders of an important, listed firm. This, then, involves a five- to ten-year building and then a quick sellout.

"What will the entrepreneur do after that? That's a good question."

But Lawrence A. Appley, recently retired chairman of the American Management Association, observes, "In the next few decades, we will have a fantastic growth in the American economy, with a gross national product of possibly 2 trillion dollars and more by the year 2000. Who will produce it all?

"Not the big fellow," he replies. "He will produce a lot of it, but hardly all. He's too conservative. True, the need for automation will mean an expansion of research and development on all fronts and this will mean more new products. But, the experience of the last two decades shows that it is the little fellow, the small entrepreneur who can turn on a dime who has driven the big boy into many new products."

As if in preparation to see who will win that battle, a trend to gear for the most effective approach to complexity and change is already well under way. The most common approach has been the delegation of responsibility simultaneous with the assignment for results. In other words, authority and responsibility have been handed down to executives in an interlocked manner.

"There is more and more of a trend toward divisionalization and decentralization," notes Harold Stieglitz, of the NICB's division of personnel administration. "These have come to be the twin answers to the problems of managing diversified, complex and ever-changing businesses. More companies have grouped production and sales activities on the basis of product, market, or region into divisions—'separate businesses'—under one man accountable for profits in his sector of the business. This organization structure is viewed as giving a flexibility to the total complex and an emphasis to its parts that is not easily attainable with the more monolithic, functionally organized company."

The effect of this new practice is to build a more elaborate corporate staff, he says, and it severs the chief executive officer from a direct contact with operations.

"The consequence is somewhat paradoxical in the sense that it places the chief executive in a position where he can think and act intelligently about the nature of something that he personally knows less and less about," adds Stieglitz.

Great reliance is entrusted to others on whom the chief executive places a large measure of authority. But, by freeing the top man from the diverse obligations of divisional responsibility, the system permits a new definition of entrepreneurial opportunity. Removed from the immediate obligations, except that he controls them from on high, the chief executive can then become a searcher for additional corporate opportunity, including that of men, money, and diversity.

Coupled with the delegation of management responsibility is a new developing process, even a science, of "forward-planning." This is an organized attempt at managing the tremendous impact of change with which every company today, and even more so in the future, is and will be afflicted.

"Many companies are learning a systematic program of planning their future. By doing so, by developing a science of market research, it will be possible to reduce the economic cycle," says Robert C. Harper, corporate vice president of the American Management Association.

"Given the realities of life, good planning can't change them but will enable business to live within the realities by preparing for the rate of change," he adds.

A salient part of the planning process is the need to constantly involve the entire management organization in it, Harper points out. This will provide a greater understanding of the corporate objectives and a better motivation for executives. It may well involve big changes in the corporate structure.

The most striking example of the top management delegation of duties into the new form know as the "President's Office," consisting of five top executives, was the major feature of GE's first, important structural change in sixteen years. The reorganization was devised by Fred J. Borch, the president of GE, to cope with the company's 60 per cent increase in sales over the previous five-year period. In other words, from that point on, the giant electronics firm would be managerially equipped to administer at least that much of a gain in the ensuing years.

The new "office" included, besides Borch, Gerald L. Philippe, GE's chairman who died late in the year, and three executive vice presidents, who previously had headed operating groups. Borch remained the boss, or the chief executive, and Phillippe the chief financial man. But the addition of the other three was to remove some of the heavy managerial load from Borch and to distribute it to the men who had come up through the operating ranks.

Aimed to streamline the reaching of decisions and to spur action, the "President's Office" was also intended to make use of the special knowledge of the three operating executives —aerospace and defense, electric utility, and consumer products—and to occasionally switch product groups among them so that the men didn't automatically become the proponent of any one group.

The restructuring plan was drafted by Borch while on a brief vacation in Spain. Like many another top executive, he does some of his deepest thinking for the company while officially relaxing.

GE had boosted its total sales $2.9 billion from 1962 to 1967, or about the total sales of its nearest competitor, Westinghouse. But, in the process, GE had suffered a severe drain on its earnings because of heavy losses in two of its ventures, computers and nuclear power. Gains in established products, however, as well as increasing volume in some new markets, had enabled the company to lift its sales an average 10 per cent in those years to a 1967 total of $7.7 billion.

But, with the heavy operating deficits in the new ventures combined with continuing large capital investments in them, Borch felt that a new strategy was vital. He was aware, too, that there was still some inside trauma and some outside stigma over the antitrust case of almost seven years earlier when more than two dozen GE executives and others from different companies had been implicated on price fixing. The men themselves had taken the onus, with GE, for one, under its then chairman, Ralph J. Cordiner, having fired or demoted them all, despite the very obvious fact that management had known of their collusion.

Beside the delegation of authority at the top, Borch decided to ease the managerial load at the lower levels, too. He doubled the number of the operating groups, and increased the total amount of divisions and departments. It also served to allow managers closer personal control, rearanged groups into a more logical and harmonious pattern, and permitted a concentration of sales impact.

In this way, the restructuring was carried all the way down the executive ranks, from staff to line, to ease the present management burdens and to gear for the future.

After Philippe's death in October, 1968, the new structure was changed a bit but its principles were retained. Borch moved up to become chairman and the three executive vice presidents were named vice chairmen. And the "President's Office" was renamed to the "Corporate Executive Office."

Two challenges of the future—the heavily encroaching burdens of corporate strategy in the marketplace combined with the pressures of social awareness—have touched off a widespread searching for new directions. One area, pointed to by AMA's Robert Harper, is that considerably more knowledge must be gained in the behavioral sciences for business. "We are all concerned nowadays," he says, "that about 97 per cent of all the research dollars are being spent on the physical sciences, on technology. The rest is being allotted to other matters, including a pitiful percentage on how to get along with people."

Taking up this challenge, the AMA has set up a subsidiary, the American Foundation for Management Research, which has as its objectives teaching management people how to become more effective and to conduct research in management on motivational aspects.

The new business environment requires a new concept of leadership. This principle was spelled out in painstaking and inspirational terms by Howard W. Johnson, president of the Massachusetts Institute of Technology, in a speech at a 1968 meeting sponsored by the National Industrial Conference Board.

By a new leadership concept, he said,

> I mean the kind of management needed to direct the activities of vast systems—public and private organizations, universities, and especially the growing conglomerate firms, whose products and services are widely diversified. There are some interesting experiments under way in a few large companies aimed at a team approach to executive responsibility. We need more of these experiments. And we need a broader framework—a new theory of management if you will—that will help us to understand and deal with the wide diversity of human choices that are available to us and to our institutions.

Outlining what he considered some basic qualities that would supply leadership in the new business environment, the MIT president cited:

> First, *competence*. By competence, I mean intelligence—native intelligence, yes; but more importantly, what I call effective intelligence—what is out of storage and into the mainstream of constant use. To use a language analogy, if intelligence units were words, what I mean is the "working vocabulary" idea.

Competence for me also includes knowledge—multidimensional knowledge of what you do (the business you are in)—and more broadly, an awareness of the environment, in the economy, in the society, and at a point in history.

Furthermore, by competence, I mean forward-thinking, imaginative ideas and creative approaches to problems—a creative competence.

Next, *direction*. And by direction, I do not mean pointing the way to a well-traveled path, but rather, I mean the forging of a new trail. Direction is goal-centered and strategy-minded. Goals are dreams and visions that are set purposely beyond one's reach. Resolve is part of goals, and it has no place for the momentary shifts of the vacillator. If heroism is "endurance for one moment more," then leadership is resolve for another day or month or year in order to achieve a worthwhile goal. And strategy is the art of translating these goals into a course of action. Rational thinking, clarity, and a sense of appropriateness describes this quality for me.

Finally, the new management will be characterized by a certain spark and sustaining vitality—by *spirit*, if you will. Spirit is a combination of personal curiosity, enthusiasm, and physical energy that welcomes challenge and accepts risk-taking ventures with a cheerful attitude.

But there is more to spirit. It is, to use a neglected term, entheos—which means "possessed of the spirit." This is a visceral form of spiritual energy which provides the element of mystery in leadership—the sign of the extraordinary. Rare, indeed, is this quality and much that passes for leadership must survive without it.

The manager today—and even more so in the future—has another important function which we generally do not recognize in our discussions on leadership. In our more complex, rapidly changing organizations, the leader must not only possess those qualities I have described; he must also be able to build and inspire and to deserve *trust*. For trust is the key to success in our changing systems. Trust relates to a sense of constructive interdependence among the members of an organization, to be sure. But, beyond that, trust means confidence that the man in charge is a man of the times—that he can relate to and understand the changing conditions of his environment, and that, understanding these conditions, he can exercise creative judgment and leadership.

3. THE NEGRO BUSINESSMAN

AND what of minority groups? Will their ambitious, educated, and zealous be able to share in the future entrepreneurial and corporate growth opportunities?

If the recent past is taken as an example, the answer must be one of qualified doubt. But, if an apparent new awareness of government and the white business community and the growing sophistication of the Negro businessman may be taken at more than face value, there is some basis for hope that the environment is brightening for the nonwhite businessman.

During the quickening racial tension that gripped the United States in the fifties and sixties, there were a number of remarkable, individual successes involving Negro businessmen. In almost all cases, they catered to the needs of their own race, benefiting from their acceptance and the lack of distrust which many Negroes have toward white businessmen. Conversely, the white money-lender and the white department store owner approaches his nonwhite customer with some trepidation, particularly the one in the most moderate income bracket. This consumer, they believe, has a considerably lower credit standing and record of payment —and is held to be generally more difficult to deal with—than the white customer or the better-income, nonwhite customer.

Joseph E. Davis, who became chief executive officer of the Carver Federal Savings and Loan Association when it opened in 1949, had the conviction that the Negro would-be borrower or depositor would respond to an institution that would cater to him.

Carver was the first savings-and-loan association to be established by Negroes in the state of New York. A group of Harlem community leaders, including Davis, founded it on a financial shoestring of $250,000, only $14,000 of which was in cash. The rest came in the form of pledges from Harlem residents.

Davis was a former shoeshine boy and tobacco field laborer in North Carolina where he was born. His early life was on a dire, poverty level; his mother was a domestic and his father died before he was born. After working his way through North Carolina College and graduating in 1929, he became a clerk with a Durham insurance company and then a teller and assistant cashier in a bank in the same city.

During the Depression, he moved to New York, and, after holding several jobs, he became a real estate appraiser for the Emigrant Industrial Savings Bank. When he was asked to become the operating head of the new savings-and-loan association, he tendered his resignation but Emigrant refused it and instead gave him a leave of absence.

At the outset, he said that Carver was being founded to serve the Negro. "Negroes, and especially low-income Negroes, were regarded as poor credit risks by white institutions," he explained. "Oh, there were token loans to a few selected Negro families, but it was no secret that many places were wary of the Negro applicant."

The bank became successful and grew to three offices, two in predominantly Negro areas, Harlem and the Bedford-Stuyvesant section of Brooklyn. The third, however, was in the Penn Station South-urban renewal project in Manhattan, where, the banker observed, "We will not be operating down there as a Negro institution. We will be competing on the same basis as any other business. The dollar downtown is just as green as it is uptown."

At his death in May, 1968, Davis left an institution which had grown to have assets of $40 million, had more than forty thousand depositors, of whom 5 per cent were white, and had lent more than $60 million to about four thousand home and business buyers.

Davis was a hard-driving executive, oriented toward setting

up a list of tasks and doggedly tackling each until he had surmounted it by delegating authority and nursing the attack along.

Other prominent Negro self-made businessmen of the fifties and sixties included William Hudgins, president of the Freedom National Bank, Harlem, a larger institution than Carver; Ewell W. Finley, a professional engineer, whose firm, Finley & Madison Associates, New York, has a substantial clientele for engineering projects; Robert Brown, president of B & C Associates, a public relations concern in High Point, N.C.; and John H. Johnson, president of the Johnson Publishing Company, Chicago, who, in 1945, founded the very successful *Ebony* magazine and other publications geared to the Negro market.

But perhaps the most dramatic success story in the past few decades among Negroes is that of Asa T. Spaulding, now the retired president of North Carolina Mutual Life Insurance Company, of Durham. "Asa," said a prominent Negro management expert, "is looked upon as the elder statesman of the Negro business community in America."

Spaulding, who was born on a farm in Columbus County, North Carolina, was educated in the county, attended Howard University, New York University School of Commerce, where he received a BS in accounting, magna cum laude, and obtained his master's degree in mathematics and actuarial science at the University of Michigan.

His rise from actuary and controller of N.C. Mutual Life to vice president and, in January, 1959, to president denoted a highly successful corporate career, but it was his exceptional demeanor in those posts and in his presidency that made him a national figure. A moderate but a progressive, he became an apostle of self-help for the Negro, combined with an active civic consciousness. An average-sized, calm, soft-spoken man, he was accepted as a leader by his own race and by white businessmen and government officials. He built his company to a preeminent position for an insurance company predominantly serving the Negro. He was elected a director of the W. T. Grant Company and of the American Management Association, represented the U.S. on several trade missions, participated in a UNESCO conference in India, and was cited by two Presidents for his public service.

Replying to a series of questions from this writer, Spaulding said that the factors that contributed most to his unusual business success were, "A burning desire for continuous growth and development from childhood; the ability to get along with people and to make friends; an interest in others, with others interested in me; trying to live by the Golden Rule and never satisfied in doing less than my best; and a willingness to attempt to do what others might consider impossible."

On the matter of future entrepreneurial hopes for Negroes, he was optimistic. "Recent leadership exercised by both the private and public sectors in providing creative and imaginative assistance to Negro entrepreneurs augurs well for their future development in a greatly accelerated manner," he said.

Asked what fields of business endeavor he would advise for ambitious Negro would-be entrepreneurs, he replied, "Any field in which they have a keen interest and aptitude and in which there is a future. With the active recruitment of young, Negro business majors by virtually all segments of the business community and the private and public-sponsored projects and programs, we find little or no restriction on business opportunities for the alert, ambitious, imaginative, and industrious Negro entrepreneurs with integrity."

Is adequate financing likely to be available for the Negro? Financing new ventures is always a problem, Spaulding said, and has been complicated in the past by restrictions based on race.

But, he said, the situation has been eased somewhat by a

recent shift in philosophy "as evidenced by the overt efforts of financial institutions, such as the life insurance industry's 'Billion Dollar Commitment,' and the tendency to make a creative approach to the consideration of loan applications presented by Negroes."

But, he added, "It must be emphasized that, although the problem has eased, it has not been eliminated."

4. SHIFTING OPPORTUNITIES

In a country which has a native flair for looking over the rainbow, too often we are prone to be set back on our heels by immediate, nagging problems. Wishfully, perhaps, the cynical side of our nature raises doubts on the long-term glow if a quarterly economic indicator or trend is negative in nature.

Yet, despite a plethora of short-term headaches in the second half of the sixties, including labor shortages, rising materials prices, investment controls, and continuing monetary problems, the nation's long-term growth potential appears to be hardly stunted.

In fact, according to one of the most detailed studies of long-term economic potential, the American economy in a fifteen-year period ending in 1982 will grow faster than in any comparable time in the twentieth century.

A study by the McGraw-Hill Economics Department made projections for each major sector of spending, including consumer, business, and government, and for many major technical and demographic trends that affect growth. And it found almost all of them good.

The study found that:

> The nation's output, or gross national product, will grow at an average annual rate of 4.3 per cent, compared with a 3.9 per cent average from 1947 to 1967 and only 2.5 per cent from 1909 to 1939.

This projects the GNP to rise from $785 billion in 1967 to $960 billion in 1972, to $1.2 trillion in 1977 and $1.5 trillion in 1982.

American per-capita income will increase by 55 per cent, against 47 per cent in Europe and 45 per cent in Canada and Australia.

A wave of consumer goods spending will find housing sales rising 122 per cent, durable goods 105 per cent, expenditures for services 96 per cent and soft goods 78 per cent.

Spending by government will become consumer-oriented, assuming an end to hostilities in Vietnam within the first third of the fifteen-year span under study. A projected cut in defense spending should lead to a 230 per cent gain in outlays for job training, income maintenance, and social security.

State and local spending will rise 142 per cent, again the stress being on consumer-oriented programs. A large part of the financing will come from federal grants to help state and local programs for roads, schools, hospitals, urban redevelopment, and social welfare.

The situation of people is also promising, not as to quantity but as to their qualities of earning capacity and education:

Total population will grow by only 21.6 per cent in the fifteen years, as compared with 26 per cent over the previous fifteen years. But it will be a population more able to contribute to the productivity growth that builds higher incomes. The dependency ratio will diminish, since the number of people in the key labor force group of twenty-five to sixty-four years of age grows faster than does the total population.

The income of the typical American family, now approximately $7,000 a year, will reach $7,825 in 1972, $8,800 in 1977, and approach $10,000 in 1982. By that time, 83 per cent of all families will earn more than $5,000 a year, against 66 per cent in 1967; 16 per cent will earn more than $15,000 against 9 per cent in 1967; and 4 per cent will go above $25,000 against only 2 per cent in 1967.

People will be far better educated. By 1982, the average American twenty-five years or older will have finished high school and have continued his education at junior college or at a university. This represents an increase in higher educational exposure compared to 1967 and substantially above that of

1952. About 1.2 million Americans will earn college diplomas in 1982, almost double that of the 1967 total and more than four times that in 1982.

The nonwhite population will increase 35 per cent by 1982, or almost twice as fast as the expected number of whites.

Other findings:

The number of workers will increase from 77.3 million in 1967 to 102.2 million by 1982, a gain which will outweigh a slight decline in the average workweek of from thirty-eight hours to thirty-five hours.

And capital spending by industry will grow 85 per cent by 1982, only slightly below the 88 per cent gain expected for the GNP as a whole. Research and development by industry will expand by 135 per cent.

What will all this and the changing business climate mean in terms of business and entrepreneurial opportunities? There are obvious answers to this question and some that are not as obvious.

One of the most obvious is that business will keep growing in the United States and that, in the process, there will be more and more giant companies. Bigness means complexity, so that the managements will be increasingly delegated to executive teams.

The team will consist of a group of generalists, who may have started as specialists (law, engineering, sales, marketing) and demonstrated such a flair for the dynamics of their jobs that they were tested in a bigger role and found to measure up well. The chief of the team will be one of these, who has pleased the directors (and the company founder, if he still survives) and to him will be entrusted the short-term destiny of the company.

He will guide it by relying heavily on his team (each one of whom will be under intense pressure) and by creating a system of checks-and-balances which will function as controls on the team's judgments. These will include not only financial and cost-accounting methods but use of outside specialists or consultants on marketing, research and development, design, sales, distribution, and manufacturing.

As the present era is being called that of the professional manager, the next few decades could, in fact, become known as "the era of the consultant." His number will be many and his influence tremendous.

Since the excellent opportunities now unfolded for the seventies and the eighties will be apparent to all, it is also obvious that competition in many of the burgeoning fields will grow to unprecedented proportions. Even in such industries where fragmentation was one of the most dominant traits (furniture, food, apparel manufacturing, home-building, and many service fields), consolidations will run rampant. The old arguments in favor of making mergers and acquisitions—buying power, market power, earning power—will be used with even more telling effect than in the big merger splurge of 1955–65.

This competition will quite obviously lead to two results, however paradoxical in nature.

One is that the American consumer will benefit greatly from the competitive attempts to please him, by the ardor with which he will be courted. The other is that because of the increasing consolidations in many important business areas, his choice of products and services will be reduced to those offerings by a smaller number of companies. To what extent this will work against the public's interest will be hard to predict. However, what is certain is that the issues of restraint-of-trade, of monopoly, and of "consumerism" will be even hotter ones in the future than they are today.

It is also obvious that the trend toward conglomerates, the containment of companies making varied types of products or offering diverse services under the same corporate shell, will continue to flourish. Their growth is already so great that only the most serious sort of financial chaos or stringent federal legislation could stunt it. The former would have to stunt all industry as well.

"The day of reckoning" for the conglomerate may come as a good many financial people predict. But, by then, the conglomerator will have learned how to weather his financial storms. A finely honed skill along these lines is already evident on the part of such practitioners as Ling, Riklis, Thornton, and Bluhdorn.

But the move toward conglomerism is hardly true only of this group. It is becoming increasingly the way of life of many public companies eager to capitalize on a tax-loss carry forward, to grow quickly, and to invest their assets or equity in a pyramid structure. The newer technique of divesting of some of their holdings in subsidiary companies in order to make these publicly held has increased the parent company's financial assets and given it new freedom to maneuver.

Catering to the explosion of business expansion will be a host of services that will boom in direct proportion to their customers' growth—and perhaps more so. Such services will include financial institutions, legal and accounting firms, advertising and public relations agencies, market research companies, and all manner of suppliers of administrative, office, and factory equipment and components.

The probable super-growth of such services may well come from the fact that while generalists will be in increasing demand by companies embarked on an unending quest for diversity, this will create a great cry for specialists to supply the services that the generalists will require to get the job done.

These general conclusions aside, what specific growth opportunities will be generated by the portended big rises in GNP, per-capita income, employment, government and domestic spending, and the improved educational levels?

Electronics and petrochemicals are two of the noteworthy

new fields of the future, says Bruce Palmer of the National Industrial Conference Board. "Another big, broad field will be the service industry, where opportunities and the number of people employed have boomed.

"Literally tens of thousands of new firms have arisen from leisure living," he notes, "and more, many more, will come. Increasing personal and leisure time create a vast area of opportunity for the enterprising businessman."

Harold Szold of Lehman Brothers believes that improving technologies will give rise to many new businesses in electronics, metals, drugs, and numerous other technically oriented fields. "On Route 128, near Boston, near where MIT and Boston are," he says, "is where the new businesses are or will come from. Find out what's going on in the laboratories and you'll know what the big, new growth fields will be."

The banker also cited the opportunities in his own field, the investment companies and the new mutual fund managers, as harbingers of growth possibilities in the world of finance.

The franchising practice will grow, he believes. "It's fundamental and emotional precepts are right," Szold says. "You, the man, are the boss, the family works with you, and you build a business. It's a good, opportunity concept."

J. Emerson Thors, a partner of Kuhn, Loeb & Company, the investment bankers, sees mass communications as an especially important field of endeavor in the next few decades. "The great basic need of the world today is education," the veteran banker says, "and the entire area of transmission of education holds promise of satisfying that need."

Along these lines, the ramifications in the space-age devices, such as the Comsat and the Early Bird satellite, are vast and diverse. "The developing nations and those that are developed all fall within the perimeter of such space communications concepts," he says.

Allied with this are the "identification" or copying and the electronic data processing fields, "where we are on the threshold of computerizing our business or our identities."

Adds Thors, "Medical electronics is another of the most challenging fields as the experts in medicine and engineering combine skills to help humanity. This is already obvious in the organ transplant area, as it is in cardiology and other specialized, intricate forms of medicine."

He also cites other "interesting areas" of future growth: the development of new food sources, such as protein food in capsulated form from the refinement of marine life; oceanography, for food and mining; air pollution control; the control of industrial waste; desalinization for the production of water; and nuclear power for fuel and research.

Entry into such fields poses problems of great magnitude, of course, particularly because of the great outlays of money and the extreme complexity of knowledge and operations that are needed. But the opportunities will exist for the enterprises with sufficient assets or the ability to raise them, while the service and supply functions may be the area of opportunity for the newer and smaller firms.

Wherever a prime contractor thrives, in other words, a zealous subcontractor may thrive, too.

The outlook for business growth and opportunity is not all glaringly bright. The next two decades hold some problems of supply and demand that will require deep thinking and deft handling, much of the difficulties arising from socioeconomic changes that have occurred since World War II. The problems are:

1. The burgeoning service field suffers from a shortage of technicians which appears due to increase in the years ahead. The auto industry, diversified consumer and industrial goods companies such as General Electric, and the technology-oriented firms such as International Business Machines feel a sharp pinch. Their engineers find that they are compelled

to spend too much time servicing the machines that they helped to create.

About 4 million new skilled workers will be needed in less than a decade, according to a U.S. Labor Department estimate. Almost one half of this amount will be required to replace retirees, and the remainder will be needed to man new jobs. About 255,000 apprentices are being trained each year, indicating that, unless the trend increases, only about 2 million craftsmen and technicians, or one half the needed amount, will be through the apprenticeship programs by 1975.

"The technical schools are not being occupied to their capacity," notes NICB's Hugh Palmer. "They are only about 70 per cent used, with overexpanded facilities and underexpanded attendance." The shortage accrues from varied causes: higher college attendance; the military draft; higher wages for unskilled labor creating less interest in long training programs; and still archaic membership restrictions by unions in some trades.

2. Despite the indicated growth of leisure time, there is a growing concern that facilities for the use of leisure time are inadequate and will become more so.

Americans by 1985 will only have to work six months a year to retain their present standard of living, according to findings by the Southern California Research Council. But a study by this business-educational group, based on a sampling considered representative of the nation as a whole, found some disquieting lacks of audience and participant facilities.

Outdoor recreational areas are wholly inadequate. Libraries are understaffed and understocked. The performing arts are sparsely patronized and "in serious financial trouble." And adult education, the study concluded, is a neglected area.

The assumption of it all is that while much gleeful talk has been heard about increasing leisure time, little action has been taken by the government and private sectors to accommodate it. Can business step into the breach? It would seem to hold great opportunities, if courage and initiative and creativity are applied, as they would under any circumstances.

3. The advent of the Negro executive is still slow and uncertain, while entrepreneurial activities by the Negro does not yet appear to be exactly a promising matter. Not many Negro self-made men feel as optimistic as Asa Spaulding does.

Business has only lately rallied to the need to employ minority group executives, but many companies remain steeped in restrictive tradition or confused at how far to go in hiring.

"The Negro cadre, the qualified business graduates, just aren't there," declared a prominent placement counselor. "The white establishment is so well entrenched and still so hidebound that, despite all the talk, it is difficult to crack the hiring façade."

Entrepreneurial activities appear to be limited to operations of smaller scope, say Negroes who have an ambitious streak. "The toughest part is to get the financing to float a new company by a Negro owner," one said. "It comes in spurts —but, occasionally, in a reverse reaction to some black militant trend of action, such as the looting and the rioting that followed the murder of Dr. Martin Luther King, there is a white backlash which dries up both white financing and white business cooperation."

4. The tremendous rate of change, of the ebb-and-flow of both consumer trends and of technology, will lead to marketing and production headaches that will take more than aspirin to cure. Mostly gone—or going—from the scene are trolley cars, newsreels, milk bottles, automobile seat covers, monaural records, crew-cut haircuts, and drug-store soda fountains. Commented the *Wall Street Journal* on the demise of Americana:

It's all due to technology and taste. Both are changing more rapidly than ever, causing a fast turnover in the artifacts of everyday life. Change is so fast that yesterday's dream is today's necessity—and tomorrow's fond memory. Indeed, this has become the era of instant nostalgia. . . .

What this means to business is not hard to determine. Under the twin prongs of rapidly changing consumer preference and constantly improving technology, the life-span of products will become hazardous in their brevity. Great successes will suddenly falter in their acceptance, while investment in products that seem to bear durability may be quickly lost because of design or engineering breakthroughs that will outmode all that has gone before them.

5. TOMORROW'S ENTREPRENEUR

PROVOCATIVE words come from the former chairman of the American Management Association. Writes Lawrence A. Appley:

> Bigness has attracted increasing attention in modern times because growth has been so fantastic. Bigness has been, and is, subject to attack from many sources. Big business, big government, big labor unions, big projects of all kinds frustrate and, many times, frighten people.
>
> There is goodness in bigness and there are great challenges to make proper use of it. When bigness destroys itself, the many services it has to render are lost through failure to understand how to deal with it.
>
> Civilization would not be what it is today without bigness. . . .
>
> Bigness supports mediocrity; it hides incompetency. The head of one of the great commercial giants of our times once told me, "Volume covers a lot of mistakes." The bigger an institution, the more mistakes it can make and still survive. . . .
>
> It has been noted by experts, authors, teachers, and others that with bigness and with success come great conservatism. There are evidences of less creativity and less vitality and less facility for change. If this be true, then there must be still another accompanying truth.

If bigness increases conservatism, then the top people in smaller institutions must be more progressive, more alert to needs and opportunities for development. Possibly, they take more risks. It must be true if there is more vitality in a smaller one.

As I listen to these matters discussed these days, and I think of them in the quietness of my study, I am convinced that nowhere nearly enough effort is being expended in the development of brand new concepts of how to handle bigness. I believe we have to discard most of our conventional organization thinking. New and different structures must be devised. Completely new thinking must be encouraged.

Possibly, top managements of big institutions are so deeply involved in fulfilling the responsibilities forced upon them by mere bigness that they are not taking enough time to stand back objectively and "brainstorm" some completely new approaches. . . .

So Appley wrote in an AMA newsletter in February, 1968. More recently, he told this writer, "We are suffering today in this country from a vacuum of leadership—in business, government, school, church, and military, or in every segment of our society."

From the business standpoint, but as much from all the others, he attributed this decline in the leadership quotient to three factors.

These were the Depression of the thirties ("We did not train reserves, men who today would be our leaders, because we were concentrating instead on survival"); World War II (which had one million casualties and "robbed us of the talents and the benefits of many potential leaders who would now be in their late forties"); and the unprecedented boom in the economy and its consequent pressure for management candidates to fill an expected quadrupling of such positions in the decade ahead.

The retired AMA chairman believes that the businessmen were the first to awaken to the challenge, primarily through their realization that they needed more knowledge. "Few others in other fields are as aware of this problem," he says. He estimated that today there were upwards of 200,000 businessmen going to various schools on a part-time basis throughout the U.S.

However, tracking his two major points against each other —the ultra-conservatism of "bigness" and the vacuum of leadership in business—Appley is convinced that a great area of opportunity exists for the rise of both new entrepeneurs and professional business managers.

Both will find their way, he is certain, through the default of others. But their common denominator will be the professionality of their business skills—a characteristic which Appley, a respected business educator, adviser, and director of numerous companies, equates with "having a philosophy as well as a technique."

Yet, there is still the overriding question that many businessmen, students of business, and others are asking themselves in this increasing age of marketplace complexity and proliferating technology. Will the classic self-made man of the nineteenth century or the variations thereof in the twentieth century be able in the future to build another General Motors, Ford, or IBM?

Stieglitz of the NICB, for one, doubts that the product creator will be able to do so.

"The future function of this type of entrepreneur," he says, "may be like the relationship of the farm system in baseball to the big leagues. He will be able to carry his growth only so far (the farm system) and then be forced by lack of managerial ability and personal assets and insufficient self-confidence to give it up to professional management in the form of the big, diversified company (the big leagues)."

But the innovator, or the dynamic user of other's skills, is more attuned to the trends and the tests of the era, he believes.

"His entrepreneurial ability grows out of his skills at

management—skills that cut across products and markets and generate the logic of synergistics with the talents that exist within the organization," Stieglitz says.

Put another way, the big trend of corporate divisionalization leaves room for the entrepreneurial opportunity of the future—that is, for the innovator at the head of a multibusiness company and for the smaller entrepreneur, the product maker, who can only go so far under his own steam until he becomes part of another company.

If that is the case, what will happen when the innovator, or the conglomerator, or the planter of the spreading corporate tree passes from the scene? This is a question, like a bad dream that keeps uncomfortably returning, that troubles bankers and other lenders who put up the wherewithal for the continuing expansion. The question is only a more recent form of the concern over the ramifications of the death of the traditional self-made man, who founded a "one-man" company.

A pertinent example worth studying here is Harold S. Geneen, whom *Forbes* magazine called "possibly the greatest corporation executive of his day." Geneen, a demanding type who relishes giving his executives almost unattainable standards to live up to, built the International Telephone & Telegraph Company from sales of $700 million in 1959 to $2.7 billion in 1967. Throughout that time, he also increased net earnings every quarter for thirty-four consecutive quarters, a feat that was not duplicated by any major American company.

Controversial because of his zealous and acquisitive nature and his driving treatment of his executives, Geneen changed the content and image of ITT from a company that obtained its income from rather unstable foreign holdings to a conglomerate containing such plums as Avis Rent-a-Car, Levitt and Sons, and the Sheraton Corporation. He hired young men who strained against frustration in their previous jobs and skilled top management who yearned for a "piece of the action." He drove them all with the lash of his tongue and with goals that strained their imagination and talents, not to mention their physical endurance.

The result was a truly amazing corporate growth story, with scarred but grimly happy executives who continued to work for him. At the same time, there was an exodus of executives to other firms where Geneen's infantry training put them across in high style.

What will happen to ITT when Geneen goes, as every man must go? The prognostication is that, despite the fact that he either deliberately or inadvertently never arranged for a successor-in-training, the conglomerate's momentum will barrel ahead and that a more formal, if less aggressive team will take over. The direction has already been clearly charted; the personality may go, but the thrust will linger on. Even when it dissipates in a few years, the size and scope of the company will be too great for it to seriously flounder. In the meantime, the waves of executives who were persecuted and badgered by the master will carry on in his tradition, if in a more subdued, more deliberate, and more gracious manner.

The replacement of the self-made man by the team of generalists who began as specialists will, in all likelihood, be the pattern of the future. But the extent or width of the opportunity gap that results from the impact of the new business climate on the shifting opportunities of the future will be less a decline in the role of the self-made man as a change in his silhouette and viscera.

Despite all the trends that seem certain to dehumanize the entrepreneur, it is more than likely that opportunities will continue ripe in many fields (different ones from the past) for the motivated, the imaginative, and those with blood in their eye.

The stereotypes will vanish, as the psychiatrists predict.

The idiosyncracies that gave the durable self-made man his style and contributed to his love-hate aura will become outmoded, if for nothing else than lack of harmony with the size of the business and its growing complexity.

His son, or his son-in-law, or some other young man with a graduate business school degree, will succeed him as the key man in the "President's Office" and probably perform in a more organized, not necessarily more capable but less dynamic manner.

Many new entrepreneurs will appear on the scene but they will be compelled to seek out the new opportunities that the big companies do not care for or detect.

And the new self-made men, being much more financially, Wall Street, and short-term success-minded, will not stay in for nearly as long a pull as their prototypes did. Turning in one's assets for a stock equity in a growth-minded public company is fast becoming a way of life in American business.

The personality change of the self-made man will be a gradual process, much as the subtle shift has taken place in other areas of American society from the highly personal leader in government, culture, and education to the more sophisticated, more worldly, less individualistic leader, speaking in well rounded, mannered tones, and behaving more like a symbol than as a human being with human qualities and flaws.

And yet—and yet, the probability of it all is not that certain, that final, that cut-and-dried. Opportunity has a way of veering off into an exciting tangent to meet the frantic dash of a hungry, sweating salesman.

One of the country's most experienced management consultants, who has worked with hundreds of companies of a wide variety of sizes and types, expressed his opinion of the future of the self-made man this way:

"If it weren't for the fact that a mousy man can grow into

a job and flex his muscles, the future of corporate life would be dim indeed. . . .

Nothing seems to come as quickly as the decline of supremacy. This means that companies wedded to the status quo, to the balance sheet, to their assets may be forgetting that business is a dynamically changing force. That is why most big businesses are not geared to change, so that they leave open great opportunities for alert, small entrepreneurs.

But, perhaps most important of all, within the next decade or two, the information accumulation will give all companies the same data, with the result that the qualities of individuality, or the qualities of the self-made man will have to come back. In other words, as competition becomes steeper and more onerous, the human equation will become more important. That should mean a great deal to the individual just as long as courage doesn't go out of style."

INDEX

Index